RETURN OF THE TALIBAN

RETURN OF THE TALIBAN

STATE, SOCIETY AND TERROR

APRATIM MUKARJI

Vitasta

Published by
Renu Kaul Verma
Vitasta Publishing Pvt Ltd
4348/4C, Ansari Road, Daryaganj
New Delhi-110 002
info@vitastapublishing.com

ISBN 978-81-19670-03-1
© Apratim Mukarji
First Edition 2024

MRP ₹ 695

All Rights Reserved.
No part of this publication may be reproduced, stored in a retrieval system, or transmitted in any form, or by any means—electronic, mechanical, photocopying, recording or otherwise—without the prior permission of the publisher. Opinions expressed in this book are the contributors' own. The publisher is in no way responsible for these.

Editorial Team Soumitro Das, A D Gnanagurunathan, Renu Arya
Cover and Layout by Somesh Kumar Mishra
Printed by Chaman Enterprises, New Delhi

*Dedicated
to
the exceptional valour of my sisters in
Afghanistan who will never give up their
fight against the brutal fundamentalist
rulers of the unfortunate country*

CONTENTS

Preface	ix
Introduction	xxv
Massoud Makes First Approach to the US	1
The Saga of the Commander	17
The 'Sins' of the Commander	24
The Scorn of the People	35
After the Taliban came	40
A Day of Panic	48
The March of Women	57
The Forebodings of A Dark Future	79
The Yankee Booty: A Friendly Gift	81
Islamabad and Kabul Can Never Gel	92
And Now on To Jihadism	114
The Impact on Afghanistan	125
Afghanistan Drawn Into the Cold War Vortex	147
Mujahideen and the Civil War	159
The Exit of the Soviet Union	178

The Rise of the Taliban	189
The Drug Connection	196
The World in a Dilemma: To Recognise or not to Recognise?	224
Tortuous Negotiations	240
Internationalising Terrorism	253
In Afghanistan, there Cannot be any Conclusion	265
Acknowledgements	*283*

PREFACE

The Taliban Islamic Front fighters—a collection of brown-skinned, tall, long-haired Afghans, attired in shalwar-kameez[1], most of them unsmiling young and middle-aged men, each of them armed with lethal weapons—marched into Kabul, the capital of Afghanistan, on the gathering dusk of 15 August 2021 as the United States completed the withdrawal process. Both, troops and diplomats scampering for their dear lives, taking the last available planes, even as the democratically-elected president of the country, Ashraf Ghani, and his cabinet barring a brave, honest Afghan Amarullah Saleh who chose to stay back and fight, fled in haste instead of providing leadership to the helpless citizens. Even the Afghan National Defence Force chose to lay down their expensive, sophisticated American weapons, leave all other militaryware behind, and flee with their lives. It was a time of national shame when leadership failed, or, rather, chose not to defend the people against the fanatical invaders.

---

1   A shalwar is a pair of loose pyjamas and a kameez is a long tunic which covers the upper part of the body

By choosing to completely abandon Afghanistan to the Taliban wolves, the United States President Joe Biden disregarded the liberal interventionist agenda. Overnight, with the terrorists taking over Afghanistan, the entire country changed. From a functioning democracy, Afghanistan became a country governed by an Islamist group determined to bring back a pure Islamic state, a task they had to leave unfinished in 2001. In the course of explaining this slide-back in the country's political culture, Professor John J. Mearsheimer emphasizes that upholding human rights, rule of law, and a broader 'rules-based international order' based on the first two principles, are typically cited as reasons for (liberal) intervention.

The political appeal of interventionist politics was obvious. In the UK, politicians have been historically weary of any foreign policy doctrine that resembles 'appeasement', the failed strategy pursued by Neville Chamberlain towards the government of Nazi Germany. David Cameron's Foreign Secretary William Haig claimed in 2009 that 'It is not in our character to have a foreign policy without a conscience; to be idle or uninterested while others starve or murder each other in their millions is not for us.' Meanwhile, the United States, as the sole post-Cold War superpower, seemed intent on a model of reproducing liberal hegemony.

Indeed, in 2002, the US National Security Report went as far as to say that 'the United States must defend liberty and justice because these principles are right and true for all people everywhere.' It is no surprise then, that the R2P (Responsibility to Protect) principles are a reflection of what the West holds close to heart.² The articulation of these principles, however, reflects a naiveté and even a chauvinism—that has turned out to be deeply problematic in practice. John Mearsheimer, the torch bearer of 'offensive realism' in international relations theory, has argued that 'You go from a modest and limited military intervention in cases of gross violations of human rights...to the decision that the best way to protect rights is to populate the planet with liberal democracies.' The logical development of the principles of R2P is extended to the kind of 'nation-building' undertaken by the international community in Afghanistan and Iraq. Despite the potential merits of such a political project these interventions failed on their own terms as a development project. The collapse of the democratic Afghan state shows that the Coalition forces failed to put in place the sort of resilient institutions capable of protecting human rights in the first place. Whether outside forces can impose Western liberal democracy in an environment unfamiliar with the concept of democracy is arguable, and perhaps even slightly

---

2 In 2005, the United Nations declared a 'responsibility to protect' (R2P). In the event of certain crimes against humanity, where a sovereign state fails to take action against or has actively permitted such acts, and where peaceful means have failed 'signatories' are prepared to take collective action, in a timely and decisive manner...on a case-by-case basis...should peaceful means be inadequate and national authorities manifestly fail to protect their populations from...crimes against humanity. The language is guarded but the implication is clear. The UN not only permits but compels states to intervene in cases where 'peaceful means' have proved inadequate. The R2P was posed as an 'answer' to the so-called (Kofi) *Annan Dilemma, the questions posed by UN Secretary-General Kofi Annan in the wake of humanitarian atrocities in Kosovo and Rwanda. 'Sovereignty, for Annan, does not just confer privileges upon states; it also imposes responsibilities on them, not least the responsibility to protect those under their rule,'* — the conflict, then, is between the sovereign state's ability to self-determine, and its responsibility to take care of its citizens. Where the sovereign state particularly fails in its responsibilities, the argument goes, the legitimacy of the sovereign is breached.

paradoxical. The feeling for many in the West is now one of fatigue. As the voting public turns against 'forever wars', the case for intervention abroad is increasingly difficult for politicians to make. The exhaustion felt by many was articulated in President Biden's withdrawal speech, with the exclamation that 'It is time to end America's longest war.' This is not to say that the United States is fully retracting the footprints it has left in the wake of the war on terror. Today, America lives in an age of 'small wars to fight in far-away places', small anti-terrorist operations carried out with light footprints in theaters of conflict that members of the public are not even aware of. Many in the West are rightly outraged about the apathy shown to people that the departing forces left behind such as, in the case of Afghanistan, Afghan women, ethnic and religious minorities, and members of the now defunct Afghan National Army and former Afghan government figures.

The question remains: How can an international community beholden to humanitarian values promote these values without the disastrous impact of forceful intervention? The well-known professor of international law, Simon Chesterman, writing in *Just War or Just Peace*, argues that liberal interventionism is a development model that answers to a false dichotomy between 'humanitarian intervention' and 'inhumanitarian non-intervention' (referring to the presumption that non-enforcement allowed states to get away with abuses), with the forceful refrain that 'unilateral enforcement is not a substitute for but the opposite of collective action'. An international legal regime able to hold states to account, without military intervention, is a far more stabilising force. As a development thesis, the doctrine of military intervention carried out under the guise of promoting liberal values, appears to be woefully inadequate, leaving behind a disastrous legacy of failed states and civil strife. While it seems that the calculus for Washington and Westminster has changed since the military adventurism of the early 2000s, the legacy of these decisions will continue to resonate in Baghdad and Kabul for generations.[3]

On 18 May 2022, under Joe Biden's presidency, the office of the Special Inspector General for Afghanistan Reconstruction (SIGAR) published an interim report confirming that the decision to withdraw American soldiers and military contractors from Afghanistan directly led to 'the collapse of the Afghan army', and consequently, of the Afghan government. The United States Oversight Authority SIGAR said the decision 'to withdraw from Kabul led to the demise of the Afghan army'. The withdrawal of the United States forces and military contractors in 2021 has been termed as 'the single most important factor' in triggering the collapse of the Afghan National Defence and Security Forces (ANDSF). The report pointed out that Washington had spent nearly US $90 billion on building the army since 2002 'in its efforts to fight the Taliban'. The new report by the SIGAR pointed to the decisions made by then President Donald Trump and his successor Joe Biden which 'thereby precipitated the collapse of the Afghan army in the month of August 2021 and the subsequent Taliban takeover of Afghanistan..Many Afghans thought the United States-Taliban

---

3 Oxford Society for International Development blog, *Afghanistan and the end of the liberal intervention*, https://www. army-technology.com/news/us-troop-withdrawal-afghanistan-august/

Agreement of February 2020 was an act of bad faith and a signal that the United States was handing over Afghanistan to the enemy as it rushed to exit the country', the SIGAR concluded. Former United States and Afghan military officials were quoted in the interim report of the SIGAR, saying that the withdrawal 'of the military contractors grounded the Afghan air force and sealed the fate. We built that (Afghan) army to run on contractor support. Without it, it (the army) can't function.' A former Afghan general told the office of the SIGAR that 60 per cent of Black Hawk helicopters 'were grounded in a matter of months in the wake of the withdrawal of contractors, including those who provided maintenance work'.

In a sparkling explanation of the American policy, in an earlier article, entitled 'Afghanistan: No More the Good War', Professor John J. Mearsheimer wrote that 'In the beginning, Afghanistan looked like a good war. The United States won a quick victory, drove the Taliban and Al-Qaeda out, and installed a friendly government. The results seemed so impressive that even before the fighting stopped, the Bush administration decided to replicate the model in Iraq.'[4]

A lot of things had actually gone wrong when the war looked 'so good' and controlled. Neither the Taliban nor Al-Qaeda were totally finished; uprooted from the soil, they had actually gone into hiding in Pakistan and there they remained until the time to resurface came. The choice of Hamid Karzai, for leading the post-Taliban Afghanistan, also proved unwise as he

---

4   John J. Mearsheimer, *Afghanistan: No More the Good War,* Newsweek, 5 December 2009.

turned out to be both corrupt and inefficient; and his repeated efforts to gain control over a divided country eventually led to his mishandling of the giant task of reconstructing a hugely damaged country, whose economy and society had been left pockmarked by tribal and religious loyalties. His successor Ashraf Ghani proved to be another misfortune for Afghanistan who spent two terms battling a resurgent Taliban, and the myriad-headed monster of divided loyalties, low moral values with the womenfolk pushed out of society.

As Mearsheimer looked at it in 2009, twelve years before the complete failure of the democratic liberal institutions put in place by the United States and backed by the international community, the most significant factor was that the Taliban were not 'decisively defeated and many of (their) leaders and fighters melted into the local population or escaped to Pakistan'. The Karzai government turned out to be incompetent and corrupt and never had much influence beyond Kabul. It was no match for the Taliban who succeeded in re-establishing themselves as a formidable force to the government. Thus, the onerous task of fighting the Taliban to the finish surfaced once again, something which was not on the calculation board before. But this time, there were major differences; first, large numbers of ground forces were required—a new factor which directly affected the American population. The US forces also changed, from being a 'liberating' force to an 'occupying' force, a different connotation altogether. And why was this new 'occupying' force in the country? To prop up an unpopular government. Incidentally, the popular disenchantment with Hamid Karzai as the leader of the Taliban-free nation was so strongly embedded in the popular psyche that after the Taliban drove out the Ashraf Ghani government, which, like the Karzai regime, carried the stigma of corruption and inefficiency, the people in a province changed the name of a high school, removing Karzai's name from the signboard of the institution, as a show of their wrath.

As more and more American troops were brought in, between October 2004 and October 2006, in just two years, United States and NATO troops spread out into every region of the country. Not surprisingly, that bigger footprint helped fuel the insurgency, leading to the dire situation prevailing in 2009 (when the article was written). 'The Obama administration spent the Fall desperately trying to find a solution. But no policy could stave off defeat in Afghanistan. Even with more troops and better tactics, the US military could not decisively defeat the Taliban because it was a shadowy guerrilla force that (could) always melt away and come back fighting another day. The local population would not side with Karzai or the United States much longer. Because they knew Karzai was a incompetent and NATO—unlike the Taliban—would actually leave.' Trying to read the future, Mearsheimer said, 'even if the US military did pacify Afghanistan, moreover, Al-Qaeda would still have its sanctuary next door in Pakistan. And Washington would face the same problem it did before 9/11; after all, those attacks could just easily have been planned from Pakistan.' The 'realist' professor then came up with a suggestion which would startle any person interested in the subject. He said way back in 2009:

> The only viable strategy for Afghanistan is thus the one President Obama will not seriously contemplate: acknowledge defeat and pull out completely. Yet that's precisely what Washington should do, while making it

clear that it will leave the Taliban alone if it keeps Al-Qaeda out. If the Taliban (refuse), Predator drones should be sufficient to keep the jihadis at bay—or, take them out. The real key to prevent another 9/11, however, is for the United States to work closely with other governments to monitor Al-Qaeda and round up terrorists before they strike. Timely intelligence and sound police work are the main reasons that there has not been another attack on the US homeland. The war in Afghanistan has done little to make Americans safer at home, and prolonging it won't either. It's been a bad war from the start and will be (so) to the bitter end.[5]

Mearsheimer, despite holding views contrary to the American foreign policy establishment, had shown limited humanitarian concerns for the Afghans. In a sense, this brings us back to the Annan Dilemma, a phenomenon we have discussed above.

Could it be argued that foreign policy determinations by the United States were usually tied to the particular moment — not necessarily denoting the fundamentals of a development— but what appeared at the moment to be fundamental to that development? This question was discussed way back in 2002 immediately after then US President George W. Bush delivered his first State of the Union address on 29 January 2002. To quote him, 'Our discoveries in Afghanistan confirmed our

---

5   John J. Mearsheimer, *Afghanistan: No More the Good War*, Newsweek, 5 December 2009.

worst fears, and showed us the true scope of the task ahead. We have seen the depth of our enemies' hatred in videos, where they laugh about the loss of innocent life. What we have found in Afghanistan confirms that, far from ending there, our war against terror is only beginning.' Bush's choice of the word 'discovery' merits attention because it exposes the wilful tendency of the world's most powerful nation to 'ignore and recognize' reality 'strictly according to its perceptions of the moment.' The intrinsic worth of fact and fiction was apparently secondary to these seemingly transitory perceptions. The American response to the civil war in Afghanistan exemplified this behavioural pattern of the US administration, which often caused misgivings in the minds of other national governments.[6]

American policy on Afghanistan has lent itself on many occasions to criticisms for the reason that Washington appeared to have deliberately left its policies not fully open to examination, especially the critical analyses conducted by intelligence agencies and the Pentagon and its myriad agencies. One major example was its dithering attitude towards Commander Ahmad Shah Massoud[7], who led the Northern

---

6 Apratim Mukarji, *Advent of the Northesrn Alliance in Afghanistan: US Policy Examined*, Journal of the Himalayan and Central Asian Studies, January-March 2002, New Delhi, pp.35-55.

7 The most informative book on Commander Ahmad Shah Massoud till date is British journalist Sandy Gall's celebrated book, "Afghan Napoleon: The Life of Ahmad Shah Massoud", published by House Publishing, in September 2021. Gall was embedded with Massoud's Northern Alliance forces in the Panjsher Valley in 1979 first against the Afghan communist government forces and then, a month later, against the Soviet occupation force. The unique features in the book include Gall's full access to the commander himself, to his diaries, and to the fighters. The information he gleaned from these first-hand sources could not be matched by any other journalist or publication.

Alliance and who had fought and defeated the massive Soviet occupation force as many as seven times in the Panjsher Valley. Massoud's allegiance to liberalism and democracy as opposed to the Taliban's abhorrence of these two qualities was self-evident, but for obscure reasons Washington never favoured the commander who was fighting a desperate struggle against the fundamentalist terrorists. However, it had seemed to several analysts that the Americans looked at the Northern Alliance or, to go by its formal nomenclature, the United Front, with severely jaundiced eyes because they did not like its spirit of independence and its penchant for taking over leadership. The latter blemish could be pardoned because Commander Massoud had repeatedly demonstrated unparalleled leadership qualities. In a country where loyalties shifted as rapidly as sand, most of his allies stuck to him through victories and setbacks, though he made a few mistakes in choosing a few of his one-time allies.

When the Taliban-Al-Qaeda (The Base) combine collapsed swiftly against the onslaught of American and Coalition forces, that was the first surprise for the international community, for this was totally unexpected, the world having been fed by predictions of fierce and long resistance by the Taliban and their ally. But, at the same time, there was a second surprise. Totally independent of the 'war on terror' mounted with the blessings of the United Nations, Commander Massoud and his forces were making rapid progress towards Kabul. The Americans were so enraged—for they had never liked the commander despite his achievements against Soviet Russia—that President Bush issued a formal warning to the United Front forces 'not to enter Kabul'. It was as if the United States presidential office was revisiting the Bill Clinton and Joe Biden eras together. A typical instance of the predetermined US perception about the Northern Alliance force was reflected in an editorial that appeared in The New York Times, 'The (Northern) Alliance's ground forces can be an important military asset in dislodging the Taliban. But its fratricidal and ethnically unrepresentative leaders must not be allowed to exploit an American-backed drive on the capital to position themselves as the nation's dominant political figures. Such a lopsided government would have little chance of gaining nation-wide legitimacy or acceptance by important neighbours like Pakistan. Many of the Northern Alliance's leaders were the same people whose murderous feuding and ill-governance between 1992 and 1996 helped to open the way for the Taliban takeover.'[8] Unfortunately, this piece of counsel typified the rigid American stance on Afghanistan, shaped to a large extent by Pakistan's machinations. What the editorial writer desired to convey to his readers was that the Northern Alliance neither represented the Pashtuns, the dominant ethnic tribe in the country with close blood relations with Pashtuns (Pathans) of Pakistan and who had traditionally presided over Afghan politics; and secondly, that Commander Massoud and his men were an anathema to Islamabad because they were mostly Tajiks, Uzbeks and Hazaras, all considered by Pashtuns as inferior to them; they were also the worst enemies of the Taliban, who were in their turn the foster-children of Pakistan. The Americans might appear oblivious to those facts, but it was a deliberate choice by the West, led by the United States,

---

8   Editorial, *After the Taliban*, The New York Times, 27 October 2021.

their governments, along with the media, to lead the campaign led the campaign against the Northern Alliance for the unacceptable four years of bloodshed, mayhem, destruction, and an almost breakdown of the law and order machinery under the Burhanuddin Rabbani government in which Commander Massoud was the defence minister. Not surprisingly, the role that Gulbuddin Hekmatyar—once a fellow-student leader at Kabul's engineering university along with Massoud—and now the blue-eyed boy of Pakistan's Inter-Services Intelligence (ISI) Directorate, who unleashed continuous bombardments on Kabul destroying district after district and killing thousands of people, forced Massoud to retreat from Kabul in order to save whatever still stood in the capital. When the Rabbani government assumed power and Massoud became its defence minister, Islamabad apparently decided not to leave them in peace and used Hekmatyar successfully to dislodge them, and in the bargain, forced them into taking the blame for their 'misgovernance'. To blame the Rabbani-Massoud duo for Hekmatyar's sins was the very height of blindfold politics and history-writing, from which the Western and even the world media at times suffered.[9] The only supporters of the Northern Alliance throughout this period were Russia, Iran and India. When Massoud was assassinated on 9 September 2001, two days before the Al-Qaeda mounted the devastating 9/11 attacks on the United States, many wilfully-shut eyes were forced to open and look at the reality.

---

9   Apratim Mukarji, Advent of the Northern Alliance…,ibid.

Members of the US Congress in both Houses had begun to question the administration's policy of sidelining Commander Massoud right from the Soviet occupation days. At that time, three Congressmen, Don Ritter (R-PA), Gordon Humphrey (R-NH), and Dana Rohrabacher (R.CA) criticised Pakistan for cutting off assistance to Massoud and Ismail Khan. While successive administrations continued to ignore and avoid the commander, there were individual Americans who kept on advocating his case for a close partnership with the United States against the Taliban and Al-Qaeda, both of whom of whom Massoud had identified as 'extreme enemies of the American people and government'.

The break out of the Ukraine war in late-February 2022 when the Russian army invaded the former and its continuance—belying the general impression that the war would be over no sooner had Russia taught Ukraine a lesson or two for daring to aspire to join the NATO—Western governments began to pressure India for not responding adequately to the Russian aggression. At that time, India took pains to remind the Europeans that just a year ago the world, and the Western world in particular, had chosen to look the other way when a 'whole civil society (in Afghanistan) was thrown under the bus (the Taliban) by the world'.[10] The point to note here is the fact that the West in particular has consciously chosen to forget about Afghanistan apart from practising tokenism by

---

10 See media reports on the Indian foreign minister S. Jaishankar's hard-hitting repartees to moralizing European foreign ministers at Raisina Dialogue Edition 2022 on 26 April 2022.

way of humanitarian aid and infrequent statements urging the Taliban to be more tolerant towards unfortunate Afghans. Whereas, in the case of invaded Ukraine, they demanded more active condemnation and active participation by India and other Asian nations; and each time such one-sided statements came, India never hesitated to emphasize that it would never betray Afghanistan and would urge other Asian nations not to do likewise. The humbug from the West has been exposed many times in many places, and in this present narrative quite a few times. But imperialist-minded Western hypocrisy seems to be boundless. They are very conscious about their rights and powers but they prefer ignorance when it comes to others.

If you want to know the best part of Afghanistan's recent history, you will have to first know this man, Commander Ahmad Shah Massoud.

INTRODUCTION

MUCH OF the text that you will go through henceforward can be explained by the definition of Afghanistan that its celebrated King Abdur Rahman Khan offered more than a century ago: 'Land of the Unruly'; 'Land of the Free'; and 'Land of Insolence'. The insolence of the Afghan, as that renowned anthropologist and historian Louis Dupree wrote, 'however, is not the frustrated insolence of urbanized, dehumanized man in Western society but insolence without arrogance, the insolence of harsh freedoms set against a backdrop of harsh mountains and deserts, the insolence of equality felt and practised (with an air of superiority), the insolence of bravery.'[11]

The geographical attributes of Afghanistan can also be described as unique in the sense that they have oriented its social, economic, political and cultural life. Perhaps what Dupree says can be further illustrated by a description of its greyness. The

---

11   Louis Dupree, *Afghanistan*, 1980 edition, Princeton University Press, Princeton, New Jersey, p. xvii.

country seems to be enveloped in this drab, non-inspirational dye that represents destruction and depression; it is literally a grey country. It does not matter which way you look, whether from the sky or the plains. To quote Dupree, 'Anyone flying over Afghanistan will be struck by the nakedness of the terrain. Bare rocks dominate dramatically everywhere above 14,000 feet or 4,270 metres.' The unbroken grey confronts you wherever you look, at the mountains, at the city, and village roads, on mud houses. It is the colour grey and the dust which invariably dominates the landscape. After a while, both elements seem to enter your body and you feel the greyness and the dust inside you. The mountains are bare, giving your eyes no relief at all from the all-pervading greyness. The famed caves at Bamyan appear to be extraterritorial with eyes fixed on giant misshapen faces. Even the permanent snowcaps offer little relief, they dazzle in the sun alright but without the soothing effect of snow in the Himalayas or the Alps or Kilimanjaro. Like the Taliban, this disturbing barrenness is also comparatively a recent development. For justifiable reasons, Afghans used to be proud of their pleasantly verdant valleys which abound in-between the high peaks of mountains. All old landscape photographs testify to the beauty that permeated this country in olden days. Fictive narratives left behind speak of scores of ideal picnic spots within accessible reach of Kabul and other cities in the North, South, East and West. Seventy odd years ago one could drive straight from the capital to the Panjsher Valley passing by unbroken greenery and waterfalls and flourishing orchards. This change was considered so serious a subject by the world community that the United Nations Environment Programme launched a scientific study on 12 September 2002 of this environmental disaster; and the necessary beautification programmes were undertaken without any delay. Experts from various countries worked together on this programme.[12]

The periodic political changes, also proved to be drastic, such as overthrow of the Sardar Mohammad Daoud government, fall of the communist governments, the end of the Soviet occupation, the reign of the Burhanuddin Rabbani-Ahmad Shah Massoud regime, followed by the first Taliban takeover—all proved to be intermittent fault-lines hindering the government in implementing projects which were aimed at improving the environment of the country. This was an important reason why the country continues to suffer from very poor environmental deficiencies, which in turn continue to affect the overall atmosphere in Afghanistan. In retrospect, it would seem that Afghanistan has always suffered from deleterious setbacks as far as political and economic stability, sustainable development and the country's ability to offer reasonably comfortable lives to Afghans are concerned. This, in turn, may have worked to enhance social and political pressure on the Taliban government that seized power in August 2021. The terrorist regime appeared to have backpedalled on several issues when the unjustifiability and inhumanity of certain situations became too embarrassing and risky. One such incident occurred in November 2021: a 14-day-old girl was sold by her parents to an old man. Traditionally, girls of even less years than the puberty level are regularly sold by their very

---

12 Apratim Mukarji, *Afghanistan From Terror To Freedom*, Sterling Publishing Private Limited, New Delhi, 2003, pp. 3-5.

poor and helpless parents in villages, especially in Southern Pashtun areas, to gangs of unscrupulous traders working in collusion with locally influential villagers. In this particular case, a similar situation occurred. The parents—though totally against parting from their new-born baby—could not escape from the clutches of an unscrupulous old man. But the incident created a sensation in social media—a phenomenon that was absent when the 'messianic terrorists' (as a perceptive analyst described the Taliban) ruled the first time—and the Taliban's attention was drawn to it. International publicity did not help the already villainous image the new rulers suffered from, and the diktat went out that not only had this sale been declared null and void and anti-Islam but also that no forced marriage would be allowed in the country anymore. But being a largely lawless country, nobody—not even the government—could ensure that such serious and unforgivable violence of human rights would not recur.

Meanwhile, four months later towards December-end 2021, the Taliban government issued a fresh order forbidding women from travelling long distances from their homes without close male relatives as escorts. The Ministry for the Promotion of Virtue and Prevention of Vice spokesperson, Sadet Akif Mujahir told the VoA, AFP and AP on 26 December 2021, women travelling for more than 45 miles (or 72 kilometres) would not be offered a taxi-ride if they were not accompanied by a close family member. Specifically, the escort would have to be a close male relative. The same order also asked people, especially taxi drivers, not to play music in their vehicles. Weeks ago, the ministry had asked Afghanistan's TV channels to stop showing dramas and soap operas featuring women actors. It also called upon women TV journalists to wear a headscarf while presenting programmes. Mujahir explained that the hijab, an Islamic headscarf, would likewise be required for women seeking transport. The Taliban's interpretation of the hijab—which can range from a hair covering to a face-veil or full-body covering—is unclear, and most Afghan women already wear headscarves. The Human Rights Watch and the US government blasted the latest decree. 'This new order essentially moves further in the direction of making women prisoners,' Heather Barr, the HRW's associate director of women's rights, told the AFP. It 'shuts off opportunities for them to be able to move about freely, to travel to another city, to do business, (or) to be able to flee if they are facing violence in the home,' Barr said. The United States Vice-President Kamala Harris told the CBS News, 'One of our big issues in terms of any conversations with the Taliban is exactly this point, which is the condition, the status and the treatment of women and girls, including for girls, access to education. I worry that the Taliban (have) not complied with what we know to be the appropriate treatment and the right treatment of girls and women. That is one of our greatest considerations and concerns.' Most ironically, however, earlier in December, the Taliban's supreme leader instructed the government to enforce women's rights. The Taliban government has since prevented most women from returning to work and schoolgirls from resuming classes across many provinces, despite pledging a more moderate rule compared to the previous time they were in power. Along with this fresh attack on women's rights came the news that the media too was being obstructed in their attempt to cover a wide range of events. The repercussions on media outlets were in line with the earlier constrictions imposed since the Taliban came to power in Afghanistan. In the first four months since 15 August 2021, Afghanistan Independent Journalists Association said 231 media outlets had been shut and over 6,400 journalists had lost their jobs during the period. Four months previously, most Afghan provinces had at least 10 privately-owned media outlets. In December, the provinces possessed no media outlets at all.[13]

Let us pause here, in this narrative of recent history, and go back to the day when Kabul and the rest of the country woke up to a long list of not 'dos' but only of 'don'ts' for women and girls. On 30 September 1996, four days after the Taliban Islamic Force entered the capital city of Kabul and took over the governance of the country, the new government issued a 10-point list of activities that Afghan women, who accounted for 25% of the total population, were hitherto excluded from. Since the publication of this list of 'banned' activities, women and girls were forbidden from doing them at the risk of severe punishment. These prohibited activities were: 1) Living without purdah: The Taliban had vowed to restore an environment where 'chastity' and 'dignity' of women were considered sacrosanct. Based on Pashtunwali beliefs about living in purdah, the burqa was made compulsory for woman in public. The regime claimed that 'the face of a women is a source of corruption' for men not related to them. Thus, girls had to start wearing burqa when they turned eight. 2)

---

13 Associated Press, Agence-France Presse, CBS News, and VoA, *Taliban Further Restrict Afghan Women With New Travel Rules*, 26 Dec., 2021.

Education: Every girl had to stop going to school when they were eight. Until then too, they were only allowed to learn the Koran. Thus, women sought education in underground schools. If caught by the Talibs they were not only flogged in public but were also executed. 3) Visit to Doctors: Women were not allowed to visit doctors or get treated by male doctors unless they were accompanied by a blood relative or husband. Many women were not even taken to doctors by family members and their illness remained untreated. 4) Showing themselves on streets, balconies and windows: Women could not walk alone on streets, without being accompanied by a blood relative and without wearing a burqa. Windows on houses situated on the ground floor and the first-floor had to be painted or screened to prevent women from being visible from the street. Women were not allowed to take a stroll in open balconies. 5) Wearing shoes or speaking loudly in public: Women were barred from wearing high-heel shoes. Reason: The Taliban did not want men to hear women's footsteps in case they got excited by it. Women were also not allowed to speak loudly in public as their voice could excite strangers. 6) Being photographed: Women's photographs were not allowed to be published in newspapers, books or displayed in shop windows. Their presence was not allowed on radio, television, or any kind of public gathering. In fact, the term 'woman' or 'women' were not to be used as a title anywhere. The names of shops that had 'woman' or 'women' on their signboards and documents were declared illegal and had to be changed overnight. The names of shops that had 'women' [like in 'Women's Saloon' or 'Women's Garden'] had to be hastily changed after the Taliban took control in September 1996. 7) Riding cycles or motorcycles:

Women were not allowed to ride bicycles or motorcycles. They could not even board a taxi without being accompanied by a close male blood relative. In fact, there were separate buses for women passengers to prevent any contact with males who were not blood relatives. 8) Freedom to marry who they want: The Taliban rule encouraged the marriage of women under the age of 16. Amnesty International reported at the time that at least 80% of women were forced into marriage before they turned 16. 9) Freedom in the domestic space: With not much freedom even inside the house, women were said to have been suffering from mental stress due to isolation. According to one of the surveys, in which 160 women took part, 87% of all women suffered from depression and 71% of them were also physically ill. 10) Applying make-up: Even wearing make-up and nail polish led to severe punishment like the cutting off of the thumb. Other punishments for breaking Shari'a law included beating on the street, striking them with metal and leather whips, and even executions.

It is in this context that we may turn briefly to Khaled Hossaini's heart-rending and utterly revolting account of life under the Taliban, *A Thousand Splendid Suns*,

'Do as you wish. But you don't get past the Taliban. Don't say I didn't warn you.' 'I'm coming with you,' Mariam said. Laila wouldn't allow it. 'You have to stay home with Zalmai. If we get stopped...I don't want him to see.' And so Laila's life suddenly revolved around finding ways to see Aziza. Half the time, she never made it to the orphanage. Crossing the street, she was spotted by the Taliban and riddled with questions— What is your name? Where are you going? Why are you alone? Where is your mahram?—before she was sent home. If she was lucky she was given a tongue-lashing or a single kick to the rear or a shove in the back. Other times, she met with assortments of wooden clubs, fresh tree branches, short whips, slaps, often fists. One day, a young Talib beat Laila with a radio antenna. When he was done, he gave a final whack to the back of her neck And said, 'I see you again, I'll beat you until your mother's milk leaks out of your bones.' That time, Laila went home. She lay on her stomach feeling like a stupid, pitiable animal and hissed as Mariam arranged damp clothes across her bloodied back and thighs. But usually Laila refused to cave in. (pp. 285-286).

In January 2022 came a statement issued by a group of human rights experts attached to the United Nations which was more damning for the Taliban than anything before. In the statement, they said that the Taliban leaders were 'institutionalizing' large-scale and systematic gender-based discrimination and violence against women and girls. 'We are concerned about the continuous and systematic efforts to exclude women from the social, economic and political spheres across the country,' the statement said. These concerns were exacerbated in the case of women from ethnic, religious and linguistic minorities, such as the Hazara, the Tajiks, the Hindus, and other communities who are even more visible and vulnerable in Afghanistan. 'Taken together, these policies constitute a collective punishment of women and girls, grounded on gender-based bias and harmful practices.' The increased risk of exploitation of women and girls including trafficking for the purposes of child birth, forced marriage as well as sexual exploitation and forced labour stood at the core of this dreadful situation. These exclusionary and discriminatory policies were being enforced through a series of measures which prevented women from returning to their jobs, required a male relative to accompany them in public spaces, prohibited women from using public transport on their own, as well as imposed a strict dress code on women and girls. 'In addition to severely limiting their freedom of movement, expression and association, and their participation in public work and to make a living, it pushed them further into poverty... Women heads of households are especially hard hit, with their suffering compounded by the devastating consequences of the humanitarian crisis in the country.' Of particular and grave concern is the continued denial of the fundamental right of women and girls to secondary and tertiary education, on the premise that men and women have to be segregated and that female students to abide by a special dress code. As such, the vast majority of girls' secondary schools remain closed and the majority of girls who should have been attending grades 7-12 are being denied access to school, based solely on their gender. 'Today, we are witnessing the attempt to steadily erase women and girls from public life in Afghanistan including in institutions and mechanisms that had been previously set up to assist and protect those women and girls who are most at risk, referring to the closure of the Ministry of Women's Affairs and the physical occupation of the premises of the Afghan Independent Human Rights Commission.'

The experts said, 'Various vital, and sometimes lifesaving, service providers supporting survivors of gender-based violence have shut down for fear of retribution, as have many women's shelters, with potentially fatal consequences for the many victims in need of such services.' Other measures aimed at dismantling systems designed to prevent and respond to gender-based violence include discontinuing specialized courts and prosecution units responsible for enforcing the 2009 Law on the Elimination of Violence Against Women and prevented aid to many women and social workers from being able to fully perform their jobs and assist other women and girls. While these measures have affected women and girls in all spheres of life, the experts highlighted their particular concern for 'women human rights defenders, women civil society activists and leaders, women judges and prosecutors, women in the security forces, women that were former government employees, and women journalists, all of them have been considerably exposed to harassment, threats of violence, and sometimes violence, and for whom civic space has been severely eroded. Many have been forced to leave the country as a result. 'We are also deeply troubled by the harsh manner with which the de facto authorities have responded to Afghan women and girls claiming their fundamental rights, with reports of peaceful protesters having often been beaten, ill-treated, threatened and in confirmed instances detained arbitrarily. We are also extremely disturbed by the reports of extrajudicial killings and forced displacement of ethnic and religious minorities, such as the Hazara, which would suggest deliberate efforts to target, ban, and even eliminate them from the country.'

The UN experts reiterated their call to the international community to step up urgently needed humanitarian assistance for the Afghan people, and the realization of their right to recovery and development. The financial and humanitarian crisis had been particularly devastating for the groups in situations of heightened vulnerability within the Afghan population, particularly women, children, minorities and female-headed households. At the same time, the international community must continue to hold the de facto authorities accountable for continuous violations of the rights of half of Afghan society and to ensure that restrictions on women's and girls' fundamental rights were immediately removed. 'Any humanitarian response, recovery or development efforts in the country are condemned to failure if female staff, women-led organizations, and women in general—particularly those from minority communities—continue to be excluded from full participation in the needs assessments as well as in the decision-making, design, implementation and monitoring of these interventions, the experts said in their statement. Significantly, women were present overwhelmingly among the UN experts who issued the broad-based statement on the treatment of women and girls under Taliban-ruled Afghanistan.

How are the people of Afghanistan faring under the Taliban rule? This question was answered in the following manner by reports on how they spent their first day of Eid-al-Fitr on 8 May 2022, three months short of the first year of the terrorist government. Thousands of Afghans had piled into buses on the day and set out down the country's once-perilous highways (the reference is to the civil war days) bound for relatives they hadn't seen for ages. Afghanistan's only national park was filled with tourists who had only dreamed till then of travelling to its intensely blue lakes and jagged mountains when fighting raged across the country. Zulhijah Mirzadah, a mother of five, packed a small picnic of dry fruit, gathered her family in a minibus, wove for two hours through the congested streets of the capital, Kabul, to a bustling amusement park. From the entrance to the park, she could hear the low whoosh of a roller-coaster and the joyous screams of Afghans celebrating Eid-al-Fitr, the holiday marking the end of the holy month of Ramadan (Ramzan). But Zulhijah could not proceed further. Women, she was told at the gate, were barred by the Taliban from entering the park. 'We are facing economic problems, things are expensive. We can't find work, daughters can't go to school, but we hoped to have a picnic in the park today,' said Mirzadah, 25. As Afghans endured the constant and random violence of the last two decades of the war, many held hopes that when peace would finally come to the country, Eid-al-Fitr would be its high water-mark, a day when families, long separated by fighting, would finally be able to celebrate the day together. Now that the war was over, people could travel freely down highways devoid of gunfire, roadside bombs and attempts at extortion. The terrifying drone of warplanes overhead was long gone. But for many the holiday that began on 8 May 2022 in Afghanistan served as a reminder of the dissonance between the promise of peace many Afghans had imagined and the realities of the end of the war. A crippling economic crisis that had slashed incomes and sent the prices of basic goods soaring forced many families to forego for the first time the Eid tradition of new clothes or dry fruit. Mosques were emptier than usual after a recent string of explosions triggering fears of the return of terrorist attacks. And many women in urban areas whose lives had been devastated by the Taliban government's restrictions, found little reason to celebrate. On 7 May, the Taliban had decreed that Afghan women must cover themselves from head to toe, expanding a series of onerous restrictions on women that dictated nearly every aspect of public life. 'To be honest, we don't have Eid this year,' said Mirzadah who spent the afternoon with her family sitting across the street from the park on a strip of grass. Most people in Kabul learned that the Taliban had announced the start of the holiday after a roar of celebratory gunfire thundered across the city on the 7 May night. Afghanistan was the first Muslim country to have officially declared the sighting of a full crescent moon kicking off the start of the holiday. The following morning, hundreds of men with prayer rugs tucked under their arms filed into the Sher Shah Suri Mosque, a huge Sunni mosque situated in the West of Kabul. Across the courtyard, they laid out the rugs in the shade of twisted tree branches while armed Taliban intelligence agents clad in camouflage pants and bulletproof vests patrolled the mosque's grounds for terrorist attack threats—a stark reminder of the threat of violence that persisted despite the end of 20 years of warfare. In the two weeks of the start of Eid this year (2022), a bloody spate of terrorist attacks on mosques, schools and public gatherings, killed at least 100 people, mostly Afghan Shiites and provoked apprehensions that the large prayer gatherings on the first day of Eid would be the next target. At the Sayed Abad Mosque, the largest Shiite mosque in the Northern city of Kunduz, more worshippers arrived for prayer on Sunday morning, 8 May 2022, more than the 400 or even 500 people who had prayed in the previous years. Many people, terrified of facing another murderous blast, steered clear of the mosque altogether.

How ordinary Afghans were conditioned to being cowed down by persistent Taliban tortures could be glimpsed through the following news that surfaced in mid-June 2022. The news was that the Taliban had detained a famous Afghan model along with three of her colleagues, accusing them of disrespecting

Islam and the Holy Koran. Azmal Haqiqi, known among Afghans for his fashion shows, YouTube clips, and modelling events, appeared handcuffed. In videos posted on Twitter by the Taliban's General Directorate of Intelligence showed the model saying, 'I apologize to the Afghan people, to esteemed religious scholars and to the Government of the Islamic Emirate.'

The statement of the United Nations panel of experts on women's rights was followed closely by the Oslo talks, the first-ever talks the Taliban held with the Afghan civil society and Norwegian officials in an initiative to normalize relations of the Taliban government with the international community. Their principal objective in joining the negotiations was, however, to earn international recognition for their government. Nearly five months had gone by since the fundamentalist force conquered Afghanistan. Once the talks started, the Taliban began to describe the event as an 'achievement in itself.'[14]

At the end of the first day of the talks on 24 January 2022, a Taliban official said the meetings were a 'step to legitimize the Afghan government.' Amir Khan Muttaqi, Afghanistan's interim foreign minister, later said, 'Norway providing us this opportunity is an achievement in itself because we shared the stage with the world.' This statement marked a divergence of outlook between the two negotiating sides, for while the Taliban were looking at the Norway talks as a means of securing recognition, the international community was contrarily interpreting the negotiations as a mechanism for channelizing

---

14 DW, *Afghanistan: How the Taliban stand to benefit from Norway talks*, 24 January 2022. https://www.dw.com/en/afghanistan-how-the-taliban-stand-to-benefit-from-norway-talks/a-60548374

humanitarian aid to ward off the looming financial, food and medical crises. It was this cumulative humanitarian crisis that compelled the world to take a fresh look at the 'untouchability' of the fundamentalist fanatical group and try to fashion a way to deal with it. For, whatever the credentials of their rulers—whom the people did not choose by themselves and whose worst victims they were—the unpleasant fact was that the Taliban were now ruling Afghanistan. The West in particular faced a unique dilemma for it was the West which had taken the initiative to undertake the task of developing a war-ravaged country in order to give a pleasant and fruitful life to its citizens. Instead, twenty years of global efforts collapsed when the Taliban smashed their way into Kabul on 15 August 2021. As the Norwegian foreign minister Anniken Huitfeldt said, 'The international community must talk to the de facto authorities in the country as it cannot allow the political situation to lead to an even worse humanitarian disaster.' But engagement with the Taliban proved to be a slippery slope for the West. The group sought recognition and financial aid for its government, and it could use the humanitarian crisis in the country as an excuse to attain that end. 'The Taliban are using the humanitarian crisis to stay relevant,' Mohammad Shafiq Hamdam, a political analyst and former adviser to the NATO in Afghanistan, said, adding that the international community should remain cautious in its negotiations with the terrorist force, 'Afghans have not recognized the Taliban as their rulers. There shouldn't be any discussion to recognize the Taliban without holding elections in Afghanistan. There should be an inclusive government respecting human rights in the country.' A Taliban representative Shafiullah Azam said, 'We are requesting them to unfreeze Afghan assets and not punish ordinary Afghans because of the political discourse. Because of the starvation, because of the deadly winter, I think it's time for the international community to support Afghans, not punish them because of their political disputes.' Shamroz Khan Masjidi, a former academic and political analyst, believed that the Taliban had intensified efforts to gain recognition for their rule.[15]

Around this time, the World Health Organization (WHO) expressed once again its concern over the basic and primary lifesaving healthcare services in the country, emphasizing that the healthcare systems were in grave danger owing to a lack of foreign financing. A report by the WHO said, 'Today, we are urging foreign contributors to step up donations and develop a new financing channel for this vital primary healthcare effort.' It said primary healthcare was the bedrock of the national health system, serving millions of citizens across the nation. The Sehatmandi programme was the pillar of Afghanistan's healthcare system. It covered nearly 64% of all public health institutions and delivered cheap, accessible healthcare to millions of citizens through 2,331 healthcare facilities in 34 provinces. However, due to the shift in Afghanistan's regime, after the Taliban took over Kabul on 15 August 2021, the Sehatmandi programme was no longer able to secure adequate financial assistance. Further, donors considered it hard to supply funds during the Taliban's conquest and substantial financing was discontinued. These crucial basic healthcare services, which were previously sponsored by the World Bank, the European

---

15 DW, *ibid*.

Commission as well as USAID, were facing major problems in the first month of 2022. In addition to this, a severe drought harmed crops as well as cattle, which led the population to suffer adversely, as per the WHO report. During the period of September-October 2021, this, along with growing food prices and the breakdown of government services, resulted in extreme food insecurity for approximately 19 million people. As the country's healthcare system continued to crumble, the Afghan Ministry of Public Health stated that it was striving to secure more foreign help for the country's health sector. Javid Hazhir, spokesperson for the ministry, revealed, 'If aid that is provided in the health sector is not distributed in coordination with the Ministry of Public Health, the crisis in the health sector may escalate and people may face many problems.'[16] The United Nations Secretary-General Antonio Guterres urged the Taliban to both recognize and uphold basic human rights 'that belong to every girl and woman.' With Afghanistan 'hanging by a thread' six months after the Taliban takeover, members of the international community had repeatedly raised concerns about the deteriorating human rights condition in the country. 'In Afghanistan, women and girls are once again being denied their rights to education, employment and equal justice. To demonstrate a real commitment to be a part of the global community, the Taliban must recognize and uphold the basic human rights that belong to every girl and woman,' Guterres said. Earlier, while briefing the Security Council on

---

16 Anwesha Majumdar, *Afghanistan's Healthcare System 'Seriously Under Threat', Foreign Donation Necessary: WHO*, 26 January 2022. https://www.republicworld.com/world-news/rest-of-the-world-news/afghanistans-healthcare-system-seriously-under-threat-foreign-donation-necessary-who-articleshow.html

the situation in Afghanistan he had affirmed, 'At this moment we need the global community—and this Council—to put their hands on the wheel of progress, provide resources, and prevent Afghanistan from spiralling any further.' Guterres also outlined actions for the de facto rulers of the country calling on the Taliban to expand opportunities and security for Afghans, uphold human rights, and demonstrate real commitment to be part of the international community. He said that Afghanistan had long been 'unfairly treated as a platform' for political agendas, geopolitical advantage, ideological dominance, brutal conflicts, and terrorism.[17]

In early January 2022, a prominent Afghan academic was arrested for publicly criticizing the Taliban government, an act which reaffirmed the universal conviction of the fanatical terrorist group's unwillingness to try to be inclusive in their handling of the administration of the country. The arrest of Professor Faizullah Jalal followed his remarks on national television made immediately after the return of the Taliban to power in Kabul, blaming them for the worsening financial crisis in the country and for routinely resorting to coercion in government. His daring acts were bound to be notorious since one of the first acts of the Taliban was to crack down on dissent of all kinds. This was the reason for the continuing suppression of women activists' street marches demanding restoration of their right to education and work and free movement. Following the professor's arrest, the Taliban spokesperson Zabihullah Mujahid

---

17 Aparna Shandilya, *Antonio Guterres urges Tan to respect women's rights*, REPUBLIC. COM, 30 January 2022.

said in a tweet that Jalal had been detained on 8 January 2022 over statements he made on social media in which he was 'trying to instigate people against the system and he was playing with the dignity of the people'. He has been arrested so that other people don't make similar senseless comments in the name of being a professor or scholar 'harming the dignity of others'. Mujahid shared screen shots of tweets he claimed had been posted by Jalal, which said the Taliban intelligence chief was a stooge of Pakistan, and that the new government considered Afghans as 'donkeys'. In one television appearance, Jalal called his co-panellist, the Taliban spokesperson Mohammad Naeem a 'calf', a grave insult in Afghanistan. Clips of his passionate criticisms went viral on social media, sparking concern in many circles that he was risking Taliban retribution.

The professor's wife Massouda, a famous personality (she was the first woman to have contested the presidency), said in a post on Facebook that her husband had been arrested by Taliban forces and 'detained in an unknown location'. 'Dr. Jalal has fought and spoken out for justice and the national interest in all his activities pertaining to human rights,' she said. A veteran teacher of law and political science at Kabul University, Jalal had long had a reputation as an uncompromising critic of Afghanistan's rulers, who, according to him, had usually fallen short of the people's expectations. On Twitter, Amnesty International confirmed the arrest of the professor. 'Amnesty International condemns the arrest of Professor Faizullah Jalal, Kabul University lecturer, for exercising his freedom of expression and criticizing the Taliban on a TV show. We call on the Taliban authorities to immediately and unconditionally release him.' TOLOnews tweeted to say, 'Professor Faizullah

Jalal has been arrested today in Kabul reportedly for making allegations against govt. departments,' a security source said, adding that Jalal is now being interrogated by the intelligence department. Jalal's family confirmed his arrest. Officials have not yet commented.[18] Such an arrest led many to question whether this government could claim legitimacy in the eyes of Afghans and of other nations as well. This question shall be examined in detail in a separate chapter. For the time being, it should be enough to say that since the violent takeover till date, no state has come forward to extend recognition to the government which is apparently ruling the country and even responding to international demands for running a normal government.

In the midst of this stalemate, there was news that surely brought a whiff of hope to the government. First, the United States government indicated that it was taking steps to start quasi-normal relations with Afghanistan. In April 2022, it signed an agreement with Qatar making the latter the 'protecting power' for American interests in Afghanistan in a very restricted manner. Then, the Indian government announced that they were considering of reopening their closed-down embassy in Kabul. In fact, the process for India started in February 2022 when a batch of security officials flew to Kabul, apparently with the permission of the Taliban government, to assess the ground situation. The change in New Delhi's position occurred when India hosted a meeting of the Shanghai Cooperation Organization's (SCO)

---

18 Dawn, Afghan professor arrested for criticising Taliban, calling intelligence chief 'stooge of Pakistan', 9 January 2022. https://www.dawn.com/news/1668502

Regional Anti-Terrorism Structure Group. India was the only country with no embassy in Kabul among the group's member-states.[19]

The case for a return to the Afghan capital was strengthened by the fact that by mid-2022, as many as 16 countries, among them Pakistan, Russia and China were maintaining their embassies in Kabul, while five Central Asian Republics had never left Kabul. The European Union (EU) also returned after the closure of the country to the outside world in August 2021 so that humanitarian work and personnel could gain a maintainable access to the Afghan people. In fact, most of the countries with functioning embassies claimed that while they were not considering according recognition to the Taliban government which was a usurper administration, they wanted a physical presence inside the country to resume their humanitarian programmes to safeguard and assist the suffering people of Afghanistan. Like all the other countries with functioning embassies in Kabul, India too emphasized that it would reopen its mission strictly to facilitate its 'liaison' work in Afghanistan and that it was not considering extending recognition to the government in power.

However, on 22 June 2022 Afghanistan was struck by the worst earthquake in the last two decades when the eastern-most province of Paktika was hit, killing, on the first count, 1,000 people and injuring another 1,500. At least 2,000 stone and mud-brick-built houses were flattened in the massive 6.1 Richter scale magnitude quake in one of the most inaccessible

---

19 Nirupama Subramanian, *India looks at reopening mission in Kabul without senior diplomats*, The Indian Express, 17 May 2022.

regions of the country, with rugged and arid mountains and almost-nonexistent roads. Poor communication systems proved to be a major blockade to the reception and distribution of aid from India and several other countries. India, incidentally, was the first country to deliver aid packages to the affected parts of Afghanistan.

The aftermath of the devastating earthquake and reaching medical and humanitarian aid to the affected people became a daunting task for the Taliban government, forcing its reclusive supreme leader Haibatullah Akhundzada to appear in public and appeal to the international community 'to help the Afghan people affected by this great tragedy and to spare no effort to help the affected people.'[20]

The extent of misery among the affected population was clear from the reports of the Bakhtiar News Agency which showed footage of people digging with their bare hands, under the rubble, for survivors. The initial estimate, that at least 2,000 houses had been destroyed, meant that counting an average of at least seven or eight members per household, at least 15 to 16,000 people had been directly affected. A health worker in a hospital in the province said on condition of anonymity that 'Many people are still buried under the soil. The rescue teams of the Islamic Emirate have arrived and with the help of local people are trying to take out the dead and injured.' However, as unsettled relations with the international community continued to persist, the supreme leader of the

---

20   Fazel Rahman Faiz, *Powerful quake in Afghanistan kills at least 1,000 people, injures 1,500*, The Indian Express, 23 June 2022.

Taliban had to clarify the government's position by declaring that in the absence of any formal relationship with the rest of the world, the Taliban government had not made any formal request for the United Nations to mobilize search-and-rescue teams or obtain equipment from neighbouring countries to supplement the few dozen ambulances and some helicopters sent in by Afghan authorities. Relief material began to trickle into the affected part of Paktika province on the following day. However, rescue and medical efforts were being hampered due to poor roads and inadequate communication lines. 'The rescue operation is finished. No one is trapped under the rubble,' said Mohammad Ismail Muawiyah, a spokesperson for the chief Taliban military commander in Paktika. Mohammad Naseem Haqqani, a spokesperson for the disaster ministry, said that while rescue operations had been finished in major districts, they were still continuing in some isolated areas. The United Nations said on 23 June 2022 that the Taliban ministry of defence had indicated as early the previous day that 90 per cent of search-and-rescue operations had finished. On 29 June, the ruler of Dubai, Sheikh Mohammed bin Rashid Al Mukhtoum sent emergency aid flights to transport life-saving humanitarian assistance which consisted of 24.5 metric tonnes of essential medicines, medical items, and cholera kits, initially supplied by the World Health Organization, from its warehouses in the International Humanitarian City, to help hundreds of thousands of people in areas of Afghanistan ravaged by the deadly earthquake. The facilitation and transport of aid came in response to the immediate humanitarian needs of the affected people. There were rumours of a cholera breakout. Giuseppe Saba, the Chief Executive Officer of the IHC, said, 'Reports indicate that this is the deadliest earthquake in two decades, further compounding the tragedy. We are accelerating the rapid response of the international humanitarian community as it rallies to come to the aid of those impacted by the disaster...Many organizations that we host in (the) IHC are working around the clock to mobilize resources, and we are coordinating with them to provide all the required support to transport relief from our warehouses into Afghanistan,' Dr. Dapeng Luo, the World Health Organization Representative in Afghanistan, said, 'The trauma and emergency surgery kits that are arriving on this flight from (the) WHO's logistics hub in Dubai's International Humanitarian City are absolutely critical to maintain our ongoing support to the people of Afghanistan as these supplies will cover the needs of at least 340,000 people. We are grateful for the vital logistics assistance provided by the UAE in support of (the) WHO's global logistics hub in Dubai.' Immediately after the earthquake, Dubai had sent 30 tons of aid, including essential food supplies to the affected country.[21]

However, while this was the general scene at the site of devastation, there were people speaking up after the earthquake how it had wiped out their homes in a matter of seconds. 'We have nothing', moaned Abdul Qadir who was digging up the ruins of his erstwhile home as he frantically kept on digging deeper and deeper. What was he looking for? His answer revealed the height of desperation that Afghans felt in Paktika. He had kept a sack of flour on the floor of the kitchen, and the quake had pushed it down somewhere under the wood and

---

21 *Dubai sends humanitarian aid to Afghanistan after deadly earthquake*, 29 June 2022, https://english.alarabiya.net/News/gulf/2022/06/29/Dubai-sends-humanitarian-aid-to-Afghanistan-after-deadly-earthquake

dust that had accumulated over the house. Like many in this desolate stretch of Eastern Afghanistan, the small bag of flour was the only food his family possessed at the time the quake hit. Half the village of Qadir lay in complete ruin.

The Afghan economy had collapsed in the aftermath of the Taliban returning to Kabul and the money flow had virtually stopped as trade had also dried up. Adir used to collect firewood and sell it in the market. Meanwhile, the price of food items had on average doubled since last August, and the poor like Qadir could no longer afford to buy food items. His debt had risen to $5,000 which he simply was not in a position to repay. In the absence of any government subsidy and no prospect of international financial aid, money would not trickle down either. There was no escape route for them any more. No shopkeeper in the market was now lending him food items. The quake had taken away six members of his family. Looking at the ruins, he said, 'This was the one comfort we still had. We have no way to get a loan, no way to get money, no way to rebuild. Nothing.' Qadir was just 27-years-old.

The extreme poverty seen in this part of Afghanistan proved that all the American and international efforts to help rebuild and reconstruct the country had not touched the people here by an iota. This was why the residents thought the Taliban rule might prove to be different and bring solace to them. That had not happened either as elsewhere in the country. And, on top of all this misery, it was Pakistan which had added more misery to the lives of people here. Pakistani militants often took shelter in this part in order to carry on their fight against the government; and the Pakistani army kept on shelling the area in order to kill them. In fact, the shelling was killing more

Afghan civilians than any Pakistani extremists.[22]

Under these extremely trying circumstances, it was extraordinary that the Taliban leadership decided to hold a three-day jirga to press the international community for immediate recognition of its government which would soon complete its first year of governance. The 3000-strong all-male gathering in Kabul issued an 11-point resolution exhorting the United Nations and its member-states to recognize the government in Kabul. It also urged the unlocking of foreign

---

22 Christina Goldbaum and Safiullah Padshah, 'We have nothing': Afghan quake survivors despair, The New York Times, 26 June 2022. On 23 June 2022 the Indian government sent a 'technical team' to Kabul where the men would be stationed at the Indian embassy to coordinate delivery of humanitarian aid. India also sent aid for the people of Afghanistan, a day after the powerful earthquake devastated a part of Eastern Afghanistan. 'First consignment of India's earthquake assistance for the people of Afghanistan reaches Kabul. Being handed over by the Indian team there,' said a spokesperson for the Ministry of External Affairs in a Twitter post, attaching a photograph of an Indian Air Force plane at Kabul airport. While New Delhi said the stationing of the 'technical team' in Kabul was meant for monitoring and coordination of delivery of humanitarian aid, it was interpreted as a first step towards reopening the Indian embassy which had lain shut since the Taliban takeover. The Ministry said in a statement on the day that 'India has a historical and civilizational relationship with the Afghan people. In order to closely monitor and coordinate the efforts of various stakeholders for effective delivery of humanitarian assistance and in continuation of our engagement with the Afghan people, an Indian technical team has reached Kabul and has been deployed in our embassy there.' This step followed the earlier delegation led by JP Singh, joint secretary in the Afghanistan, Pakistan and Iran desk in the ministry to Kabul on 2 June 'to oversee delivery operations of our humanitarian assistance to Afghanistan and met with senior members of the governing Taliban, who were otherwise considered pariah by India. However, as India by slow measures was advancing restoration of relationship with the people through aid and earthquake assistance, the pitch was suddenly queered by an attack on the lone gurudwara standing in Kabul on 18 June which was later claimed by the Islamic State-Khorasan Province, killing two and injuring three others. In an immediate response to this incident which the Taliban government had failed to prevent (of course, even attacks on mosques in the capital and other cities continued with the government unable to stop) New Delhi granted visas to 111 Sikhs in Afghanistan.

aid while pledging to take 'valuable steps in the direction of realizing national interests and people's welfare and preventing poverty and unemployment'. 'We call the United Nations and other international organizations, especially Islamic countries and organizations, to recognize (the) Islamic Emirate (Afghanistan) as a legitimate system, interact positively with it, remove all sanctions from Afghanistan, free the frozen funds of the Afghan nation, and promote economic development and reconstruction of our nation,' the resolution said according to the state-run Bakhtiar News Agency. In the resolution the Taliban also pledged allegiance to Mawlawi Haibatullah Akhundzada, the group's reclusive supreme leader, whom the resolution referred to as the 'leader of the people'.[23] 'Thank God, we are now an independent country. (Foreigners) should not give us their orders, it is our system, and we have our own decisions,' Akhundzada added. Speaking to the clerics, Akhundzada reaffirmed his commitment to the implementation of the Shari'a Law, Islam's legal system derived from the Quran, while voicing his opposition to the 'way of life of non-believers'. His words brought back to memory the unspeakable horrors of harsh punishment meted out to those who were found guilty of various offences (more women than men) and who, after judgement, were either stoned to death or executed for their 'sins'.

---

23   CNN, *Taliban labels Islamic State affiliate a 'false sect'*, Sahar Akbarzai, Ehsan Popalzai and Ivana Kottasova, 3 July 2022.

CHAPTER 1

Massoud makes first approach to the US

IN A deliberate move, I propose to introduce Commander Ahmad Shah Massoud at this early stage of this narrative in order to outline a different approach to the study of Afghanistan. Massoud strikes an observer as a man who was faultlessly dedicated to the uplifting of his country from the morass of backwardness and push it towards modernity. It is an absorbing story. We follow him as he negotiates delicate balances between conflicting parties and probable external benefactors like the United States. The latter was crucial in bringing about meaningful changes in his fortunes as a freedom fighter struggling to preserve Afghanistan's integrity amidst clouds of suspicion, conspiracies and the underhand tactics employed by his enemies such as the unrelenting Inter-Services Intelligence Directorate (ISI-D).

In addition, the treatment that Massoud received at the hands of the United States tells the story of how the most powerful country in the world failed to help this man who found himself out in the cold in the fight against the Taliban. By consciously pushing out Massoud from its Afghan perspective, the United States in effect facilitated the Taliban's return to power twenty years after their defeat. It is a moot point why Massoud was alone when his enemy, Al-Qaeda struck at him and easily did away with the man who was the single biggest obstacle against the complete domination over Afghanistan. The aftermath of Massoud's assassination took the shape it did because the United States for the first time felt the heat of global terrorism within its homeland in the aftermath of 9/11 and had to act decisively to save its own people. Thus, by his death, Massoud in a way, proved his importance in the fight against religious obscurantism and rank terrorism both in Afghanistan and the United States.

Years ago, when he was fighting the Soviet (Occupation) Army on Afghan soil, even that early he was planning to forge unity among the divided guerrilla factions in order to fight more effectively. We get a complete picture of his efforts in the unification campaign in those early days in 1986 in the diaries of his close confidant Masood Khalili, later translated into English and published as *Whispers of War*. Massoud told Khalili,

> 'Without unity and coordination, it will be very hard to win the war sooner than expected. The enemy (the Red Army) has one command and one strategy; we have lesser unity and almost no strategy. The enemy's resources are limitless but ours are much less than we require. In a guerrilla war, we need, not just to organise our warriors, but to mobilize our civilians too. This is why I try my best to mobilize the people in their own areas. If you lose the people, you lose the war. I am purposely training

some young educated fighters to do this job and also ask my commanders to always keep good relations with the common people.'[1]

'Along with everything else, we need an army for the future of Afghanistan and my goal is to lay the foundation of that army today. No doubt, it takes time, money, and a lot of sacrifice but we have to start it now. Today's organised guerrilla force should be tomorrow's army of a free Afghanistan.'

However, the United States' enduring lack of trust and, in some quarters, plain hostility towards Massoud ensured that his dream would never come to fruition and the country would have to wait to get its first modern army only after the United States and its allies put their minds and money towards that goal. It was, as was seen later, a very well-equipped and well-trained army but it preferred to lay down their arms and surrender to the Taliban when the time came to successfully conclude its campaign. We may well ask the question whether Massoud's planned army would have behaved in a similarly shameful manner. Our familiarity with his fighting history and his capacity to think ahead of events tell us that that army would have been a true army of independent Afghanistan. Before we move on to other subjects, we may recall the United States' strict directive to those who were on the ground that irrespective of what happened, Massoud's fighters must not be

---

1   Masood Kalili, *Whispers of War An Afghan freedom fighter's account of the Soviet invasion*, p. 132, trans. By Mahmud Khalili, Sage Publications India Ltd. 2017.

included in the united mujahideen force to fight the Soviet occupation army.

Khalili's account informs us that Commander Massoud was acutely aware of one major deficiency he suffered from: he was a Tajik among Pashtuns who constituted the majority in Afghanistan. He told Khalili that he and his men had to be 'as close as possible' to the Pashtun commanders of different parties. He added that he had already built close relations with some important Hazara and Uzbek commanders and that the political office of the Jamiat (the party he headed) should be closer to all other parties of all the different ethnic groups. He repeatedly and confidently told Khalili that ultimately 'we should win the war but we have to work day and night to prepare the nation and ourselves for that day'.

Commander Massoud also revealed that he had built an 'effective' spy network to infiltrate the enemy (the Soviets). He mentioned that 'some of the Kabul communist regime's commanders' were cooperating with him and had helped him to learn more about what was going on within the regime's army and police force. He mentioned Dr. Abdul Rahman and two or three others who were working very effectively in this field and added, 'A war without intelligence is like a room without windows.'

Commander Massoud analysed the strong and weak points of the Russians and of the communist regime in Kabul and said,

> They are united and have a plan, are determined, well-equipped and rich but they do not have the support of the people. We are determined and full of faith, we fight for a great cause and have the full support of the people

but we are not united, not well-equipped, and are very poor (emphasis added). Despite our deficiencies we win, because God, people and time are on our side.

He informed Khalili that he was concentrating on his upcoming operation against the Farkhan government garrison. He was confident that this would be the first government garrison to be captured by the resistance fighters. 'Its success would, Inshallah, enable us to boost morale and provide experience for the offensive phase of the war.'[2]

This author was impressed when, while visiting Commander Massoud's vast library at his home in Panjsher Valley, he found poetry books dominating the collection. All the poetry books were of course in Persian. It was, therefore, no surprise when Khalili began to note in his dairies that after the two of them had talked about the war against the Soviet occupation, the commander smiled and suggested, 'Khalili Sahib, let us read poetry. That is what relaxes us and fills our hearts with joy. Politics never ends, life does. Let us take care of the second, first.'

At his request, Khalili began to recite from memory the following celebrated poem by Hafiz:

Come, come, Oh my Beloved!
Bring me a cup of wine,
Our Life is fast, founded on the wind,
The castles of our desires are founded on the sands
Believe in no promise,
From the promise-breaking universe,

---

2 Masood Khalili, *ibid*, pp. s133-134.

> *This old window is the bride of a thousand grooms.*
> *Under the blue sky*
> *I am the slave of the one who is not dependent,*
> *Upon anything, upon anybody.*

Khalili noted in his diaries that after the recitation was over, Massoud continued to lie down on his mattress, repeating the words, not dependent upon anything, upon anybody. Then, he asked, 'Are we not fighting because of that, Khalili Sahib?' 'It is deeper than that,' Khalili responded. 'It is not only a question of freeing a piece of land but freeing our hearts as well.' He winked at the latter, and said, 'One at a time.'

One day, Khalili asked the commander point-blank, 'Commander, in the last two or three days you told me so many things about your activities on the ground but please tell me honestly, do you really believe we can defeat the Soviet army?' He did not answer for a few seconds and then replied, 'I believe with all my soul, spirit, heart and mind that we will be victorious.' The room seemed to become even more silent as his words faded into it. After a minute, he sat up in his sleeping bag and asked me in a deeper voice, 'Did you hear me, Khalili Sahib?' 'Yes, I did but tell me do you have any time limit for reaching our goal for freedom?' Quietly and calmly he replied, 'I cannot answer that question because I do not know.' Khalili sat up in his sleeping bag too and said, 'Okay, Amir Sahib, I agree that we will win the war but what do you think will happen after?' With a kind of unique intensity, he went on, 'That is exactly why we should work very hard to lay the foundations of peace in a post-war Afghanistan. It will not be easy at all. Every post-war situation is harder than the war itself, especially in Afghanistan with its strategically important but geographically difficulty location. Undoubtedly, the fight for freedom is difficult but when you finally win freedom, you need stability and stronger leadership.'

Speaking in 1986 (which we have described in part so far), Massoud was asked what had been the 'most important operation' for him so far (till 1984), and without pausing, he answered, 'It was the time of the ceasefire. It was a political, military, civil, and intelligence operation. For the most part, my forces were weak, immobilized, not very well equipped or trained, poor, and inexperienced, at least in comparison to the Soviet troops. The first thing that came to my mind was (that) if the Russians attacked, it would be nothing short of a complete massacre of my forces and of the civilian population in my (Panjsher) valley. On the other hand, the perception was that I was strong, organised, experienced, well-trained, well-equipped, and well-funded. I was in a dilemma. Now, the Russians wanted a ceasefire. As you know, I had two people in the Intelligence Ministry of the communist government in Kabul named Tajuddin and Kamran. They clearly told me that the Russian reasoning behind the ceasefire was ultimately to attack the Panjsher valley and the Shamali plains and destroy my forces. (Therefore) I had to act (swiftly). I called the Counsel of Religious Scholars, my fighters, commanders, and the elders of the people. After a week of discussions, the majority gave me their consent for a ceasefire.'

Massoud continued to speak.

'The day of the signing of the ceasefire agreement arrived. Soon after, high-ranking Russian officers came to the Panjsher valley and we signed a ceasefire agreement. We both wanted more time. They needed time to prepare for an attack and I needed time to train my men more and lay down defensive positions. As soon as we signed, the propaganda against me started. Everyone called me a traitor. The Russians were secretly spreading the rumour that they had bought me and I was their puppet. For my part, I showed everyone that I was upholding my side of the ceasefire. In the meantime, I started to send false reports to them through my double agents that we were not preparing for battle and everything was normal in the valley. Six months passed.

'I received concrete intelligence that the Russians were ready for their attack. They had all the intelligence they needed for the Panjsher valley and my forces. I was the one who had given them all the military maps of the positions and coordinates through my double agents. The Russians were going to drop commandos on each and everyone of my 34 military bases throughout the Panjsher valley. They were confident they would win. My strategy was to evacuate the common people from the valley in such a way that the Russians would not know. If they did, they would instantly attack before their planned date. The safety of the people was the most important thing. There were probably about 150,000 people living throughout the valley. The mountains were full of snow and the weather was freezing. Would the people agree to leave their homes and their valley? Would they cross the mountains with their women and children to the other side of the Hindu Kush range? The brave and loyal people accepted. It was going to be an unprecedented evacuation. It had to be done and it had to be kept secret.

'On the military side of things, I told my men to plant hundreds of mines in the places around my military bases where we thought the Russian commandos would descend. All along, we never let on that we know that they were going to attack. We got word from Kabul that in three days the Russian siege would start. I immediately called the commanders of the bases and told them to make sure that their populations were evacuated except a few that were kept back to show that everything was normal. On the day of the attack, first came the reconnaissance planes flying overhead and then the thundering sounds of dozens of attack helicopters could be heard heading toward our location. The skies of the Panjsher valley were soon filled with these sinister flying machines. Now, it was time to see if my plan would work. Would they land where I guessed they would? Would our forces be able to defend our positions? Would we have many fatalities? The helicopters began to descend and the attack started. The shadows of their combat choppers fell upon each corner of the valley as they circled and dropped their men. Each one was filled with fully-armed commandos. One group of helicopters landed in the part of the valley where the local population had their homes. Simultaneously, the others landed behind the fighters' bases. As their feet hit the ground, they triggered the mines my men had planted weeks before. My fighters, who had taken defensive positions around the drop zone, gunned down those who had not stepped on the mines. The Russians were dying. My plan was working. It was then, through the distant sounds of exploding mines and machine gun fire that the Russian generals realized (that) they had fallen into my trap. My people were safe; their commandos were ambushed. As we watched all this unfolding, Radio Kabul was announcing over and over again that my forces had been defeated, I had been killed, and that the

Panjsher valley had been overrun. They did not know yet that our poor fighters had successfully defended against the attack. Those Russian commandos who could retreat did so. Those who could not were either wounded or killed. Thank God, my forces suffered very limited casualties and (the) total victory was ours'. Massoud was silent on his role in the operation, and when I asked which was the most decisive factor, he responded in his own way, 'The people's support gave us the strength to fight better. We fought for our people and we won for them'. Then, he paused, thought for some time, and resumed speaking, 'Write in your (Khalili's) diary that there was an old man with a sick and injured son. They were evacuated one cold night with hundreds of others. He struggled to climb the snow-filled mountains with his son on his back. People offered to help him but he refused. With his back hunched with the weight and his body exhausted from the climb, he crossed the excruciatingly high wheel of the key pass. When they crossed the pass, everyone was exhausted. Each person tried to rest somewhere. The children were running around, happy to be no longer climbing. Suddenly a loud mournful cry erupted, so great that it seemed to shake the whole pass. Shocked, everyone looked around and saw the old man tenderly laying his son on the ground. He gave him a kiss on the forehead and looked at him for a long while. People gathered to see how the boy was doing, still hearing the loud cry of the father echo across the mountain top. The old man looked around, tears flowing from his eyes and said, 'I kept two things secret in my heart in order not to bring down the morale of the women and children: the death of my beloved son and the cry of my own soul.' It was here that the father announced that his son had died on the other side of the mountain. Everyone cried for both and they buried the son where the father had tenderly laid him down. One day, if we have time, we will go to see the grave of that young boy and tell him about the bravery and heroism of his father for the love of freedom.'

Khalili replied, as he wrote in his diary, 'Love and sacrifice were born together.'

Khalili, later describing how the commanders convened by Commander Massoud were reacting to his questions and advices, recorded that one of them was curious to know Massoud's mind about some of the topics they (Massoud and Khalili) were discussing, especially the policies of the West and of Pakistan towards Afghanistan.

In response, this was what the commander said, 'The time for scattered fighting, party politics, thinking individually and operating separately, is over. We have to believe sincerely in mobilizing the people and organizing our fighters to make them believe that they are one and the same. The enemy is united and we have to be united too; the government in Kabul does not sleep and tries to do whatever it takes to defeat us.'

He stopped for a few seconds and looked at each of his commanders and then resumed speaking, 'We have to do more. We have to reach out to other parties and encourage other commanders to support our efforts. We cannot do it alone and should not do it alone. Success lies in the unity of the resistance fighters. No doubt, it is a holy war (jihad) but blessings do not come without moving forward. The Russians are bringing thousands of soldiers and spending millions of dollars to win the war. We cannot defeat them until and unless we are organised and united.'

While commander Massoud had parted ways with Gulbuddin Hekmatyar and other Pakistan-sponsored Afghan mujahideen leaders and charted his lone and honest path to fight the Taliban, he made several attempts to get a sympathetic hearing from the United States. However, the substantive support he was receiving from Russia, Iran and India—all of whom were anathema to the United States—stood as an obstacle in achieving this purpose. In 1998, Massoud formally reached out to the United States in the form of a press release which was widely publicized. It was a lengthy document on the strengths and weaknesses of the Northern Alliance. It reviewed Massoud's two-decade-old struggle against the Soviet occupation, Pakistanis, the Taliban, and Al-Qaeda. The mistakes made in the past were also enumerated, with the following comment, 'Our shortcomings were as a result of political innocence, inexperience, vulnerability, victimization, bickering and inflated egos.'³

He added that his country was at that time 'entering a new stage of struggle and resistance for its survival as a free nation and independent state.' He accused 'governmental and non-governmental circles in Pakistan of sending '28,000 Pakistani citizens' as well as military wings to fight alongside the Taliban. Massoud claimed in the letter to have captured more than 500 Pakistani POWs. 'For the second time in one decade,' he wrote, Afghanistan was once again 'an occupied country.' Speaking on behalf of the freedom and peace-loving people of Afghanistan,

---

3   Ahmad Shah Massoud, *Letter to the People of America, 1998*, www.afghan-web.com/documents/let-masood-html.

he lauded '…the mujahedeen freedom fighters who resisted and defeated Soviet communism, the men and women who were still resisting oppression and foreign hegemony, and in the name of more than one and a half million of Afghan martyrs who sacrificed their lives to uphold some of the same values and ideals shared by most Americans and Afghans alike. This is a crucial and unique moment in the history of Afghanistan and the world, a time when Afghanistan has crossed yet another threshold and is entering a new stage of struggle and resistance for its survival as a free nation and independent state.'[4]

He further wrote to say that he had spent the last 20 years of his life which included most of his youth and adult life, along with his compatriots, at the service of the Afghan nation, fighting an uphill task to preserve their freedom, independence, right to self-determination and dignity. 'Afghans fought for God and country, sometimes alone, at other times with the support of the international community.' Against all odds, the free world and Afghans halted and checkmated Soviet expansionism a decade ago. But the embattled people of Afghanistan did not savour the fruits of victory. Instead they were thrust in a whirlwind of foreign intrigue, deception, great gamesmanship and internal strife. 'Our country and our noble people were brutalized,…We Afghans erred too. Our shortcomings were as a result of political innocence, inexperience, vulnerability, victimization, bickering and inflated egos. But by no means does this justify what some of our Cold War allies did to

---

4   Ahmad Shah Massoud, *ibid*.

undermine this just victory and unleash their diabolical plans to destroy and subjugate Afghanistan.'

Today (in 1998) the world clearly 'sees and feels the results of such misguided and evil deeds'. South-Central Asia was in turmoil, some countries were on the brink of war. Illegal drug production, terrorist activities and planning were on the rise. Ethnic and religiously-motivated mass murders and forced displacements were taking place and the most basic human rights and women's rights were shamelessly violated. The country had gradually been occupied by fanatics, extremists, terrorists, mercenaries, drug mafias, professional murderers. One faction, the Taliban, which by no means 'rightly represents Islam, Afghanistan, or our centuries-old cultural heritage, has with direct foreign assistance exacerbated this explosive situation. They are unyielding and unwilling to talk or reach a compromise with any other Afghan side'.

Naming Pakistan directly for the first time in the letter, Massoud wrote that unfortunately, this 'dark' accomplishment could not have materialized without the direct support and involvement of influential and non-governmental circles in Pakistan. Aside from receiving military logistics, fuel and arms from Pakistan, 'our intelligence reports indicate that more than 28,000 Pakistani citizens, including paramilitary personnel, and military advisers are part of the Taliban occupation forces in various parts of Afghanistan'. At the time of writing the letter, Massoud informed Americans that 'Northern Alliance forces were holding more than 500 Pakistani citizens including military personnel in their POW camps. Three major concerns—terrorism, drugs and human rights—originated from Taliban-held areas but were instigated from Pakistan, thus forming the inter-connecting angles of an "evil triangle".' 'For many Afghans, regardless of ethnicity or religion, Afghanistan, for the second time in a decade, is once again an occupied country.' Massoud cautioned the international community that it would be pointless to expect a Taliban-led Afghanistan to enjoy 'stability, peace and prosperity in the region.'

The goal was clear, Afghans wanted to regain their right to self-determination through a democratic or traditional mechanism acceptable to the people. 'No one group, faction or individual has the right to dictate or impose its will by force or proxy on others. But first, the obstacles have to be overcome, the war has to end, just peace established and a transitional administration set up to move us toward a representative government.' Inviting other stakeholders to get together to start affirmative discussions towards that objective, as spelt out above, Massoud once again reminded the United States and other democracies of their responsibilities towards fulfilling the democratic aspirations of the Afghan people, and not tolerate any more the divisive, anachronistic, fanatic and intolerant forces that were pushing Afghanistan away from peace and democracy.

The letter was a clarion call not only to the government and people of the United States but also to the rest of the world which had somehow been lackadaisical in respect of his country.

But an unwieldy United States scarcely responded, which made Massoud's political adviser, Daoud Mir, say in an interview to Le Figaro that 'the US should intervene in Afghanistan…

Quite simply, they have no choice'.⁵ But such impeccable logic accompanied by rhetoric failed to open the closed doors of the US, Department of State, forcing the commander to shift his attention to France and the European Parliament. He wrote a letter to Vice-President Dick Cheney in early 2001 reiterating his request for assistance. Unbelievably, this letter remained unacknowledged and unanswered. In March 2001, just weeks after this letter was written, the Taliban targeted the Bamian Buddhas and left only tale-tell holes on the face of the hill.

---

5 Patrick de Saint Exupery, *The US Envoy Bill Richardson in Kabul: Afghanistan is at the heart of the Great Game*, Le Figaro, 17 April 1998.

CHAPTER 2

The Saga of the Commander

THE 'LION of Panjsher' Massoud's manifold exploits also included a plot, hatched jointly with an equally patriotic and independent commander, Abdul Haq, the 'Lion of Kabul', to topple the Taliban by organizing a country-wide military campaign under the tutelage of the National Commanders' Shura (Council) and restore Afghan independence. Simultaneously, Zahir Shah, the former king then living in Rome, would be encouraged to lead a campaign to build a political leadership to run alongside the National Commanders' Shura in order to prepare the field for a civilian government to be installed after the defeat of the Islamist fundamentalists. The idea was that while Massoud was playing a stellar role in uniting Tajiks, Uzbeks, Hazara and other ethnic minority groups in the war against the Islamist fundamentalists, Haq could do likewise with the Pashtuns, the country's dominant community, and motivate them against the predominantly Pashtun Taliban. But there were flaws in the composition of this joint front for complete trust was missing between Massoud and Haq. In 1992, when Najibullah's government was tottering, Massoud had brushed aside Haq's proposal to join forces, to form an 'inter-ethnic' front, to protect Kabul from marauding mujahideen. The incident was still fresh in Haq's mind. Therefore, the idea of a combined moderate Pashtun-Tajik leadership to counter the Taliban, comprising of Massoud, Haq and Karzai, appeared to be standing on unstable ground.[6]

The plot that Haq unfolded at a meeting with 'unofficial' Americans with access to the US State Department, worked upon and gave shape to in June 2001 just two months before 9/11, involved former King Zahir Shah, and some Pashtun and Tajik leaders, such as, Hamid Karzai, Abdul Haq and Ahmad Shah Massoud; but first a loya jirga (general council) of representative stakeholders committed to fighting jointly against the Taliban had to be convened and the plot approved. This was the traditional Afghan way of reaching an inclusive agreement over a local, regional or national issue. Here, the issue was how to oust the Taliban by a joint military campaign to be conducted by the Military Commanders' shura which would involve the entire country and its people who did not want the fundamentalists to continue further. The loya jirga's task was to establish an alternate political narrative and re-establish an Afghan army and prepare a constitution. These ideas were expostulated by Massoud who said, 'As I see it, all favour a constitutionally-based, democratic central government. Political parties will contest elections and represent their communities at the centre. All ethnic groups should have a place in the interim government.' By a historic quirk of fate, all these democratic

---

6   P. Tomsen, *ibid*, pp.558-585.

institutions would come to be established after the Taliban and Al-Qaeda had been ousted not by the National Commanders' shura but by Operation Enduring Freedom involving the United States and its allies and the whole world through the United Nations. It would take another twenty years, till August 2021, for the Taliban to be back in office in Kabul, by which time Commander Massoud had been removed from the scene.[7] Experts on Afghanistan will surely remain grateful for the gems of intimate information that dot Tomsen's book, *The Wars of Afghanistan*. His frankness in exposing the awful shallowness of junior-level American diplomats and intelligence operatives is simply astounding; but in choosing this process he continues to enable us to get a fuller picture of foreign policy formation at Washington, a piece of knowledge that also helps us to understand why the coordinated devastating aerial attacks on the American soil happened despite the availability of abundant intelligence inputs. Tomsen writes devastatingly in a telegram sent to the State Department roughly two months before the Al-Qaeda-engineered attacks:

> 'Aside from Massoud's success in building coordination among several important commanders, there is not yet tangible evidence that he, Abdul Haque and other anti-Taliban Afghans can construct a nationwide alternative to rally support against the Taliban and, in a transition period, avoid the conflict among regional commanders which occurred in 1992-1996. Haq and Massoud plan to increase consultations with other anti-Taliban and Afghan

---

7   P. Tomsen, *ibid*, pp.574-578.

leaders in the weeks ahead. The US should encourage this process. While a long shot, the success of moderate Afghans in replacing the Taliban regime in Kabul would be the most effective way to address the terrorist, radical Islamist and narcotics problems menacing the world from Afghan territory.'[8]

And how did this effort, involving at least two other American citizens and some of the most distinguished Afghans including the former King of Afghanistan and the Italian government of the day, come to nought? The efforts of these gentlemen across three continents met with a stony silence after Tomsen briefed the then US Assistant Secretary for South Asia, Christina Rocca. But we had better listen to Tomsen himself: 'Rocca did not respond. She ended the conversation after fifteen minutes by saying that her next appointment was waiting.'

Steve Coll, however, lets us glimpse a unique example of the cross-purposes at work within the US establishment across various presidencies regarding Commander Massoud. During President Bill Clinton's time, Massoud was clearly and seemingly permanently out of favour. President Clinton agreed with his team that (by 1999) Massoud had been reduced to a 'spent' force, his Northern Alliance was 'tainted and in decline'.

However, reflecting the deep division between the President's office and the Department of State and the Central Intelligence Agency (CIA) on the advisability of aiding Massoud, the CIA and especially inside the Counterterrorism

---

8   P. Tomsen, *ibid*, pp. 574-575.

Centre, career officers passionately described the commander by 1999 as the United States' 'last, best hope to capture or kill Osama bin Laden in Afghanistan before his Al-Qaeda network claimed more American lives. 'Massoud might be a flawed ally,' they declared, 'but bin Laden was by far the greater danger.'[9]

The one act of alleged perfidy (because Massoud later insisted he never received the money in his hand) committed by Massoud was in respect of a cash payment of $500,000 to the Northern Alliance. In 1990, the CIA's secret relationship with Massoud 'soured' because of a dispute over this payment. Gary Schroen, a CIA officer then working from Islamabad, Pakistan, had delivered the cash to Massoud's brother in exchange for assurances that Massoud's forces would attack Afghan communist forces along a key artery, the Salang Highway. But the forces never moved, so as far as the CIA could tell. Schroen and other officers believed they had been ripped off for half-a-million dollars. This alleged breach of faith along with old records of massacres of rival mujahideen fighters and involvement in drug smuggling continued to vitiate the relations between the US administration and the commander but by and large, the contacts between the CIA, its Counterterrorism Centre and Massoud survived and even managed at times to be quite warm and frequent. As Coll later wrote, 'the mission codenamed JAWBREAKER-5 which flew to northern Afghanistan from 1999 onwards was targeted to revive secret intelligence and combat operations against Osama bin Laden in partnership with Commander Massoud. We have

---

9 Steve Coll, *Ahmad Shah Massoud links with CIA* 'The CIA had pumped cash stipends as high as 200,000 a month to Massoud and his Islamic guerrilla organization'

a common enemy, said the team leader, later identified upon personal consent, as Gary Schroen, meaning bin Laden. But Washington's sole target was the destruction of Osama bin Laden and his Al-Qaeda and consequently, the Taliban, the main enemy of Afghans, was not on the agenda at all. This would be revealed to Massoud and his men at every step as negotiations for further cooperation continued. Despite his utmost efforts, the commander could not succeed in his efforts. The US government rejected the concept of a military confrontation with the Taliban or direct support for any armed factions in the broader Afghan war. Instead, US policy focussed on capturing bin Laden and his lieutenants for criminal trial or killing them in the course of an arrest attempt. If Massoud helped with this 'narrow' mission, the CIA officers told him, perhaps it could lead to wider political support in the future.

Thereafter, regular help flowed to Massoud in the form of 'formal' groups from the CIA, the first of which was codenamed NALT-1, while three more teams delivered strategic equipment and funds to the Afghan side by the summer of 1999. The electronic intercept equipment they delivered allowed Massoud to monitor Taliban battlefield radio transmissions. In exchange, the CIA officers asked Massoud to let them know immediately if his men ever heard accounts on the Taliban radio indicating that bin Laden or his top lieutenants were on the move in a particular sector. But this round of collaboration remained strictly bound to the bin Laden issue; all mention of Taliban was forbidden. President Bill Clinton was fixated on restraining Massoud's role to assisting the US in tracing bin Laden and his top aides and that was all because the president was convinced that the commander was not up to defeating the Taliban and ruling Afghanistan from Kabul. At a critical juncture, this donkey-oriented policy prevented an early destruction of the Taliban, who would be destined to rule the country once more from 2021 onward. Throughout the relationship between Commander Massoud and the American government, a common thread was the massive mismatch between the aims of the two sides, with the US administration chasing only the specific target of capturing Osama bin Laden alive and Massoud's pursuit of a military confrontation with the Taliban. This mismatch sometimes produced hilarious results some of which were faithfully detailed in Steve Coll's excellent and exclusive account. The outcome is well-known, documented many times over, and Afghanistan continues to pay a heavy price even now. Massoud used to lament that the US policy on the Taliban was 'all wrong', and there cannot be any other description.

CHAPTER 3

The 'Sins' of the Commander

NO DISCUSSION on Commander Massoud can be comprehensive without referring to his tally of 'sins' drawn up in official American eyes. Here is the list provided by Coll: Massoud's deep links with the Russians usually prevented him from taking a stand against them. This was a result of America's denial of aid, funds, and equipment; denial coming from the White House and State Department levels. Also Massoud had entered into a secret pact with the Soviets, a fact exposed by a former Soviet army general. Besides, there was Amnesty International's condemnation of the execution of six people by Massoud's fighters and the massacre of 85 educated men in the Panjsher Valley where Massoud's writ was the only law during his war with the Soviet occupation army and the Taliban. A 'serious' sin was committed when Massoud approached India and the latter agreed to help him in various ways; and yes, Russia gave 'three' helicopters to Massoud in which CIA men flew on several pro-Massoud missions; in February 1993, five thousand were killed in 25 days when the capital was being defended by Massoud's militia; 10,000 were killed in eight months in

Kabul; Massoud was accused of giving shelter to 'most wanted terrorists'. After Massoud's men entered Kabul in 1992, they used their guns (!); public executions were conducted by the Burhanuddin Rabbani-Ahmad Shah Massoud government in 1992; and perhaps the truly heinous crime when Massoud's men burned books after raiding Kabul University in 1993. Finally, the US establishment continued to raise two questions: Was Massoud comparable to the Angolan freedom fighter and leader of the African country's 'total' revolution Jonas Savimbi and was Massoud a deserving candidate for the Nobel Peace Prize? The two questions raised mainly by the Americans show that they remained enormously sceptical of Massoud's 'genuineness' as an example-setting and universally inspiring figure. On the other hand, Afghans who commemorate Massoud's assassination day as the 'Massoud Day' were shocked to hear of the American objection when a group of French parliamentarians recommended Massoud for the Nobel Peace Prize a year after his assassination in 2001. On 9 September 2002 the Interim Administration headed by Hamid Karzai organised an international conference on the commander; and there, as has been recounted in the Acknowledgement of this book, Europeans in particular did not hide their boundless admiration for Massoud.

All analysts of the United States' Afghan policy have zeroed in on the State Department's invariable penchant for backing America's enemies and disfavouring its friends. The ISI of Pakistan, which followed a persistent anti-American policy in Afghanistan, was much favoured in Washington while all pro-American Afghans were habitually looked down upon, and this illogical propensity was extended even to former American diplomats, defence and intelligence officials. One of them, Tomsen, writes:

> I began to question basic assumptions underlying US Afghan policy and advocated change. Before the Tanai coup,[10] I had grown increasingly convinced that Pakistan was playing a two-faced Afghan policy. The Pakistani foreign ministry's criticism of Beg[11] and Gul's[12] support for an Afghan military victory in Afghanistan, echoed by Edmund MacWilliams and other disgruntled US embassy diplomats, was the first sign of fundamental differences on the United States' Afghan policy. During the following eight months up to the Tanai coup (referred to earlier), the ISI's blatant favouritism for Hekmatyar, the assassination of moderate Afghans in Peshawar, and the ineffective irremediable AIG also indicated that our Pakistani ally was playing a double game. I thought that the Tanai coup attempt could not have a rogue operation. The ISI was firmly inside the Pakistani military hierarchy and General Beg was Pakistan's military commander. (However) CIA officers objected to my assessment that a battlefield stalemate existed in Afghanistan. They claimed

---

10 P. Tomsen, *The Wars of Afghanistan...*, pp.394-397. Shanawaz Tanai, a Pashtun, was a feisty Khalqi commander who later challenged President Najibullah in 1990 and, when cornered, escaped to Pakistan and came under ISI patronage, through which he eventually joined the Taliban.

11 Tomsen, *ibid*, Mirza Afzal Beg, Pakistan army chief of staff (1988-1991), worked closely with the ISI director-general Hamid Gul to install Gulbuddin Hekmatyar through whom he worked to influence Afghan politics to the detriment of Afghan interests.

12 Ib, Gul Agha Sherzai, a powerful, corrupt, Pashtun warlord, close to the ISI, was governor of Kandahar province (1992-1994), after the defeat of the Taliban was appointed a minister and special adviser in the President Hamid Karzai cabinet.

the mujahideen were winning. Others advocated... a Najib-Mujahideen power-sharing coalition government. These discussions, talks and back-talks among American legislators, military, CIA, and diplomats in essence led to a continuation of the traditional American policy towards Afghanistan and Pakistan.

The Taliban ultimately came to power in 1995-1996 and were in turn ousted in November 2001. But as this book is a history of the Taliban's second coming to power, US policy lies exposed as being incapable of formulating an effective Afghan policy. Otherwise, its ignominious 'escape' (officially 'withdrawal') from Afghanistan, leaving the country and its people to fend for themselves, leads to only one conclusion: Afghanistan is the burial-ground of America's Afghan policy.

In a scintillating and revealing analysis of the United States foreign policy and the behaviour pattern of the 'liberal' establishment in Washington including members of the Republican and Democratic Parties in Congress, their relations with the foreign policy establishment in the Department of State, the defence establishment in Pentagon, and media and academics all leaning towards 'liberal' ideas, James Carden seeks to explain the anomalies and results thereof. He starts by quoting the mid-20th Century Protestant theologian Reinhold Niebuhr to the effect that he could have recognized the 'irony of a foreign policy that continually enters into alliances (both covertly and overtly) with groups and causes that are themselves the very antithesis of the values that the US foreign policy and defence establishments claim they are defending the world over. Over the past several years, the weaponization of 'woke' politics has had numerous ramifications across the United States. And among the most ominous of these has been the burgeoning alliance of woke liberals and progressives and the unaccountable careerists who staff the US foreign policy bureaucracy and the military-media-defence nexus that has cynically adopted the language and mores of the woke opposition in the service of American global hegemony'.[13] We will resume discussion on this topic in a later chapter but it should be mentioned at this stage that John J. Mearsheimer had first identified this malady and has since consistently analysed American foreign policy in the light of this theory, but Carden's use of the word 'woke,' meaning 'in torpor; or 'ceaseless sleeping' admirably captures the mood of the entire situation of continuous bungling.

Soon after the United States invaded Iraq in March 2003, the messy aftermath began to chasten the administration and forced it to realize that America lacked troops and international backing to force North Korea to abandon its demonstrably more advanced and threatening nuclear weapons programme. Slowly Washington began to give out signs of appreciating anew the awkward compromises that had governed relations among nation-states since the Treaty of Westphalia in 1648. Thus, in the name of catching Osama, President George W. Bush preferred to ignore Pakistan's nuclear sins.

The Bush government realized that getting to the bottom of Pakistan's nuclear proliferation programme would put General Pervez Musharraf into serious trouble and embolden the powerful Islamist political parties which shared power in

---

13 James Carden, *The irony of America's 'woke' foreign policy, Asia Times* 2 February 2022. https://asiatimes.com/2022/02/the-irony-of-americas-woke-foreign-policy/

the Musharraf government and ran militias with long-standing associations with Al-Qaeda. As had already happened in Saudi Arabia, the most likely alternative to the questionable regime in Islamabad were the very jihadis who had been tolerated so long. As a matter of fact, Bush was just following the policy that his predecessors had adopted over the previous two decades. In the 1980s when Washington's sole aim was to dislodge the Soviet occupants of Afghanistan, the United States kept its eyes closed to Pakistan's so-called 'Father of Pakistani (or Muslim) Bomb' Abdul Qadeer Khan and to the Pakistani establishment's pursuit of nuclear weapons and delivery systems.

For the United States and of course for the rest of the world, the direct consequence was that jihadis in Pakistan became enormously influential in Pakistani society, forcing successive governments to go soft on these terrorists. The first and foremost consequence was the Pakistani jihadis' uncontrolled forays into Afghanistan to further promote Pakistan's Afghan policy. The Indian state of Kashmir was equally affected with Pakistani terrorists trying to push their agenda to disturb peace and stability in the Indian state.

Thus, the Pakistani nuclear weapons programme aimed at promoting Islamabad's interest in two neighbouring states, Afghanistan and India. Pakistan and its President Musharraf were living happily in this conducive atmosphere but Osama intervened—most inconveniently, one would say—obliging Musharraf to execute what has been colourfully described as a '180 degree turn'.[14]

---

14   Jonathan Randal, *Osama The Making of a Terrorist*, Alfred A. Knopf, New York, pp.288.-290.

However, despite this state of affairs, the sole aim of American foreign and defence policy was capturing or killing Osama bin Laden. As Washington looked at it, after the airborne assaults on American soil had shattered peace and tranquillity all over the United States and had taken the lives of nearly 3,000 Americans, no alternative was left but to ensure the survival of the Bush administration and finish off the world's most feared terrorist. Even the deplorable conditions in which American troops were fighting in Iraq caught in a deadly quagmire were ignored and the entire attention was focussed on the mastermind of 9/11 and its other perpetrators. However, an American revenge on Osama could lead to unfathomable repercussions in Pakistan where the authorities in Islamabad could only cooperate with Washington up to a certain limit and no further. The strategy, therefore, was to exploit the weakly-placed Musharraf to achieve their goal: getting at Osama (preferably dead). However, the problem was how to locate American troops and FBI and CIA agents on Pakistani soil without causing a political upheaval in the country? For, Washington did not want to jeopardize Musharraf in any way. That was a given.

However, despite the open declarations of revenge against Osama, it was not conclusively made clear if removal of Osama would lead to durable peace and put a stop to jihadi activity. A perfect example was available in Iraq where Saddam Hussein's capture and death did not end the insurrection against the West. Saddam Hussein's death merely changed the colour of the resistance, from one weighed down by Saddam's 'terrible legacy' to a single-minded resistance to a Western occupation force. Above all, Osama made his discovery as difficult for Americans as possible by not just moving from place to place but also because there was the persistent suggestion in jihadi circles that the Emir had instructed his bodyguards to martyr him rather than allow his capture. Not for him the videotaped humiliation of Saddam's medical inspection for lice at the hands of an American military doctor. Osama had no desire to finish his days as a 'caged prisoner' to be exhibited in his enemy's capital. Washington also might as well prefer to have him dead rather than put him on trial in an American court and run the risk of inspiring the world's 1.2 billion Muslims with tales of bravado. At stake was the future of the myth he had come to symbolize. Beyond the mechanism of perpetuating his legacy, Osama had succeeded in isolating the United States internationally in ways which even the Soviet Union had not been able to achieve in its heydays. Eventually, the Bush government had to acknowledge that its 'muscular' foreign policy and military interventionism had worked greatly to the disadvantage of American prestige and foreign policy so thoroughly that to put it in the words of one commentator, 'it will take us (the US) many years of hard focussed work to restore America's international standing.'[15]

The conclusion that Randal reached about the supreme folly of President Bush was to indelibly identify his country with

---

15 Margaret Tutwiler, in discussing her new State Department job in charge of public diplomacy, Edward Djereji, former American ambassador to Israel and Syria, concluded that 'the bottom had indeed fallen out of support for the United States' after submitting a report on the problem the previous October at Congressional request. As reported in The New York Times, 5 February 2004.

Israel, the Arabs' 'worst enemy'. Israel was also mentioned by John J. Mearsheimer and James Carden, both already discussed in the text above. The fact is that throughout many decades the United States and the powerful Jewish lobby in America had succeeded in persuading successive American governments to turn a blind eye to Israel's anti-Arab and anti-Muslim policies, thereby permanently stamping their policy towards the Arab and Muslim world with a strongly committed pro-Israeli stance. An example was available when in 2006 Israeli extremists celebrated over two days the 60th anniversary of the deadly bombing of the King David Hotel in Jerusalem by Irgun, the Jewish group then led by Menachem Begin (later to become Israel's prime minister) in which 90 innocent boarders including 28 Britons were killed. This was during the tenure of Binyamin Netanyahu. The celebration was tolerated by the Israeli government which ignored Britain's official and public protest.[16] However, as Sayid Seleem Shahzad has pointed out, the 'neo-Taliban', the Taliban who had made a spectacular but very well-calculated and executed comeback in Afghanistan over the previous two decades since their 'eradication', had established and prepared the launching-pad for exporting jihadism to newer pastures, particularly in Muslim countries where popular disenchantment with their ruling establishments had reached a dangerous level of frustration. Pakistan was ripe for ranking in this category of Muslim countries; and the 'neo-Taliban [the 'new' Taliban are assessed to be distinctly different

---

16 Hasan Saroor, *Celebrating terror, Israeli style,* The Hindu, 24 July 2006.

from the 'old' Taliban who were almost entirely indoctrinated in Islamist ideology and received military training in the North-West Frontier Province of Pakistan (today's Pakhtoonkhwa)] were already moving to expand their areas of control inside Afghanistan's South and East. According to an anonymous senior member of the Taliban, cutting off NATO's supply line from Pakistan was an important element in the terrorists' strategy. 'If it is correctly implemented (the year is 2008), NATO will have to leave Afghanistan in 2009, although we may need an extra year.'

This strategy took the Taliban far from its traditional bases in the port city of Karachi and the supply line connecting it with Kandahar and Kabul. On 9 May 2008 the Pakistani manager of the container fleet that took oil supplies from Karachi to Kabul was kidnapped and his whereabouts were not known at the time Shahbaz was writing his article. In August 2008 about 30 Taliban members attacked a weapons convoy as it was leaving Karachi, which attested to the quality of the group's intelligence. A Western security expert explained that some Taliban bases in Southern Afghanistan were running on almost empty fuel tanks and were forced into 'stopping all movements and offensive operations because of fuel shortages'. Observers agreed that Pakistan remained central to Al-Qaeda and Taliban strategy.

'The neo-Taliban's immaculately planned victories in East Afghanistan has enabled (them) to devise the next stage. Since the number of tribals in East Afghanistan has dwindled because of migration to Iraq, deaths and arrests, a new core formed from other nationalities has taken over the task. Their stated goal is to remove the Western coalition from Afghanistan and

Iraq, and lay the foundation for the liberation of Palestine. And ensure new battles as part of the vision of the arrival of the Mahdi.'¹⁷

The question is what lay behind the astonishing growth of Al-Qaeda and other Islamist terrorist groups? It was the Drug Connection, about which more particulars will be available in the following pages of this book.

---

17 The Mahdi (the Guided One) is an eschatological Messianic figure in Islam who is believed to appear alongside Isa the Prophet (Jesus) and establish the divine kingdom of God on earth, *Wikipedia*,

CHAPTER 4

The Scorn of the People

BEFORE WE wade through the hope-filled, hate-soaked social media posts in order to get a glimpse of how Afghans, mainly the young educated ones in Afghanistan and in exile abroad really felt, we will have the simplest possible explanation of why the Taliban, despite the people's ample fear of their ideology and performance, succeeded in coming back to power. Let us listen to Masood Khalili, about whom readers are already aware. Khalili writes in his celebrated diaries, *Whispers of War*, 'You might ask, What are the reasons for the situation remaining the same and the poor people of Afghanistan not seeking peace in their war-torn country?' Let me try and make it easy for you. The corrupt Afghan government's lack of honesty; absence of trusted leader(s); insufficient rule of law; political instability; open interference of neighbours, especially Pakistan, by sheltering, encouraging, training, financing, and arming terrorists; the poorest economy in Asia; global terrorism; and the gradual weakening and even relative withering away of international interests for Afghanistan are sadly the causes pushing the situation for the country to look even scarier and more brutal'.

Now, we are ready to look into social media and see what has been happening there after the return of the Taliban on 15 August 2021. How do you assess, from the outside, what is happening inside and how Afghans are reacting to the situation while all access to the country is barred? As the Taliban closed down Afghanistan after seizing power in August 2021, social media became a great means of venting anger and frustration for Afghan citizens. The young tech-savvy generation which was well-aware of the benefits of modern education nevertheless had many in their ranks who preferred to 'sincerely' follow the mullahs. This dichotomy appeared to represent the real Afghanistan as it adjusted itself to an indefinite rule by the Islamist forces. But the majority of netizens one did come across in certain websites and chat groups brought into focus daring and honest persons who anonymously took their new rulers to task. Najmia Khatibi wrote in Facebook, 'Mysterious murders of women in Afghanistan; the body of a young girl in West Kabul. On 8 March 'International Women's Day,' the mysterious murders of young girls in Afghanistan have increased. Public sources in Western Kabul confirm that the body of a young girl with closed hands (Sunday, 1937) was found in the alley of the Evolutionary School in the Barchi Plains. Sources claim that the girl was also sexually assaulted. In images published on social media of the girl, she shows her hands and legs closed on occupations. 'The identity of this girl has not yet been established. Taliban officials in Kabul security command have not said anything about this so far. This is while a few days ago, two young girls were murdered mysteriously in Balkh province. Their bodies were found on Thursday (Thursday, 1398 HUT) in the vicinity of the happy

Tangi of Mazar-e-Sharif. Ahmad Mohid wrote on the same page in defence of the 'Islamic' system that the Taliban had brought to Afghanistan for the second time in twenty years, 'The Islamic system is the result of the blood of thousands of martyrs that have been shed in the past 20 years to form the Islamic system. No one is allowed to break the Islamic system and still from Afghanistan there is no threat to any country in the world and we also ask from the countries of the world that out internal affairs should not interfere (should not be interfered with?) and discuss issues that cannot be discussed with us before the divine sovereignty of Afghan culture because they are not negotiable.' A woman, no doubt very bold, Skokriya Amiry was sharp in her counter-comment, 'This system is not Islamic system. These violent groups are made by the United States and the West, they are created to secure the interests of the United States of America and the West.' But the logic of her argument seemed to be lost in the resultant complexities of ideologies. Another post in the Facebook page of the chat group, 'Friends stay connected', cited the murder of a Special Forces officer of the Ashraf Ghani government, allegedly by the Taliban: 'The everyday crime of Taliban. Faizal Shirzai, a special Special Forces, who was arrested by the bloody Taliban group about a month ago, died of torture and mental pressure today (8 March 2022). His relatives have said the Taliban injected him with shots during interrogation so that he could slowly die. Shiraz's family could not see him during his period of incarceration. The probability of the drug injection is strong. He could not talk. The T(aliban) knew he won't be able to talk. So they released him.' Benafsha Sayeed Zada, an English major and teacher, advisor and psychologist, and a former Psychological Counsellor at War Child Canada for a brief period, ran her page with the arresting tagline, 'Raise your daughter like a queen.' This must have attracted a good deal of attention in a country where traditionally women and girls have been subjected to unmitigated deprivation of everything that makes life worth living. Around 6-7 March 2022, on the eve of the International Women's day, she posted the following: 'If life was a rainbow! Women are the colours of this rainbow… Today is the day we celebrate your existence. I wish you the beauty and charm of gold. May you blossom…' Another post by a netizen read, 'Long live Ferrari Baba' in a sharp rebuke to a senior Afghan leader.

More rarely, finer sentiments crept into the Facebook posts, like a son posting on the International Mother's Day in early May 2022: 'Mother, I love you. A man whose faith and separation tremble at the approach of a woman, who is shaken and provoked, is not a man but a devil(s)…' It is obvious that as the Taliban rule was going to last, their suppporters inside Afghanistan were growing bolder and more challenging in their verbal exchanges with those who were critical of the Taliban or lived abroad. Here is an exchange between two such men, Naziz Durrani, a critic, posted a number of photographs showing Taliban fighters hooting and celebrating raucously while standing atop a few vehicles running along a road, and commented: 'The whole filth is emanating from them (the Taliban), they should cleanse their filth and then repent.' Jawad Azimi, a Taliban supporter, hit back, 'They did not put filth in your mouth.' Naziz Durrani responded, 'Your dad ran away and now you are sleeping in the corner of the house.' Shaheen Popalzai, another Taliban supporter, came on the scene, 'Whether we want it or not, the country belongs to the Taliban. What did they do in Ghani's government? You tell me. Don't be afraid of the truth. You either don't understand politics or you (just) don't know. So don't talk unjustly. Tell me who was stealing and who was killing people?'

Following the Facebook posting of a photograph showing Uzbek-Afghan leaders in Ankara in mid-May 2022, the social media users burst forth in stinging satire and ridicule of their leadership's quality. Homara Sharif, in all probability an assumed name, wrote, 'Oh no, all the moustaches are now gathering behind the curtain. They don't trust each other and, therefore their promises are worth nothing! They killed, robbed and plundered with impunity! Have they already drawn the map of a fragmented Afghanistan? None of them is ready for a long drawn-out guerrilla warfare; they have learnt nothing. It is again the sons and daughters of the poor and the deceived who will die! What service can be rendered by this group of traitors? People want freedom from ignorance and poverty, they want to dream and to find happiness, they certainly do not want the Abu Jahi group! These people are not the answer to our question! Baji Zekriya Ahadi, seemed to be astonished, 'Great God, all of them are in Ankara. If they are not worthy of guidance, may they be destroyed so that our poor nation gets rid of them.' Reqab Wahedi, too, was unsparing, 'God damn these wild animals.' Sharafuddin Arash joined in, 'Marshal Babe (a pejorative for Marshal Abdel Rashid Dostum) used to be very popular among non Uzbek people, now it's over.'

CHAPTER 5

After the Taliban came

AS THE world media grew fixated on Afghanistan where the old Devil—the Taliban fighters and the world's most dreaded terrorist group—took control, Afghans braced themselves to endure the nightmares they had been through once before, twenty years ago. Before the day was out, it was already clear that the country's fate was already sealed—it was never in doubt as the Taliban had advanced territorially over several years defeating government and international forces—that the Afghan government would not be able to withstand the Taliban who were advancing towards the capital with a demonic force. Most of the provinces had already fallen, or rather, surrendered, though there were pockets where honest generals, commanders, and soldiers continued to fight bravely. However, by the time the insurgents reached Kabul, they had made sure there would be at the most, insignificant counterattacks from the hinterland. News from Afghanistan began to dominate the world media over the following months as the fanatical terrorists seemed to have established their sway over most of the country. Every day brought increasingly depressing news about what was happening in Afghanistan, what was pulverizing the equanimity of international diplomacy. Western nations, the entire South-Central Asia, and China and Japan which had invested heavily in the reconstruction and development of the war-ravaged country looked on helplessly as the Taliban quickly accomplished their mission and barged onto the world stage like a bad dream come true.

As Kabul fell and the news spread that President Ashraf Ghani and his cabinet had taken a flight out of the country in the nick of time, with the sole exception of one of his deputies, Amarullah Saleh, who refused to flee and stayed back to give leadership to an incipient resistance movement, numerous stories appeared of the sheer panic that gripped the city and the country. The Kabul airport came to witness unprecedented scenes of traffic jams, of desperate searches for seats on the waiting planes, of fisticuffs, of serious law-and-order problems, and of Afghans clinging to the bodies of planes that were trying to fly away to safety. The police force had disappeared with the entry of the Taliban, and the terrorists took their time to tackle law-and-order issues. The media was deluged with human interest stories; gradually the world realized that it was not just the dreaded return of the Taliban but the beginning of a gigantic humanitarian crisis enveloping Afghanistan. Food became scarce, medicines were not available, and cash shortages hampered daily life with the Taliban imposing a ban on bank transactions to prevent Afghans from escaping the country. Malnutrition, which had been traditionally endemic in rural Afghanistan, began to haunt Afghans in villages and towns. Two consecutive droughts had sapped the vitality of the country. The sudden closure of hospitals and severe shortages of doctors and nurses, jeopardized the functioning of medical care facilities. One of the first signs of near-normalcy occurred when the Taliban realized that hospitals and front-line healthcare workers like doctors, nurses and supporting staff, must be allowed to resume duties immediately otherwise, they would have a first-rate crisis on their hands in no time.

Beginning 15 August 2021 up to the first two months of 2022 as many as 500,000 jobs were lost. The United Nations International Labour Organization (ILO) said in a report that more than half-a-million people had lost or been pushed out of their jobs since the Taliban takeover. In a warning, the organization said that the economy had been 'paralyzed' and there had been huge losses in jobs and working hours. The ILO Asia Pacific tweeted that 'there have been huge losses in jobs and working hours in #Afghanistan since the change in administration with #women workers especially hard hit'.[18]

One question that troubled the global community was why Afghanistan had remained so poor and undeveloped after twenty years of a global initiative, led by the world's richest country, the United States of America, backed by the developed nations of the West and Japan. Statistics laid bare this harsh truth but, at the same time, questions were also raised as to why, with the return of the Taliban, Afghanistan must lose the enormous benefits that the reconstruction and development efforts had brought to the country and its people.

---

18 United Nations News (/en) Global perspective Human stories, *Economic Development* /en/news/topic/economic-development, *Afghanistan: 500,000 jobs lost since Taliban takeover*, 19 January 2022. The details of the report are available in the following text. Both were posted on 28 February 2022.

As months went by, it became clear to many Afghans, especially the young and the educated, that at the core of this extraordinary story of a relapse into chaos and deprivation after having been introduced to development and a democratic life lay a failure of the Afghan people itself. The kind of frustration that young Afghans felt could be gauged from the following post on Facebook. Zaher Wardak wrote, 'My dear country, everyone has participated in this destruction. Each one of us, regardless of black and white, red and green, is responsible for this catastrophe. First we oppressed our own people, then we mistakenly denounced them, then we allowed the foreigners to take over our house. We are the worst, the most mendacious, the most cruel, the most brutal people on the planet. In looting, stealing, lying, accusing, backbiting, devilishness, murder of innocent people, we reign supreme. A special international court must be set up to try all the monsters who have done this: the president and the king, amir and sultan, politicians, even the ghosts of Plato and Socrates, Ramprahov, Baba, the first and second deputy, Massoud, Hekmatyar, that is every murderer and savage directly. Don't say you did it, I am clean. Say I am a murderer and impure.' The original post was in Persian, and Google translations are always inaccurate. But the netizen's frustration was inescapable, and reflected the mood of the young population as their country settled down to a reign of terror. Another Facebook post by another netizen, also in Persian, began dramatically, 'The difference between yesterday and today. Yesterday, they were Minister of Defence, Minister of Interior, and Chief of National Security; along with them were the governors of several provinces, security commanders and hundreds of generals, all of them were Panjshiri. They were trying to destroy the houses of the people with foreign forces and dogs. Kabul had private prisons, it was called good work and defence of the system. But, today in broad daylight, in the presence of the world's camera, people stand at the gate of justice and demand houses. You are called men by men and women by women. Why question??????' Ashraf Ahmadi wrote, 'May your house be destroyed, old cow. People will never forgive you. You have handed Afghanistan over to the terrorists with your own dirty hands.' Sotoda Frotan added a different perspective, 'Khalilzad (the US Representative on Afghanistan Reconciliation) played a role in the surrender of power to the Taliban but he blames the government, the people, and the soldiers of Afghanistan.' Muhammad Salem Almas wrote, 'Repent to God. If you write Vladimir Zelensky on Google, the name of Ashraf Ghani with his picture will appear immediately. V Zelensky also thanked Muhammad Ashraf Ghani, the president of Afghanistan in a press conference, and said, "Your escape made me a hero, otherwise I would not have gained such fame in the war with Russia."' All these posts, ringing deep with frustration, sarcasm and hopelessness, appeared on Facebook in the first few days of March 2022 when the war was raging in Ukraine and Afghanistan had retreated to the back of the world's consciousness with little news coming out of the country, no doubt giving the Taliban rulers a respite from constant attention. Thus, social media handles provided a window, as authentic as permitted by the abnormal situation in the country, to the Afghan public opinion under Taliban rule.

However, it seemed as if Afghan netizens gradually became aware of the increasing dangers of going online to inform the public of incidents and Taliban policies which were not available publicly. Both sides were aware that Afghanistan in 2021 was not what it was in 1996. By 2005-2006 the Taliban had established the Al-Emarah website in Dari, Pushto, Urdu, and English. Besides, a Pushto language app was made available on the Google play store in 2016. The chief Taliban spokesperson, Zabihullah Mujahid opened his Twitter account but it was suspended. This was quickly followed by a second Twitter account in 2017 which was still functioning in 2021. These steps were being taken by the Islamist fundamentalists- who were ideologically opposed to modern technology and had prohibited the use and spread of such technology in 1996. By the time they came back to power, they had realized these were tools which could be used to spread their own ideology. The impressive response the website and the app received since their launch indicated that there was enough curiosity in Afghanistan and the world to learn about the Taliban ideology. As far as Afghan citizens were concerned, while brave souls continued to vent their grievances and openly talked about specific misdeeds of Taliban fighters and members, there was also a rising fear of reprisal. Still, in 2022, it looked as if the Taliban would take time to bring under control mobile phones which were, at that point being accessed by an estimated 70% of citizens.[19] However, it would seem that Afghan netizens residing in the country are fast losing their battle against their rulers. There were reports available a little after the Taliban takeover in August 2021 that the new rulers and their co-travellers were keeping an eye on their online activities.

---

19 Saif Khattak, *The dual role of social media in Taliban-controlled Afghanistan*, https://dtrac.org/en/202109/28/deco-talibans-use-of-social-media.

The very group that abhorred all channels of communication and entertainment like radio and television came to establish the Voice of Shari'a not just to broadcast news, but also to use it professionally as an additional propaganda machine. A multilingual organ using English, Pushto, Dari, Persian, Arabic and some other languages, the radio was positioned to play a major role in convincing a large number of listeners that the Taliban was a 'nationalist' and a 'progressive' force which was playing a 'stellar' role in reuniting the nation and developing it into a modern strong country. The contents were tailored to suit and appeal to each segment of the audience. Religious ideas were presented in Arabic and English publications; appeals to legitimize the fundamentalists were made in Persian; and Urdu was used to deal with local political issues. Internationally, the Taliban described themselves as a 'national' and 'radical Islamist group' that sought social justice and self-determination while fighting 'imperialism.' A common thread throughout was the theme of legitimization of the Taliban as a viable political alternative to the government in Kabul. Their military competence was highlighted, and strategic victories were played up in order to enable the Taliban to position themselves as a significant regional power.[20] Howsoever clever, calculating and determined the fundamentalist terrorists could be, Afghanistan, under their control, lacked one supreme element of the modern state: freedom to think and to freely express that thought. In private, Afghans, if they were so inclined, now had the means

---

20 Weeda Mehran, *How social media helped the tech-savvy Taliban retake Afghanistan*, The Guardian, 24 August 2021, https://www.theguardian.com/commentisfree/2021/aug/24/tech-savvy-taliban-afghanistan-propaganda-fundraising-recruitment

of reaching out to the world to convey their assessment of the new government; and this they have been doing with gusto. This also involves intense risk to freedom and life, and a large number of such rebellious individuals would not disclose their identities. Nevertheless some of them were betrayed by their acquaintances and were thus exposed to the risk of arrest or execution. They could also be identified through the web which made their endeavours even more daunting. All these unfortunate developments were later documented in the Human Rights Watch World Report 2022, which apportioned a certain percentage of responsibility and blame for illegal and abusive treatment of citizens upon members of the Afghan National Security Forces (ANSF) along with the Taliban and Islamic State-Khorasan Province (IS-KP), while the Taliban were held responsible and condemned for large-scale cases of 'unlawful killings, enforced disappearances, and violations of the laws of war'.

The HRW World Report 2022 quoted a United Nations report to the effect that the Taliban were responsible for at least 40% of the civilian deaths and injuries committed during the first six months of the year 2021, although many (similar) incidents remained 'unclaimed'.

CHAPTER 6

A Day of Panic

WHAT KIND of a day was 15 August 2021? If you asked the people of Kabul, would they recall the day as a hot and humid one or would they remember the weather as being balmy? No, they would remember the day as one on which the greatest catastrophe overtook them. The Taliban had returned and henceforth the Afghans would be told how to live, what to eat, read or write. Men, women and children would have to live exactly as the Taliban ordered them to. Afghanistan was being pushed back from the 21st century to a mythic medieval past.

There was panic in the streets of Kabul on the 15th of August 2021 as rumours spread thick and fast throughout the Afghan capital that Taliban fighters had entered the city gates. People went crazy, there were maddening traffic jams that expanded faster than one could imagine, hundreds of thousands of commuters were in a hurry to reach the safety of their homes in a suddenly congested city. Associated Press quoted two young men who were among those trying to rush home. Economics student and a resident of the city, Ali Sina said, 'I think the government has surrendered Kabul to the Taliban. I think it's good for the people because there will be no fighting.' When he was asked if he would be able to continue with his life and studies, Sina said, 'I think so.' But Hamidullah, who only gave one name due to security concerns, said, 'I'm afraid of (the) Taliban controlling all of Afghanistan. I worked with (the) US military and if (the) Taliban control Kabul, they'll try to kill me if they know about me.'

On that fateful day when fast-paced developments were adding to the general air of panic, the most ominous rumour was that ethnic, battle-weary fighters had entered the city and could start looting and killing people at any moment. As people grew more and more desperate and managing the unceasing crowd was beyond human capability, the Taliban's interim interior minister Abdul Satar Mirzakwal said that Kabul was not under attack and would not be attacked, and urged the residents not to pay attention to propaganda. He said that a peaceful transition of power would take place in Kabul under an agreement entered into with the previous Ashraf Ghani government. A senior aid to the former government, Matin Bek, who was a member of the negotiating team which had meetings with the Taliban delegation in Doha (the team is usually known as the Doha shura) and had since abdicated its power of governance to avoid unnecessary bloodshed also urged the people not to panic. A Taliban spokesperson tweeted, 'The Islamic Emirate instructs all its forces to stand at the gates of Kabul, not to try to enter the city'. By early afternoon, Taliban spokespersons announced that they were not entering Kabul forcibly and wanted a peaceful transfer of power. A general amnesty for all, especially for employees of the former government and soldiers of the former Afghan army, was also announced as a guarantee that there would be no revenge killing.[21] It should be noted here that Islam forbids parties and individuals to dishonour their own commitments and says that under no circumstances a state or a people or an individual should break its or his undertaking on any matter. That would be unIslamic. The Koran says, 'O ye who believe. Why do you say that which you do not, most displeasing is it in the sight of Allah that you should say that which you do not. (61:3-4).'

This law to the following: Another source of international conflict is the divergence between proclaimed intentions and policies and actual practices and actual conduct, which is bound to cause irritation and distrust. Doubts concerning motives and designs are bound to be raised in respect of a state whose conduct is inconsistent with its undertakings and its proclaimed policies and aims.

The chaos and panic that marked the change of government in Afghanistan could only imply a major failure—perhaps not accidental but a deliberate, calculated accomplishment—for which both the United States government and the Taliban could be held responsible. The most glaring fact about the so-called peace deal was that the legitimate government of Afghanistan was isolated and kept out of it, and yet a peace deal was born! As he concluded the eighth-round of negotiations with the Taliban in Doha on 12 August 2019, the United States Special Envoy for Afghanistan, Zalmay Khalilzad did not quite say that a deal allowing the extraction of American troops was done. But he came close. After 'productive' discussions in

---

21 / Various contemporary media reports.

Doha, the two sides were down to 'technical details', he said, it had taken a year of formal meetings 'to arrive at this point (and years of quiet chats before that). But it is too soon to celebrate. Those details will be devilish.' The talks involved a relatively straightforward bargain. America would start pulling out its 14,000 troops from Afghanistan. In return the Taliban would promise that Afghan territory would not become a safe staging ground for international terrorist groups like Al-Qaeda and the Islamic State. That would satisfy the main demand of Taliban insurgents and would address the problem that led America to invade 18 years ago (counting from 2001). 'I hope this is the last Eid where #Afghanistan is at war,' Khalilzad tweeted, referring to the major Muslim festival then approaching. 'But those negotiations were the easy part,' said Laurel Miller, a former State Department official and later with the International Crisis Group, a think-tank. Khalilzad was also desirous that the Taliban agree to a ceasefire. He also expected the Taliban to talk to other Afghans about a political settlement and, by early September 2019, agree on a loose 'road-map' towards achieving one. It is clear that the Americans hoped at the time that such an arrangement, mutually agreed among the Afghan parties including the Taliban, would obviate the need for a presidential poll that was scheduled to be held on 28 September, and that might be a workable means to avert the usual bickering over alleged electoral fraud and whoever would be elected president would be the common target of the rest and the Taliban would be very likely to exploit the development to their advantage. While Khalilzad's fond hope to see all these elements being part of the package, unfortunately, clashed with what America's red lines were; and this would add further to the air of uncertainty and vagueness over the effectiveness of whatever peace deal was finally signed. In retrospect, as has been discussed elsewhere in this narrative, Washington D.C.'s psychology to get out of Afghanistan as fast and as completely as possible jeopardized the non-Taliban Afghan forces to a dangerous extent; and writing in the comfort of later history, it is quite plain to see that it was the Taliban alone who profited by the peace deal, and that the subsequent withdrawal of American and international troops in August 2021 could only strengthen the conditions for takeover by the fundamentalists. The sense and image of the Taliban's invincibility and their inevitability to rule Afghanistan appeared to be almost a major part of the entire peace process. Even the American withdrawal was chaotic to the extreme; and the United States under President Joe Biden became a universal laughing stock.[22]

How horrific the return of the Taliban was could be glimpsed through the story of a fast-food restaurant owner in Kabul. The name of the restaurant owner was Mujeburrahman Musleh who ran a successful restaurant business. After the Taliban's victory, running his popular restaurant grew very difficult. The business, following the Taliban's return, dropped by 80 per cent, after which further running the business became absolutely impossible as his customers dried up. The last stage was reached when he did not have enough money to pay his staff. There was only one step left, shutting the restaurant. This he eventually did and started looking for a job. But even in the job market, Musleh said, the prospects were 'gloomy'.[23]

---

22 The Economist, *Security in Afghanistan Exit Strategy America and the Afghan Taliban appear closer to a deal,* 18 August 2019.
23 Zehra Tayeb, Business Insider India, 1 May 2022.

As the days quickly followed each other, it became clear that the Taliban had no intention to honour any of these assurances and guarantees. For example, while they invited back employees of the Ashraf Ghani government and its departments in the capital and in provincial capitals, and the soldiers of the disbanded National Defence and Security Forces of Afghanistan, the former army and police forces, none of them were either taken in or they themselves were too nervous to rejoin the new dispensation. The latter seems to have been the more likely option.[24]

The most important feature of the change in government that was uppermost in the minds of the international community and of the people in the country was a "peaceful transfer of power". The United States, backed by the international community, pressed on this condition while the Taliban Islamic Movement too harped on it. But in truth nothing of the sort happened, and the concept of a peaceful transfer of power was given a go-by. Later analyses backed by further substantiated information showed that simultaneously with the victory over the enemy, the Taliban fell in a serious dispute with their partner Haqqani

---

24 Thomas Gibbons-Neff & Mujib Mashal, US, *is quietly withdrawing its troops in Afghanistan*, The New York Times, *Kabul, 21 Oct., 2019:* Michael Crowley, *Bagram Airfield, during visit to Afghanistan reopened talks with Taliban, says Trump*, months after ending them, 29 Nov., 2019; The New York Times, *Definitive End to America's "Forever War" Biden to pull US troops in Afghanistan by Sept. 11*, 13 April 2021; Phil Stewart & Steve Holland, *Biden on Afghanistan: It is time to end America's longest war*, The New York Times, *14 April 2021*; Robert Burns, *As US Moves To End Its War in Afghanistan Pentagon preparing for Taliban attacks during US troop withdrawal*, Associated Press, 30 April 2021; Agence France-Presse, *Washington, 'Surge in attacks on Afghan army'*, 30 April 2021; Reuters, *Brussels/ Berlin, 'NATO to exit Afghanistan along with US'*, 15 April 2021.

Network. While the Taliban had negotiated with the Americans over a peaceful transfer of power, they had also negotiated with the Haqqanis over the acceptability or otherwise of an "inclusive' government to be set up in Kabul, a concept which the entire international community including their friends Pakistan, Saudi Arabia, Iran, Turkey, Russia and China were promoting. While the Taliban led by the prospective interim Prime Minister Abdul Ghani Baradar was batting for this concept, the Haqqanis fought tooth and nail against it.

This development in turn led to various incidents which gave a bad name to the new rulers and fuelled the general repugnance that Afghans felt for the Taliban. The new government, even after its formation and a formal announcement, was not sworn in and installed formally. The eleventh of September was considered to be the right date for the inauguration and the Taliban planned to make a great show of it aiming to embarrass the United States, but they backtracked at the last moment and only a minor ceremony was held to mark the occasion with no mention of the swearing-in of the new cabinet.

If the Taliban government's first task and promise was to establish law and order effectively and allow public life to flow once again in a normal manner, it failed miserably on this score as well and this came to the fore very soon. On the very first day when young Taliban fighters had entered Kabul with a vainglorious state of mind, there soon broke out disputes with strangers on the streets, and soon fires were shot, injuring civilians. A report filed one week after the Taliban takeover of Kabul said after they violently fought their way to power overthrowing the Ashraf Ghani government, the Taliban 'were still putting out fires breaking out across the war-torn nation as a result of resurrected memories of their previous rule. Expats were making a beeline for the Kabul airport, desperate to be evacuated out of the country. Foreign embassies had all but emptied out. Women were out on the streets fighting for their rights.' Towards the end of December by when four months were almost over and the rulers had got enough time and opportunity to establish that they were faithful to international law and norms of diplomacy, came the shocking news that the Taliban had seized a British aid worker, Grant Bailey in his 50s, and put him in jail but despite their utmost efforts the British government had not been able to locate him. This incident reinforced the impression—by then shared by the entire international community—that the Taliban were not interested to behave as was expected in a civil society but would run Afghanistan as they willed. As a matter of fact, the British authorities wondered what motive this man, Grant Bailey, could have in returning to the most dangerous place in the world after fleeing to the outside world when the expatriates were escaping from Afghanistan at the last moment. By returning to Kabul, Bailey virtually ensured that he would be in danger very soon. Reports at the time said he was detected and picked up during a security clampdown in Kabul. 'We were quite surprised he went back to Kabul after the Western withdrawal as the security situation there is obviously much worse. Added to that, the Taliban government is making it very difficult for the few expats working there, making it very difficult to travel,' said an official in London.[25]

---

25 The Daily Mirror, *British worker Grant Bailey missing in Afghanistan after Taliban seized him at gunpoint,* 24 December 2021, wionnewsweb@gmail.com (WION Web Team)

The United Nations General Assembly was in annual session when the Taliban returned to power in Afghanistan, and the reaction of the international community to the Taliban take over reflected in its deliberations. While US President Joe Biden announced his government's decision to engage more closely with the world in a departure from his predecessor Donald Trump's policy of withdrawing from the UN and other international organizations and concentrate on his home country, almost all other member-states emphasized the utmost necessity of strengthening democracy in the face of a new surge in terrorism and an enforced role assumed by non-state actors such as the ISIS-Khorasan which became very active in Afghanistan following the victory of the Taliban. In almost all exchanges of ideas and policies between national leaders and their aides, this theme of strengthening world peace and countering terrorism effectively echoed time and again.[26]

---

26 Nirupama Subramanian, *After US exit from Afghanistan*, The Hindu, 15 April 2021.

CHAPTER 7

The March of Women

WELL INTO the first year of their return to power, the Taliban took a major step to wipe out any sign of compassion in their treatment of women when, on 7 May 2022 they announced that henceforth women must wear the full-length head-to-toe burqa while going out in public. This represented two developments. It appeared that the Taliban had decided to be more hard-hearted than before because they had realized that their efforts to be perceived by the international community as a reasonably reformed and liberal force had not borne the desired results, and that it would be a waste of time and would give a wrong signal to women if this policy were continued. It seemed to have also been intended by the rulers to send the signal that the Taliban would no longer care to have normal relations with the international community. By issuing the latest decree on women's public appearance, the Taliban reinstated their policy of the 1996-2001 vintage. 'We want our sisters to live with dignity and safety,' said Khalid Hanafi, acting minister for the Taliban's Vice and Virtue ministry. 'For all dignified Afghan women wearing Hijab is necessary and the best Hijab is

Chador (the head-to-toe burqa) which is part of our tradition and is respectful,' said Shir Mohammad, an official from the Ministry for the Propagation of Virtue and the Suppression of Vice. 'Those women who are not too old must cover their face, except the eyes.' The decree emphasized that if women did not have to perform any important work outside their homes, it was 'better' for them to stay at home. 'Islamic principles and Islamic ideology are more important to us than anything else,' Hanafi elaborated. Senior Afghanistan researcher Heather Barr of Human Rights Watch urged the international community to put coordinated pressure on the Taliban. '(It is) far past time for a serious strategic response to the Taliban's escalating assault on women's rights,' she wrote on Twitter.[27]

Earlier in 2022, the Taliban decided against reopening schools for girls who were studying grade 6, reneging on an earlier promise and opting to appease their hard-line base at the expense of further alienating the international community. At the same time, they appeared to have downgraded their efforts to win recognition as an equal partner on the international stage with other sovereign nations. The implications of this further regression in Afghanistan carried the message as well that apart from recognition as a state and qualified to be a member of the United Nations, the Taliban did not care much on the ground for further alienating donor countries for the Afghan people would continue to suffer deprivations of the most unkindest kind ever since August 2021.

---

27 Associated Press, *Afghan Taliban order women to cover up head-to-toe in public*, Kabul, 7 May 2022.

However, soon enough signs appeared that Afghanistan had changed a lot internally even if the Taliban, the tormentors, had remained the same as before. On 19 May 2022, the Taliban authorities asked television broadcasters to ensure that women presenters on local stations cover their faces when on air. The order came days after women had been asked to cover their faces in public, in a return to the policy the fanatical terrorists followed in their previous regime. 'Yesterday (18 May 2022) we met with media officials…they accepted our advice very happily,' Akif Mahajar, spokesperson for the government's Ministry of the Propagation of Virtue and the Prevention of Vice, said adding that this move would be received well by Afghans.[28] The Taliban also stated that the order was 'final' and 'non-negotiable'.[29]

However, perhaps for the first time something unique happened, publicly voiced criticisms uttered in plain language flowed. On 21 May 2022, Mahira (a women TV anchor) appeared on the TV screen wearing a black mask over her face in the wake of the Taliban government order for woman anchors to cover their faces while being on air. '[Saturday] was one of the hardest days of my life. They made us feel as if we had been buried alive,' she told the TV news channel Al Jazeera. 'I felt like I am not a human. I feel like I have committed a big crime

---

28 Reuters, *Taliban say women Afghan TV anchors must cover face on air*, 19 May 2022. https://www.reuters.com/world/asia-pacific/taliban-say-female-afghan-tv-presenters-must-cover-face-air-2022-05-19/
29 Ajeet Kumar, *Ex-Afghanistan president Hamid Karzai says burqa has nothing to do with Afghan culture*, 21 May 2022, https://www.republicworld.com/world-news/rest-of-the-world-news/ex-afghanistan-president-hamid-karzai-says-burqa-has-nothing-to-do-with-afghan-culture-articleshow.html

which is why God made me a woman in Afghanistan,' choking back her tears. 'Which law in the world requires women to cover their faces on TV? Even in [other] Islamic countries, female news anchors or presenters do not wear masks,' she said, the anger evident in her voice.

Sosan, a 23-year-old TV presenter, shared Mahira's anger. She started working in the media in 2019 with hopes of following in the footsteps of the brave Afghan women reporters she had watched reporting from the length and breadth of her country. 'We had achieved so much, and had a robust free media, with growing presence of women in every sector. But look where we are now…in a country where I can't even choose what to wear or what topics to report on,' she said, referring to an earlier decree of '11 rules' for journalists', that was promulgated. The Taliban's latest edict, announced on 19 May, was seen by many as the latest sign of escalating restrictions on women's freedom and a return to the repressive rule experienced during the 1996-2001 period.

In a magnificent gesture of solidarity with their endangered female colleagues, male TV anchors also began to cover their faces immediately. Two of them, Hamed Bahram and Naser Nabil of TOLO News wore masks while reading news on 22 May (the order was actually finalized on 20 May). Netizens on social media also burst upon the latest Taliban sacrilege, castigating the fanatical fundamentalists for their extreme depravity. It was interesting to see how a decree which affected only a handful of women anchors in fact triggered a much larger social media response. That was perhaps because the decree dealt a powerful blow to a visible symbolic mark of progress Afghans had made in two decades (2001-2021) of Western-backed rule: women on television authoritatively presenting information.[30]

Human rights activists saw the developments as gradually narrowing the space for women in the country, saying that the Taliban's moves were aimed at 'removing women from public life' and that it was 'clear they intend to enforce the latest decree on face coverings'. 'Women journalists on television are highly visible. Their continued presence gave girls and women some small shred of reassurance, on deepening attacks on women's rights, that some women were still able to do their jobs, to hold important roles, to appear in public,' Heather Barr, associate director of the Women's Rights Division at Human Rights Watch, observed.[31]

A leading Afghan human rights activist who was living in exile, said, 'The Taliban's micropolicing of women in a country grappling with multiple humanitarian emergencies provided an insight into the Taliban's worldview. In one of the poorest countries in the world, a country where children are regularly victims of explosive remains of war, no country still battling polio, explosives, disease, there was a campaign against hunger but one against women.

The latest Taliban decree also raised a host of concerns, not only about women's freedom of expression but also about whether they would be able to continue to do their jobs.

---

30   Rachel Treisman, *Male Afghan TV anchors cover faces in solidarity with women after a Taliban order*, Al Jazeera, 24 May 2022. https://www.aljazeera.com/news/2022/5/22/afghan-women-tv-anchors-forced-to-cover-faces-under-taliban-order
31   Zuhal Ahad and Ruchi Kumar, *Afghan women journalists defiant as Taliban restrictions grow*, Al Jazeera, 24 May 2022. https://www.aljazeera.com/news/2022/5/24/afghan-female-journalists-defiant-as-taliban-restrictions-grow

Some women began questioning whether the 'veiling' order was a prelude to being ordered off air entirely, because many conservative Muslims considered a woman's voice to be 'sexually arousing', and therefore should not be heard in public. There was mixed compliance at first, which provoked the Taliban to begin a strict implementation of the order over the weekend. The Ministry for the Propagation of Virtue and the Suppression of Vice declared that 'The decision was final and there was no room for discussion.' The news readers were certainly confused because the same ministry had not yet implemented its earlier broader decree on women and pubescent girls covering their faces or wearing a burqa in public.

The speculation at the time was that the ministry may have wanted to first set an example of women who appeared on airwaves, whose numbers were negligible. Associated Press reported that most women TV anchors were being seen on TV screens wearing masks in consonance with the government order. Apart from male Afghan TV anchors and news readers, male journalists in several other countries also joined in the protest and wore masks as a proof of their solidarity with the unfortunate Afghan female anchors. Human Rights Watch urged diplomats at the time to express their solidarity with the Afghan female anchors by covering their faces while conferring with Taliban ministers and officials. 'Women journalists are just the latest casualties in what has become the most serious women's rights crisis in the world,' the organization added, 'But the Taliban are not immovable, and coordinated pressure has the potential to impact their decisions.' Many TV anchors expressed their concern at the time that they would not be able to perform their jobs 'adequately from behind a mask'. Two female TOLONews anchors, for example, said it would be difficult to lead hours of programming with their faces covered. One questioned how much a mask would affect her ability to breathe and speak, while another said, 'We are not ready mentally and morally that such things should be forced on us.' How would this new practice affect their performance as clear presenters of news and analysis and the viewers' experience of this new spectacle? Human Rights Watch expressed similar concerns. 'The rule blatantly violates women's rights to freedom of expression as well as personal autonomy and religious belief,' it said. 'It will also prevent access to information for people who are deaf or hard of hearing who lip read or rely on visual speech cues to help them understand people speaking.'

In a video an unnamed female journalist explained how important it was for anchors to feel calm while delivering the truth to viewers and said presenting news while the face was covered with a mask would have the 'opposite' effect. 'If such decrees are issued and imposed on women, the women across Afghanistan will be eliminated', she added. 'As we see now, that women are being gradually eliminated.' As it was, scores of women journalists had been eliminated from the profession of journalism under various circumstances, which included open threats, physical assaults, murders, pressure on their employers, and family pressures. As a matter of fact, while the Taliban completed their victory in August 2021, their malevolent influence on female visual and print media journalists had begun at least one year ago. From December 2020 and by 15 August 2021, just 100 out of a total of 700 women journalists were still working in Kabul's private TV and radio stations, as reports by Reporters Without Borders and the Centre for the Protection of

Afghan Women Journalists informed at the time.

The compulsion for women to wear the burqa was also challenged by no less than former President Hamid Karzai who pointed out that this apparel had nothing to do with Afghan culture. When the nation-wide anger and strong criticism of the edict broke out, Karzai argued that covering faces was not the 'tradition of Afghanistan'. He said 'covering faces is not Hijab' and the use of the burqa was not 'Afghan tradition'. Burqa had come to Afghanistan probably 200-300 years ago. 'Women began to cover their faces since then, and the apparel had come to Afghanistan 'from other countries, it is not an Afghan tradition', Karzai emphasized. He added, stressing the women's right to ignore the latest fundamentalists' diktat, that 'No, they shouldn't, no, they shouldn't because that has got nothing to do with Hijab—that has got nothing to do with Afghan culture either. They should not obey this…The Taliban leadership must resent this decision, whoever made this decision. It hurts Afghanistan, it hurts Afghanistan's reputation, and it is not Afghan at all,' he told TOLONews TV channel.

Traditionally, as Karzai put it, Afghan women used to take a 'huge chador,' which was actually a huge scarf on the head but not as a burqa. He described the current government's order to women to wear masks while presenting news and other programmes on TV, as 'wrong' and 'unfair'.

The women's march—the second in as many days in Kabul—began peacefully. Demonstrators laid a wreath outside Afghanistan's Defence Ministry to honour Afghan soldiers who died fighting the Taliban before marching on to the presidential palace. 'We are here to gain human rights in Afghanistan,' said Marian Naiby. 'I love my country. I will always be here.' As the protesters' shouts grew louder, several Taliban officials waded into the crowd to ask what they wanted to say. Flanked by fellow demonstrators, Sudaba Kabiri, a 24-year-old university student, told her Taliban interlocutor (that) Islam's Prophet gave women rights and they wanted theirs. The Taliban official promised that women would be given their rights but the women, all in their early 20s, remained determined to continue their march. As the women reached the presidential palace, a dozen of Taliban special forces ran into the crowd firing in the air and sending demonstrators fleeing Kabul. The Taliban have repeatedly promised an inclusive government and a more moderate form of Islam than when they ruled during 1996-2001. But a sizeable section of Afghans, especially women, are deeply sceptical and fear a roll-back of rights gained over the last two decades.[32]

---

32 The Living Conditions of Afghan Women under the Taliban force https://graduate. way.com/living-conditions-under-afghan-women-taliban-force.. ; The Taliban and Afghan Women Majority Foundation https://feminist.org/our-world-afghan-women-and-girls-taliban-afghan-women... ; List of Taliban Policies Violating Women's Rights in Afghanistan https://www.hrw/news/photos/2021/09/29list-taliban-policies-violating-policies-violating... ; A Look At The Life of Afghan Women under Taliban rule https://www,moneycontrol.com/news/world/a-look-a-the-life-of... ; The Plight of Afghan Women Under The New Taliban rule https://globalvoices,org/2021/08/24/the-plight-of-afghan-women-under... Afghan Women's fate under the Taliban https://the-annapurna-express,com/news/news/afghan-women-fate-under the ... Women in Afghanistan and Girls : Taliban To Restrict Their Education https://www.nytimes.com/2021/09/20/world/https://www.nytimes.com/asia/afghan-girls-schools-taliban-html Afghan Women Demand Their Rightsunder Taliban rule/News HTTPS:www.dw.com/en/afghan0women-demand-their-rights-under-taliban.

However, the Taliban and the concept of inevitability seem to travel together. True to this truism, the first expansion of the cabinet in Afghanistan since the formation of the interim government in the third week of August 2021 showed that the rulers had stuck to their principle of excluding women—irrespective of their merits—could not be made ministers. Deputy Minister for Information and Culture, Zabihulla Mujahid said on Tuesday, 21 September that several ministers had been drafted in the expanded cabinet though no women were among them. However, 'minorities 'had been made ministers in order to bring 'inclusiveness' to the Taliban government. It was apparent that the Taliban were trying to ignore the insistence by the international community to make the government 'inclusive' while stressing the necessity of including women in governance. The identification of the 'minority' ministers was not available in details; therefore, only their names were announced and not the ethnic groups they represented.

Following the successive restrictions imposed on women, the United Nations Security Council issued a press statement dated 25 May calling upon the Taliban government to swiftly reverse its policies and practices which were restricting the basic human rights and fundamental freedom of Afghan women and girls, including through the imposition of restrictions that limited access to education, employment, freedom of movement, and women's full, equal and meaningful participation in public life and emphasized that these restrictions contradicted the expectations of the international community and the commitments made by the Taliban to the Afghan people. The Council members further expressed deep concern regarding the announcements by the Taliban that all women must cover their faces in public spaces and in media broadcasts, only leave home in cases of necessity, and that violations of this directive would lead to punishment of their male relatives. They also expressed concern regarding the decision to dissolve several key national institutions. The volatile situation prevailing in the country also attracted the Security Council's deep concern including political, economic, social and security challenges and their impact on the lives of the Afghan people. The UN body made special mention of the 'continued terrorist attacks targeted at civilians and civilian infrastructure, including on religious minority communities across Afghanistan and of the cultivation, production, trade and trafficking of illicit drugs'. The Taliban must 'swiftly reverse' the policies and practices that had severely constricted the human rights and fundamental freedom of Afghan women and girls. The international community as represented in the Security Council also reiterated on the Taliban to adhere to their commitments to reopen schools for all female students without further delay.[33]

Any student of modern Afghanistan should be immensely impressed by the sheer guts shown by the country's women who are supposed to be belonging to the so-called weaker sex but are in reality stronger than their menfolk. What explains this unexpected and surprising characteristic of Afghan women? In this book there are examples of women whose lives should be

---

33 Press Trust of India, United Nations, *UN Security Council concerned over erosion of respect for human rights of women in Taliban-ruled Afghanistan*, 25 May 2022.

helpful in understanding and appreciating this phenomenon but the author will be more keen to present the story of a woman who lived in 1000 AD and left behind an unparalleled tale of bravery, love and versatility.

Her name was Rabia Balkhi (914-943 AD), a medieval poetess from Balkh, located in the present-day Northern Afghanistan. Rabia is one of the most venerated female figures in the Afghan imaginary. She is credited with having been among the first practitioners of New Persian or Parsi-ye-Dari (Persian of the Court), the language that flourished in the 10th century after two centuries during which the Islamic conquest transformed the region's cultural and linguistic composition, infusing the Middle Persian (Pahlavi) with new vocabulary and a new script. Rabia was a poet princess in the Balkh court where her father served as Emir. She fell in love with her brother's Turkish slave (in another version, he was the commander of Balkh's army), Baktash, and would write poetry to him. Her brother discovered his sister's secret love when one such poem landed in his hands, and he cast Rabia into the hamam, her private bath (but generally speaking, public baths for women). Rabia slit her wrists (in the other version, her wrists were slit when she was imprisoned in the hamam) and with her blood she wrote her last love poem until her death.

We now reproduce the last poem she wrote for her lover:
I am captured by your love
trying to escape is not possible
love is an ocean without boundaries
a wise person would not want to swim in it
If you want to love until the end
you must accept what is not accepted

welcome hardship with joy
eat poison but call it honey.
Here is a tribute paid to her by Sufi poet Farid al-Din Attar in Ilahi-Nama:
The moon-faced beauty struck blood with her fingertips
Many poems stemmed from her agonized heart
When no walls remained in the hamam
So, too, a few drops of blood remained
As she covered the walls with poetry
She collapsed like the fragment of a wall
Amid blood, fire and tears

Her sweet soul swiftly left her body with a hundred desires.[34]

One of the many manifestations of this norm of 'strict implementation' was the 26 September 2021 banning of driving schools for women. Driving had become particularly popular among Afghan women during the previous twenty years, and this was obviously a long-identified target of the Taliban. Women were being systematically bowed down by the new rulers as part of their agenda of re-establishing an Islamic Emirate of Afghanistan. There was another side to this development. Women were facing a growing regime of harassment, both hysterical and mental, which in fact graduated to torture and could therefore invite international strictures on the government. But in this particular development, the statement and several warnings were issued from time to time to

---

34 Munazza Ebtikar, *The Story of Rabia Balkhi, Afghanistan's Most Famous Female Poet*, Ajam Media Collective. Ebtikar is a Ph.D. candidate at the University of Oxford.

that effect but the ultra-conservative and fundamentalist group did not pause to take any notice of those cautions. Instead, they sought to countermand these warnings by reiterating that the ground reality was different and that Taliban ground troops had been 'disciplined.' However, the truth was to the contrary, and almost seven weeks after the victory, the Taliban leadership once again decided to issue the sternest warning to unruly fighters to take care of their behaviour or they would be severely punished and thrown out of the force.

However, Afghan women had never cared to place trust in any such assurance by the Taliban. All that the people noticed was that unlike the Taliban 1.0 this time the Taliban leadership had made several attempts—all of which at least at face value—appeared to be genuine attempts to bring discipline to the ranks. Interestingly, women journalists started leaving their jobs as early as March 2021, nearly four months before the Taliban conquered the country. Nearly twenty per cent of Afghan women journalists quit or lost their jobs in the past six months—that making it a full year before the Taliban won the war. The Afghan Journalists Safety Committee, a professional body of journalists, said on 7 March 2021 that 300 women had left the industry in recent months, citing the 'wave of targeted killings' as one of the main reasons along with financial difficulties caused by the coronavirus problems. A few days ago three women employees of the Enikass TV were gunned down by militants in the Eastern city of Jalalabad; later, the killings were claimed by the Islamic State-Khorasan. In December last, another woman was murdered. After four of its women employees were killed, the TV station said it had asked all its women employees to stay home until the security situation improved. The AFP report quoted a woman TV presenter, Nadia Momand, saying ' I love journalism but I also love to live. I am not going to go out again unless they send me an armoured vehicle.' The TV channel's director Zalmai Latifi said, 'There is no protection for them. We also decided not to hire any additional women employees.' The media watchdog said in a statement, 'Afghanistan is celebrating the International Women's Day this year at a time where security threats against journalists and media workers, especially women, in the media, have intensified.'[35]

As we remain saturated with reports of the Talibani restrictions imposed on Afghan women forcing them to restrict their movement strictly within the walls of their homes and minimizing their presence in the outside world, it may prove surprising to learn that from among their ranks have come some of the bravest poets of most erotic and revolutionary poems written anywhere in the world by women. Here are some sparkling examples:

The name of my lover is written on my body
I don't want to wash
in case his name disappears.
Tomorrow is a celebration day
everyone wears clean clothes
I wear the same unwashed ones
they carry the scent of my lover.
Kiss me with your lips
but let my tongue be free

---

35 AFP, *Afghan women leave journalism in droves*, 8 March 2021, https://www.thehindu.com/news/international/afghan-women-leave-journalism-in-droves/article34022550.ece

I want to tell you so many untold stories.
One night I dreamt of your death
in the morning my lips were cracked with dryness.

The extent of the audacity of the Taliban in their sustained attempts to suppress Afghan women can be conjectured from the fact that despite their minimizing the women's social role and activities, women continued to compose and publish erotic and revolutionary poems, more of course abroad than at home. What happens when a woman poet dares to stay in Afghanistan with her husband and still decides to publish her poems? Nadia Anjuman, a young married woman and a well-known poet and journalist, was murdered by her husband in Herat, in 2005, reportedly for writing poetry, just any type of poetry! Such cruelty towards women poets forces them to hide their talent or for the brave ones, use male pen-names to conceal their identity. Therefore, there are many George Eliots in Afghan literature who have maintained a male identity until death. We find out about such women poets years after they have been buried, when the dust has truly settled.[36]

It is not clear whether the women who wrote these poems were really brave enough to have affairs with their lovers, but it is clear that they were brave enough to produce poems like these in a country where strict rules prevent women from having lovers. While women poets in Afghanistan still live in fear of being punished for describing their feelings, Afghan women

---

36 PEN Transmissions, English PEN's magazine for international writing, *The erotic and revolutionary poetry of Afghanistan*, 19 June 2014, https://pentransmissions.com/2014/06/19/the-erotic-and-revolutionary...

who live in the West do not have such fears. The internet has created opportunities for Afghan women to write freely, to write about explicit matters that even some Western women might not dare to address. 'Is this a reaction to centuries of not being able to write freely and not even having the basic right to a formal education?' asks PEN Transmission.[37]

Bahar Saied is one of the poets who lives in the West. She first published her poems in Iran before the Iranian revolution, also in Afghanistan prior to the Soviet invasion (1979), and in the West after she had left her homeland. Her poems are direct in criticizing a society in which women have almost no role and where everything is decided by men. These poems attack religious leaders for using religion as a tool. One of her poems follows:

> He kissed me once and stole my lips
> and robbed me from sleep
> I am scared if he touches my body
> my patience will be invaded.
> I have come to you to taste your body
> my lips fall on yours, tasting your mouth
> with my fingers I tear off your shirt
> I taste the nakedness of your chest
> I am inhaling the perfume of your breath
> and touching your body with my breast
> tasting the burning of your body with mine.
> Come and carve me, my body is yours
> carve me in your heart in the night of dreams

---

37   PEN Transmission, *ibid.*

come and carve me until morning
with beautiful touch and kiss.
I love the buttons on your collar
which ask me to open them
and throw myself on you.

Sanam Ambarin is another poet who has published a book of poetry titled 'I was writing about you'.

When my shirt
does not feel the rhythm of your heart
blood's current
stops in my heart.
(…)
It is not a sin
if my lips are red with love
laugh at me or not
open the window or not
I don't believe in winter's subject matter
I know my way
if you come with me or not
I know my way alone
I know how to build a bridge between dawns.

And before we turn off this subject, we must listen to Anjila Pagahi, who lives in Germany and writes revolutionary poems against the Taliban and fighting for a better Afghanistan:

With the words of Allahu Akbar on your lips
you shed blood this way
your hands have the smell of hell
I know you follow Satan, you barbarian.

After the Taliban planted a bomb concealed in a copy of the Quran (Koran) in a mosque, Pagahi wrote:

> You have made bomb out of the Quran
> you cause so much misery.

The Afghan women poets who live in the West have been able to write openly but that doesn't mean that those women who live in Afghanistan have been quiet. The fall of the Taliban (2001) gave women the space to address social issues, criticize injustice and to write about the evil of the Taliban era (i.e., the first regime 1996-2001). Karina Shabrang writes about the soldiers fighting with the Taliban in the following poem:

> I found you again soldier
> in your own country
> like the lost unity
> I found you again soldier.

The political situation in Afghanistan could be blamed for much of the misery in the country. Samira Popalzai, a poet from Kabul, wrote about the politics of Afghanistan:

> The shadows of politics
> once again raised their flag
> colourful with the blood of our young men
> this endless cruelty
> breaks our bones
> deceives us.

The involvement of Afghanistan's women poets in their country's politics was so emphatic and wide-ranging that they could find enough to say even about elections about to be held, utilizing the opportunity to exhort the people to exercise their voting right to strengthen the democratic set-up which was put in place by the international community after the Taliban and Al-Qaeda were eradicated from Afghan soil in end-2001, and democracy with free elections and franchise for all citizens was enshrined in a constitution. At that time, the Taliban tried their best to disrupt the electoral process and frighten the voters so that the exercise came a cropper. The first elections came through well enough, Parliament was established and began to function, and there would succeed two more presidential and parliamentary elections, but all these good things could not stop the Taliban who came roaring in and powered their way in August 2021. But, in the intervening twenty years, women poets had their day traversing the entire canvas of life in Afghanistan.

The Taliban had consistently tried to disrupt the elections with the aim to discourage voters from coming out of their homes on election days but always failed. Rahela Yar, who lives in Germany, published three books of poems, entitled 'Bud of Songs', 'Why the River doesn't talk about our tears', and 'The Sadness of Song', wrote on the 2019 elections in the following poem:

Someone brings material for explosion
someone is a suicide bomber
someone has cut off my finger for voting
God would you listen to my pain?

And Karima Shabrang, a poet from Northern Afghanistan, wrote about her pride in being a woman:

I am a woman
a woman who is not unable
a woman who lives with pride
a woman who fights for her rights
I am a woman who would never surrender.

The point, the author hopes, of citing so many examples of erotic and revolutionary poems is not lost, and these should be taken as facilitating the phenomenon of the unparalleled bravery and honesty of Afghan women, both ancient and contemporary.

There is another type of poetry in the Afghani Pashtun tradition, called Landai, anonymous and daring. Landai is a poem with two verses, shorter than a Haiku. It expresses forbidden erotic words and feelings, and often criticizes authority and rigid religion. Even married women on occasion have resorted to Landai to declare their forbidden love with invitations 'come to the spring where I collect water. My husband is away'. This type of poetry, no matter how disturbing to society is tolerated as entertainment, even though it often addresses serious subjects. Since nobody claims ownership of these poems no reaction is required. 'There is no known target to hang or stone to death,' remarks PEN Transmissions sarcastically.

In the mid-June of 2022, when the Taliban government had been running the country for eight months, the United Nations came out with a damaging report on Afghanistan. The United Nations Human Rights Commissioner Michelle Bachelet told the Human Rights Commission that the people of Afghanistan were passing through some of the 'darkest moments' in a generation.

On 15 June 2022, almost a year after the Taliban reconquered Afghanistan, Michelle Bachelet told the Human Rights Commission, 'In the wake of years of conflict, and since the takeover by the Taliban in August last year, the undermining of their (women's) human rights in the critical situation continues under the repression of the Taliban's codes of conduct'. The UN High Commissioner further cited a school ban affecting 1.1

million secondary school girls as well as other decrees including the enforcement of the hijab rule and restrictions on women's access to jobs. 'Let me be clear: what we are witnessing today in Afghanistan is the institutionalized, systematic oppression of women,' she said. The task of supporting the restoration and preservation of human rights of every Afghan, and particularly of women, affected by the 'concerted work by the de facto authorities, renewed space for civil society and support by the international community' to safeguard the human rights of everyone in the war-torn nation. 'The representation of all Afghans in policy and decision-making processes will be crucial' to this end and require 'listening to the voices of women and girls' as well as 'heeding the calls of religious and ethnic minorities', she outlined.[38]

---

38 Anchal Nigam, *Afghanistan facing 'The Darkest Moments' With Institutionalized Oppression of women: UN*, https://www.republicworld.com/--world-news/rest-of-the-world-news/...

CHAPTER 8

The Forebodings Of A Dark Future

BELYING ALL hopes for a stable democratic Afghanistan, the Taliban fighters recaptured Kabul on 15 August 2021, and what were till then the dark forebodings of a dark future manifested themselves in reality. A year more would pass since then, and still neither the people of Afghanistan nor the international community could glimpse even a single ray of hope. By August 2022 another year would pass, and the Taliban would be ruling with an ease of mind because they knew neither the Afghans nor the international community had the guts to confront them. On the contrary, the international community was falling in line, one country being followed by another, to cultivate the fierce uncompromising fanatics, either on humanitarian grounds or in search of means to retrieve and continue their vast investments in Afghanistan's mines of precious metals.

As was experienced during 1996-2001 in the entire country so in 2021-2022 Afghans passed through different levels of intimidation, torture and killings; their experiences were more or less at the same level. But here comes a different kind of story altogether. Boy fighters recruited by the Taliban merely presented a slightly different focus. Little boys were being recruited by the Taliban even during the reign of the democratically elected government of President Ashraf Ghani and of his predecessors. A media report spoke about 47 boys imprisoned in Badam Bag juvenile detention centre in Kabul as 'national security threats.' Such detained boys ranging in ages from an unbelievable 8 to 17 belonged to the 'Suicide bomber squad' and were generally deployed as fighters in battlefield. This again violated a major international norm of not using young boys and girls for war-like activities.

After the newspaper requested an interview with the jailed boys at the Kabul prison, 47 responded positively with all insisting that they be identified only by their first names and the names which were common in the country. During the interview, a ministry official and a counsellor were present, as the newspaper explained. One of the interviewed was Muslim. Among the significant points made by him was a firm denial that he was a suicide bomber. When Nordland approached him, he was reciting in a high-pitched beautiful voice a Pushto poem—a capella elegy—on the prison floor, and he was reciting the following, 'And do not come to us for Eid, for we are not free to welcome you/ I don't want you to look at my chest/ for there are no buttons on my shirt/ Don't come to this asylum, for we are all lunatics here'.

CHAPTER 9

The Yankee Booty: A Friendly Gift

THE FIRST few months of the second Taliban rule oscillated between disbelief and a slice of reluctant belief but not of trust. The people continued to refuse to trust their rulers, for they had seen too much. Recollections of the unbelievably cruel years of the earlier period never stopped flashing through the people's minds. They had good reasons for thinking so. Even if ordinary Afghans had scant reason to remember this, but leaders and intellectuals may recall then US Vice-President Dick Cheney's triumphal declaration on 7 December 2001, that 'The Taliban is (are) out of business.' What lay behind this astonishing story of the most fearsome terrorist group's first rise, followed by a resounding retreat and then this resurgence? The success rested mostly on building up a solid fighting prowess, and to achieve which the terrorists gathered all the essential ingredients like the latest weapons, high-power artillery, fast-moving armed vehicles which are more than mere vehicles, and also tiny versions of arsenal equipped with the very latest firing capability. According to a 2017 report—the latest available on the kind and extent of highly-developed military equipment in the United States arsenal. They include the following: Light tactical vehicles 42,604 in number armed with rifles; Humvees 22,174 in number armed with pistols; MTVs 8,998 in number armed with machine guns; APCs 189 in numbers armed with shotguns; total key vehicles 75,898 in number armed with total key weapons; and—for the first time and the lack of which had bothered the Taliban forces enormously through the insurgency—A-29 aircrafts (number not disclosed). Besides, the American weapons handed over to the Afghan army and which fell into the hands of the Taliban include 126,299 pistols AC 208; machine guns 12,692 C-208; shotguns 12,693. Quite a formidable force, one must admit and thanks to the inability or indecision of the Afghan commanders and soldiers to carry or not to carry them in their final and irrevocable fleeing from the battlefield. As if they had learnt their lesson from the ex-president and his government and decided to follow their example![39]

It is however unclear exactly how much 'usable' military equipment has been seized by the militant group during 2021, although it is possible to estimate the size of the potential arsenal using data that show the transfer of US weapons to Afghanistan over the past few years. According to a 2017 report, from the Government Accountability Office (GAO), the United States transferred around 75,898 vehicles, 599,690 weapons systems, and 209 aircrafts to the Afghanistan National Security Forces

---

[39] Thomas Gibbons-Neff, *Even As US officials Publicly said Their Mission in Afghanistan Was Successful Documents Reveal American Officials Misled Public Over Afghanistan*, The New York Times, 9 December, 2019.

from 2003 to 2016. A later report from the Special Inspector General of Afghanistan Reconstruction (SIGAR) revealed that over 7,000 additional machine guns, 20,000 grenades and 4,700 Humvees were transferred to the ANFS.[40]

A study of the progress of the Taliban Islamic Movement forces throughout the nearly two decades of democratic rule in Afghanistan naturally has to delve constantly into events that happened during that period; and here we may take a look at a report on how the government forces were tackling the insurgents at the time. Mirwais Harooni of the Reuters News Service reported in July 2015 that Afghan security forces and militant fighters were locked in a battle for control over a portion of Northern Afghanistan. Police and local officials evacuated their compounds in the central district of Yamgan in Badakshan province as militants laid siege to the area, provincial governor Shah Wadiullah Adib informed. 'But they are now fighting to take back control of the district. We have enough forces to take the district back and keep it in future. The casualty figures given by the two warring sides invariably varied; while the Interior Ministry spokesperson Seddiqi tweeted that 'Six militants were killed by Afghan security forces during the clearance operation', the Taliban who owned responsibility for the attack claimed that their fighters had killed 18 security force members but the Reuters man noted that the militants' claims were 'often inflated.'

---

40 Polly Bindman, *The US military arsenal now available to the Taliban,* The New Statesman, 31 August 2021.

In retrospect, it seems surprising that the world could be caught unawares when the Taliban swept into Kabul on 15 August 2021. A SIGAR report at the time said, 'The Afghan government has lost control of nearly 5 per cent of its territory to the Taliban since the beginning of this year (i.e. 2016). The area under the Afghan government's control of influence decreased to 65.6 per cent by the end of May (of the same year) from 70.5 per cent (in 2015), based on data supplied by American forces in Afghanistan. That accounts for a loss of 19 districts.

The commander of the US forces in the country Army General John Nicholson said most of the areas the Taliban controlled at the time were rural. 'They believed they were going to be able to seize and hold terrain, and they failed to do so,' Nicholson told a Pentagon briefing via video link. Afghan officials said that the exact figure could not be measured as the fight against the Taliban and other armed groups was an on-going process. 'It's not just the Taliban but many other insurgent groups in Afghanistan battling to gain territory, and we are fighting to push them back, so we cannot really measure how many areas are in control of the Taliban or other insurgent groups,' General Dawlat Waziri, spokesperson for the Afghan Defence Ministry told Al Jazeera from Kabul. 'However, we can confirm that the Taliban seem to be present mostly in rural districts and not in strategic cities.' The Afghan forces who were so badly humiliated by the Taliban Islamic Forces in 2021 and were for all practical purposes obliterated from the soil of Afghanistan were trained and equipped by the American forces. The purpose of the Americans to spend so much money and so many man-hours in preparing them to fight the Taliban 'on their own' was to facilitate and fructify the United States' declared policy of withdrawing their own forces from the Afghan battlefield by a certain date. Why had the Afghan forces not been able to fight back the insurgents? American forces, based on their field experiences, reported that the loss of control had been occurring because Afghan forces were 'deployed' from lower-priority areas to 'conduct offensive operations, gain and maintain the initiative, exploit opportunities and consolidate technical gains.' They considered, and quite correctly, that the deficiency of their Afghan counterparts lay precisely in these areas of military offensive operation. It was an indication of how Afghanistan was reshaping the United States' plan to eliminate the Taliban from Afghanistan for a second time that then President Barack Obama acknowledged that the security situation was deteriorating by saying he intended to leave 8,400 American troops back after completing withdrawal of the main forces, which was an increase from his previously announced number. He also authorised American troops to accompany Afghan forces while allowing greater use of air power. Earlier, General Nicholson was permitted to take action against the Taliban only if they posed an immediate threat to American or coalition forces or if Afghan forces faced a 'catastrophic failure.' A 2013 study by the Asia Foundation found that as the United States began to draw down 'surge' troops in 2012 followed by further withdrawals the following year and transferred security authority to Afghan troops in June 2013, 'the Taliban-led insurgency escalated'.[41]

---

41 Sriram Lakshman, *'Political settlement alone won't end violence in Afghanistan*, The Hindu, 23 November, 2019.

The report made two important points. This offensive was more intensive, aggressive and widespread than their previous assault in Badakshan's Jorm district in April. And, 2015 was the first year when the security forces faced the insurgents 'on their own, after most foreign troops withdrew at the end of last year (2014) and the new NATO-led mission shifted its focus to training and advising the military and government'. In the first four months of 2015, the United Nations recorded 2,937 casualties nationwide, a 16 per cent increase over the same period in 2014. These figures clearly marked the changing pattern of the war as the Taliban kept gaining confidence despite far more superiority in weapons for land and air fighting and the most valuable presence of foreign military prowess and experience. The Taliban, on the other hand, were depending on their strength and Pakistan's tactical and moral support.

All through this demoralising history, one would notice that the most fundamental deficiency in modern-day Afghanistan, which peaked during the twenty years of democratic rule (2001-2021), was perpetuated by almost a continuous failure of the state to follow and implement the reconstruction and rehabilitation programme fixed for the country. However, this programme was run alongside an equally important programme of democratisation and bringing in stability in order to achieve peace, a kind of peace that would last for a relatively reasonable time. Unfortunately but not unpredictably, both programmes could not be implemented fully and satisfactorily and thus the results which should have been there at the end of the programmes were not achieved. Let us take a closer and clearer view of what went wrong, for we must know what went wrong to explain why the Taliban could manage to come back to power after twenty years of democracy. Such a bad turn had seldom happened in history.

In 2005, just four years after the Taliban were replaced by democratic institutions, an elected president (2004) and a Lower House of Parliament (2005), the ousted fundamentalists were not just back in strength but were also creating considerable mischief in the Eastern provinces. The people were talking about rampant corruption in government ministries and provincial departments, jobs were being sold and bought in markets, and arms and ammunition were in evidence in plenty but then the latter were a part of traditional Afghan life. On the other hand, the successful holding of presidential and parliamentary elections along with provincial council elections was certainly a major achievement for a fledgling government still on probation but, here again, the credit rightfully went to the people. It was evident that the Taliban were not welcome back as far as the people were concerned. And yet, they did come back in another 16 years, and we are trying to understand why and how that happened. 'It was widely acknowledged that the the real winners in the two elections was not the Bush administration but the people of Afghanistan who were immensely proud to have voted for the first time in their history and thereafter to have exercised their right to vote for a second time within a year.[42]

---

42 Apratim Mukarji, *Challenges to Democratization, Peace and Stability in Afghanistan*, incl. In K. Warikoo ed. *Afghanistan The Challenge*, issued under the auspices of Himalayan research and Cultural Foundation, New Delhi, Pentagon Press, p.27.

A second important feature of these elections was the virtual absence of violence, especially when all participating parties and their leaders were maintaining battle-hardened fully-armed militia. This was a very unusual feature in a democratic exercise but still the elections passed off peacefully. There was, however, a major hiccup. Human rights activists pointed out that the electoral success of so many warlords and their hench men, tainted with previous records of numerous atrocities perpetuated on the people during the mujahideen days and the civil war, indicated a serious defect in the democratic system being developed. In normal conditions, these people should not have passed through the nomination stage, not to speak of being allowed to contest the elections. But they did all that and most of them won the electoral battle too. It was obvious that the electoral mechanism used in the country was considerably defective.

The most damaging feature of this period—when the war had ended, relative peace was achieved, and a new state and government had taken over—was that the whole reconstruction and democratisation process was essentially an American show; and that President Hamid Karzai was nothing more than an instrument which the Americans were using to meet their ends. From this was born the impression which slowly spread among the people that their president was merely an 'American puppet', an epithet that the Taliban used effectively to ridicule and downsize his successor Ashraf Ghani's government. People's worst fears were confirmed when the United States government opened peace negotiations with the Taliban, in 2019, bypassing the elected government.

The rapidity with which the Taliban began its campaign

to recapture the country and its consequences were reflected in the fact that even by 2005 the government's writ did not run beyond the main cities of Afghanistan. President Karzai went by the derisive nomenclature of 'Mayor of Kabul'. Could there be any worse insult for the president of the Afghan nation? All objective analyses including those of the United Nations and international aid and human rights agencies of the time pointed to the 'patently defective and inadequate policies' being pursued at the time by the US-led Coalition in restoring normalcy in Afghanistan. These were, in fact being perceived as countermanding the normalisation process to a considerable extent. Those assessments underlined the inadvisability of relying on military solutions to the menace of extremist violence without effectively attacking the sources that fed it. They also pointed out the opportunistic but self-defeating policy of utilizing warlords and militias, known to be connected with narcotic drugs smuggling, in the campaign to neutralize extremists operating in Southern and Eastern Afghanistan. Apart from these, international aid agencies in particular took strong objection (in the wake of killings of several aid workers) to the policy of US soldiers dressing in civilian clothes and driving around in white Land Cruisers typically identified with the aid agencies.

The growing complexity of the situation and the inadequate response of the US forces was amply demonstrated when on 5 July 2005 rebels attacked a US medical team as it was helping villagers in the same region of Eastern Afghanistan where an American air strike had earlier killed 17 civilians, forcing the Afghan government to rebuke the US forces. The reprimand failed to convince the people who could see that the government was totally subservient to the Americans. The Americans' inadequacy in the face of the highly complex situation was well-reflected in the words of a US military spokesperson when he blurted out that, 'It's incredible to us that the enemy would attack our forces while we are providing innocent Afghans with healthcare.'[43]

What ultimately happened in August 2021 can be better understood when, as many as four years after the democratisation, normalisation and development processes had begun in right earnest, with the blessings of the Afghans and the world, these processes reached a crossroad. The people were waiting for a signal towards the next step, but none came. For instance, the process of democratisation went forward with presidential and parliamentary elections being held successfully to the applause of the people and the world. However, at the same time, the traditional malady of non-state actors still played its nefarious role in undermining those very institutions. In a very real sense, the multiple benefits of the development of democratic institutions remained confined to urban areas as the traditional lawlessness continued to prevail over the vast countryside. Private armed groups continued to lord it over helpless citizens, and central government agencies remained unable to provide sustainable security and protection to their lives and properties. How would we look from today's perspective at the tentacles of the vast illegal drugs trade that ran through every segment of Afghan society and kept on undermining the newly-

---

43 Daniel Cooney, *US medical team attacked in Afghanistan*, www.boston.com, 6 July 2005.

emerging democratic establishment in Afghanistan? What was the real picture of development in the country? As the Asian Development Bank pointed out in its Development Outlook 2004, even the construction boom easily visible in Kabul was driven in large part by the international community's spending and emergency assistance efforts while in services, numerous hotels and guesthouses were renovated or opened since 2002, clearly to cater to foreigners. Retail trade, auto repair shops, and restaurant businesses burgeoned, and taxis, trucks and donor vehicles 'now clog Kabul's streets'. Clearly, the four years of international and Afghan efforts at rebuilding the country had little to show in substance. Back in the early 2000s, all future assessments of the potential of Afghanistan ended somewhat in the following fashion: everything depended 'on the realization of the hopes for peace, security and further stability'. As the daily brutalities in Iraq continued to be televised across the world and as the Taliban, Al-Qaeda and the motley groups of insurgents were able to strengthen the threat perception they represented, one recalled Osama bin Laden's words uttered in 2001, 'My life or death does not matter because the awakening has started.'[44]

---

44 Apratim Mukarji, *Challenges to Democratization…*, ibid, pp.45-47.

CHAPTER 10

Islamabad and Kabul Can Never Gel

THE REFERENCE to Pakistan's covert and open support of the Taliban cause was often contradicted by Pakistanis. The following report from a Pakistani to a post indicating the neighbour's involvement reflects the mood in Pakistan. Ali Effendi wrote on 7 May 2015 in response to an article published by the Institute for Defence Studies and Analysis, New Delhi, that 'Pakistan is busy with an insurgency on its own border which is its top priority. In fact, the success of the Pakistani operation can be ascertained from the fact that the militants are pouring over the border into Afghanistan. The author does not explore the possibility that the Afghan security forces may be overstretched and consequently struggling to deal with these insurgents? A compelling explanation to the security challenges being faced because of the myopic reaction to call for operations to be undertaken in the Pakistani area whose security forces are coping quite well in their anti-insurgency operations.' A reply came from Major-General (Retd.) V. Mahalingam advising Ali Effendi to look up the following publications: 'Statement by the Leading Council of the Islamic

Emirate (meaning the Taliban) regarding the inauguration of Spring Operations called "Azm" (Resolve), Voice of Jihad, 22 April 2015; Bill Roggio's article in the Long War Journal, 27 April 2015; Sheikh Ayman al-Zawahiri's "Guidelines for Jihad", As-Sahab Media in WorldAnalysis.net, 14 September 2013; Associated Press report Rahim Faiez's "Afghan officials warn of insurgents from Pakistan", 29 April 2015; David J. Lynch's "Afghan Forces Suffered Heavy Toll in First Taliban Battles", Bloomberg, 3 May 2015.'

The Pakistani reaction was identical to that of his government's and his fellow-nationals' responses to all claims by Afghanistan that the latter's efforts to contain extremists were being hampered by direct and indirect assistance from the Eastern neighbour; that the Afghan security forces were being compelled to fight two enemies, and not one, in the form of the Taliban and Pakistan's policy of assisting the insurgents while increasing their significant interference in affairs of Afghanistan. This policy still continues unabated and with evident success, and even the United States is forced to respect Pakistan's heft in the Taliban-ruled Afghanistan. The Taliban government is also subservient to Pakistan despite some appearances to the contrary.

Afghans had always taken pride in their spirit and unsullied history of independence from any outsider, and had always resisted colonialism. This sentiment lay at the roots of the fierce opposition that Afghans offered to the Soviet occupation for nearly ten years, a most ill-considered policy formulated by the Soviet Union as part of its expansionist policy. In truth, the Taliban would not possibly have grown on the soil of Afghanistan if the Soviets had never occupied the country.

The same hardened sentiment and proud history resurfaced in 2021 when, following the Taliban forces' triumphant entry into Kabul on 15 August, Pakistan felt that it must not hesitate to remind the new government of its obligations to its benefactor. This was a terrible mistake and Pakistan was condemned to pay for its error for several years to come.

Among the various minor rifts that had arisen between the two neighbours, the most significant one was related to the formation and character of the new cabinet. For several reasons the Taliban Islamic Movement's High Council decided to form only an interim government in the beginning. It wanted to test the durability and capability of the cabinet ministers appointed in the first phase. However, the choice of individual Taliban leaders was securely based on the determination that the first Taliban government would be an inclusive government. This decision was taken because at the time, the Doha Shura was calling the shots in continuance of its status during the three-year-old negotiations with foreign powers led by an immensely impatient United States government. The latter had lost heavily in its misadventure to eradicate the Taliban and other fundamentalist groups, in putting hundreds of thousands of its own servicemen and women on the front line, and in pouring down billions of dollars to maintain its dominance on Afghanistan. Contrary to the United States' calculations, the Taliban 1.0 had not actually ended with their defeat in November 2001 but has continued with the Taliban 2.0. Instead of being finished forever, the terrorists have risen phoenix-like from the ashes to retake power in August 2021.

To return to our point of discussion, the United States is not the only country to be disappointed over the turn of events but Pakistan is another. Pakistan's expectation that the Taliban 2.0 would be grateful forever to it has also proved to be an illusion. As Afghan history had forewarned, even the Taliban group has never assented to playing second fiddle in their own country. They certainly remain grateful to Pakistan for its enormous and continuing bounty; but they know that this munificence shall last only as long as Kabul implements all the orders that its superior hands over to it.

Islamabad raised a strong objection to the decision to have an inclusive government which would have been composed of Taliban and opposition leaders plus representatives from the ethnic minorities. There was also a special provision for inviting the former President Hamid Karzai and the former Chief Executive Officer Dr. Abdullah Abdullah in the new cabinet in order to prevent a separation from the ousted elected governments. The reason why the terrorists were interested in including these two political leaders was to placate the international community which was insisting on their inclusion so that the new government could be trusted. There was also a clearly defined desire on the part of the Taliban not to break completely with the past so that the process of seeking continuation of the Afghan state could be made easier. But this was completely unacceptable to Pakistan and to the Quetta Shura and the Pakistan-based Haqqani Network. Therefore, Pakistan, the Quetta Shura and the Haqqani Network banded together and put such pressure on the Taliban leaders that they had to back down from their initial determination, and the Doha Shura was superseded by the Quetta Shura, thereby changing the complexion of the new interim cabinet. The reformed cabinet became one of pure and unspoiled Taliban hard-liners' club, and for good measure almost all senior and junior ministers figure among the world's most wanted terrorists. A cabinet of some distinction, indeed!

After the tussle over the issue of inclusiveness and exclusiveness was forcibly settled, the Taliban Islamic Movement leadership announced the finalisation of the cabinet formation: Mullah Mohammad Hasan Akhund was declared the head of state of the Islamic Emirate of Afghanistan with Mullah Baradar Akhund and Mullah Abdus Salam as his deputies. It was learned confidentially that Mullah Akhundzada had recommended Mullah Hasan Akhund for the post. Sirajuddin Haqqani of the Pakistan-based Haqqani Network was given the vital post of interior minister with the power to appoint all provincial governors, thus reflecting the fruition of the Inter-Services Intelligence Directorate's desire to control Afghanistan by setting up the Haqqani Network to be almost as powerful as the Taliban themselves. Therein lay the seeds of flare-up between the two sides almost immediately after the appointments which also marked the triumph of the Quetta Shura over the Doha Shura and Pakistan's tightening grip over the government.

An assertion made at the time by former Afghan Vice-President Amarullah Saleh made a major impact. He said that the Taliban were being 'micromanaged' by the ISI as Islamabad was effectively in charge of Afghanistan. He also claimed that the government's official spokesperson was receiving briefings from the Pakistani embassy in Kabul 'by the hour'. Pakistan had now promoted itself into a colonial power, he added. The ISI seemed to confirm Saleh's assertion while making a public statement that…ISI is working overtime to bring its own person as Afghanistan government head. No one is talking about government in Kabul right now. Some leadership for Kabul is also likely.

The reorganised cabinet included such United Nations-sanctioned notorious Taliban criminals who were imprisoned in the infamous Guantanamo Bay prison of the United States on the suspecion of involvement in the 11 September 2001 attacks on the United States. At least 14 of the cabinet ministers are on the United Nations Security Council blacklist. They include acting Prime Minister Mullah Mohammad Hasan Akhund and both his deputies. Specially designated global terrorist Sirajuddin Haqqani, who carries a reward of $10 million on his head, is the acting interior minister while his uncle Khalil Haqqani is the acting minister for refugees. Acting defence minister Mullah Yaqoob, acting foreign minister Mullah Ameer Khan Muttaqi and his deputy Sher Mohammad Abbas Stanikzai are all listed under the UNSC 1988 Sanctions Committee, also known as the Taliban Sanctions Committee. 'At least 14 members of the Taliban's interim government are on the UNSC Security Council blacklist.'[45]

So much for the eligibility of the Taliban government to sit along with the representatives of over 190 member-nations of the United Nations and to participate on an equal footing with leaders of other countries! In fact, the history of the Taliban shows that their leaders have always been adept in exploiting given situations in order to further their cause and to bolster the impression that it is foolish to oppose them. The Taliban

---

45 BBC Urdu section.

initially received genuine support from the people in Southern and Eastern Afghanistan where they were victims of rampant corruption, failed governance and looting and murdering on highways by hired goons of the warlords. In contrast, in provinces where the people were satisfied with the governance of the Burhanuddin Rabbani-Ahmad Shah Massoud duo, they made little headway.[46]

In the media report on the triumphant entry of the Taliban into Kabul on 26 September 1996 we get sufficient evidence of Pakistan's deep involvement with the rise of the Taliban as a formidable military force. The report tells us how Baharak, a village in the Northern Afghanistan's Panjsher valley played a major role in exposing the presence of Pakistani regulars among Taliban fighters which helped win the war against the Burhanuddin Rabbani-Ahmad Shah Massoud's army. Since the fundamentalist Taliban swept the Burhanuddin Rabbani regime from Kabul, in September, fighting spread from the capital, North to the mouth of the 100-kilometer-long Panjsher. In August 1996, the forces of Burhanuddin Rabbani's partner-in-the-compromise-government Ahmad Shah Massoud counter-attacked and the war shifted back towards Kabul. Apart from the 350-plus who died or were wounded, more than 700 Taliban fighters were taken prisoners and locked up in Panjsher. Among them were 37 men who conceded that they were Pakistani citizens. 'If you want proof

---

46 See Antony Davis, *How the Taliban became a military force,* in William Maley-ed. *Afghanistan and the Taliban The rebirth of fundamentalism?,* Penguin Books, 1998, pp.43-71.

that Pakistan is actively interfering in our country, go to Baharak,' Massoud told Asiaweek. Clad in a shalwar-kameez and chequered head-scarf, Hasan Abu Hamid's sturdy build and dark complexion marked him as unmistakably Punjabi. As were several of his compatriots. Hasan's road to Afghanistan was smoothed by the Jamiat Ulema Islami (JUI), a Pakistani religious party. Son of an alim (religious scholar), Hasan studied under a local JUI leader named Maulawi Mahmoud. 'He told us that in Afghanistan and Kashmir (Indian part of the divided valley) sharia was not being enforced and it was our duty to fight. After Afghanistan and Kashmir, we would ensure that sharia was properly enforced in Pakistan.' Earlier in 1998, the 24-year-old underwent training in a camp in South-Eastern Afghanistan near the town of Khost. 'There were about 40 of us in the group,' Hasan said. 'We were trained by a Pakistani man called Safiullah and two assistants in the use of small arms—pistols, rifles, rocket-propelled grenades.' Ultimately, Hasan's new-found military skill was of little use. In mid-October, he and six other Pakistanis operating with a force of some 60 Afghan Taliban were ambushed by Massoud's troops on the winding Salang highway. 'We were attacked from two sides as darkness fell. We abandoned the armoured vehicles and ran. We moved at night across the mountains and next morning came down and surrendered.' The former Kabul authorities found it less easy to present clear evidence of the involvement of Pakistan's military intelligence. The ISI, for years the sharp end of Pakistan's Afghan policy, is also believed to have helped the Taliban logistically and advised them on strategy. Shortly before the fall of Kabul a Taliban military transport landed in Massoud-controlled territory. On board were five Pakistanis.

They were held in Panjsher under suspicion that they were ISI officers. The leader of the group Omar Faruq, a grey-bearded man in his early 50s, insisted that he was a religious teacher. His group he claimed wearily was merely visiting a shrine in Afghanistan and were the victims of a frame-up. But analysts were in little doubt that the ISI had links with Pakistani religious parties that provided volunteers for jihad in both Kashmir and Afghanistan. 'It is part of the privatization of an earlier operation run by the ISI for the Kashmir conflict,' according to a Western source. 'Beyond that, these religious factions were sending youth to fight and the authorities have done nothing to stop it. That certainly gelled with what the Panjsher POWs had to say. When groups finished training for Kashmir ISI officers would issue them with weapons, ammunition and 2,000 rupees ($50) a man.'[47]

However, when the Taliban regained power in August 2021, and the new government was able to revamp the domestic security system, the issue of border management in the East became paramount for this was the entry point of Pakistan's ISI agents and provocateurs. It did not take long for clashes to flare up between the two sides. Islamabad apparently had expected unfettered entry and exit with its own creation, the Taliban, in power in Kabul. But the Taliban leadership had already looked at the dark side of Pakistan's 'unstinting' help in seizing power. Pakistani actions seemed to imply that the ISI expected its earlier arrangement to continue. But that was a

---

47 Anthony Davis, Baharak, The Not So Hidden Hands: How Pakistanis Help the Taliban crusade, Asiaweek, http://edition.cnn.com/ASIANOW/asiaweek/96/1129/nat3.html

different time altogether as there was no governance in the last days of the Ashraf Ghani government. The new government would not permit the old haphazard border management to continue at any cost.

On 17 April 2022, Pakistan shot off a stiff warning to the Taliban government in Afghanistan to stop sheltering home-grown Pakistani Taliban militants who were lately staging increasingly deadly attacks against the Pakistani military. The warning followed Afghan reports that Pakistani aircraft had carried out bombing raids late on 15 April night in Eastern Afghanistan's Khost and Kunar provinces, killing civilians. Pakistan kept quiet for the time being, and on the contrary brought fresh allegations that the Taliban government had taken a hands-off policy towards Pakistani Taliban's depredations. 'Terrorists are using Afghan soil with impunity to carry out activities inside Pakistan,' the Pakistani Foreign Ministry said in a statement, but it chose such a harsh language that it immediately attracted wide attention.

This episode contrasted sharply with the picture that prevailed before the Taliban swept to power in Afghanistan. That time, barely a year ago, everything was hunkey dorey between the two. The Taliban of Afghanistan were nurtured by Pakistan on its own soil, sheltered in innumerable camps, all financed by the United States and Saudi Arabia, trained by the Pakistan Army and the ISI, armed, and then pushed into Afghanistan through its Eastern border. When the Taliban 2.0 sat on the throne of absolute power in Kabul, Islamabad deliberately projected the ISI and its army as the creator and protector of the new rulers. The cabinet formation could not be done without the ISI's approval. But, soon the brotherly relations soured and towards the end of 2021 Kabul began to protest publicly about Islamabad's intransigence in hindering proper border fencing to prevent easy access from Pakistan. Clashes and mutual firing became a routine affair throughout the last few months of 2021; and then further proof that the Taliban regime and Pakistan were not yet in a mood to stop low-scale hostilities was available in the beginning of 2022 as well.

The Taliban's first conquest of Afghanistan primarily represents a clever application of the Islamic concept of holy war to wage a war against a legitimate state on the pretext of rampant corruption and serious deviation from the correct Islamic path. This concoction apparently proved successful in the first experiment, and various circumstances were efficiently exploited by the fundamentalists. The second application of the concept of jihad as a weapon against a targeted enemy was apparently a different case altogether. It was no longer an experiment. On the contrary, jihad played a restricted part in the war and much more importance was attached to strategic and tactical warfare along with adequate weaponry, money power and fighting spirit. It was a war in its full implication. That an 80,000 strong army of the Taliban Islamic Movement could defeat a mythical 300,000-strong Afghan state army brought little credit to the Talibs' fighting skills. The fact must not be forgotten that the invaders were fully and efficiently supported by a modern state with a highly efficient army and by Pakistan's devilishly clever spy agency ISI. On their part, the Afghan state and its army remained friendless throughout the war even though backed by a large American army and by a NATO-led coalition force with sufficient military supplies. But the outcome of this international military assistance eventually came to little as in the first place, a major deficit of trust bedevilled relations between the home army and its benefactors. Besides, the Afghan governments of the first President Hamid Karzai and his successor Ashraf Ghani never enjoyed an easy, intimate and trustworthy relationship with each other. The growing corruption despite strong international warnings only served to strengthen this trust deficit. Ghani's image both in his country and in the world at large plummeted when US President Donald Trump arranged direct negotiations with the Taliban excluding the Afghan president. It was too much for him and he lashed out at his American counterpart, even though his publicly expressed anger and frustration was of no avail.

The bitter relations between the two presidents, Donald Trump and Ashraf Ghani, and their administrations came to a head when a startled world, the United States and Afghanistan included, learned to their utmost shock, that Trump and his administration and the Taliban had come to an agreement in a peace deal in which American troops would be withdrawn from Afghan soil in instalments with the first drawdown to take place in May 2019. In return, the Taliban would ensure that they would issue counterterrorism measures in order to protect the withdrawing American soldiers. In this utterly surprising and thoroughly undiplomatic agreement the Afghan president and his administration was nowhere in sight. The news, which broke in February 2019, also shocked the Afghan people. After the scandal broke out, Trump said it was time to bring their people back home. Immediately after his administration signed the deal with the Taliban, 5,000 American troops were brought back home, even as Trump said, 'maybe I'll invite Taliban leaders in the near future'. However, he did not specify the date for such a meeting. He added that the White House had been trying to reach an agreement for a long time and had faith in the deal because everyone is tired of war. 'I really believe the Taliban (want) to do something to show we are not wasting time. If bad things happen, we will go back with a force like no-one never seen (sic).' The deal was signed between the Special Presidential Representative for Afghanistan Reconstruction, the Afghan-American Zalmay Khalilzad, and the Taliban Political Chief Mullah Abdul Ghani Baradar who acted on behalf of the Taliban at the Doha talks. Another media comment asked if a peace process could ever work when the government of the country was excluded from the conflict-resolution process. 'We may be finding out. Both the US and Russian efforts excluded the Afghan government.' A third media report said that Trump had disclosed in a tweet that he had arranged a meeting between President Ghani and the Taliban at Camp David. The latter had counter proposed severe restrictions on terrorist attacks. But the Afghan government had been kept ignorant about it. A further report asked if 'the suspicious move was motivated by Trump's penchant for a dramatic spectacle. The plan was put together on the spur of the moment.' The newspaper said that the US government and the Taliban negotiators reportedly came together on a broad agreement. American troops would be withdrawn and the Taliban would publish counter-terrorist assurances. The Afghan government was excluded from the peace process. Yet another report quoted a former top-ranking security official in the Trump administration who said Trump 'never intended to withdraw American troops by 1 May because the deal was a ruse. True to form Team Trump, there was no due diligence and the usual National Security Council process was dispensed with. This disclosure made it clear that the United States not only excluded the Afghan government from the negotiations but also hoodwinked the Taliban who were perhaps happy to play along in the hope of striking it rich.

President Ghani was easily cornered by both the Trump administration and the Taliban because he was holding on to his highly-questioned presidency. The manner in which he refused to take seriously his rival candidate Dr Abdullah Abdullah's claim to the top job because of the controversial voting and vote counting process, was widely reported among opposition groups, and in the media and the general public. A US report commented, 'the capacity, transparency, legitimacy, and cohesiveness of Afghan governance are crucial to Afghan stability as nearly all international forces exited Afghanistan by the end of 2016. The size and capability of the Afghan governing structure has increased significantly since the Taliban regime fell in late 2001, but the government remains rife with rumours of corruption and ethnic and political tensions among the major factions. Its recent elections have been marred by allegations of vast fraud and post-election political crises. Hamid Karzai who served as president since late-2001, was constitutionally term-limited and left office when his successor Ashraf Ghani was inaugurated on 29 September 2016. The inauguration represented a resolution of a presidential election dispute which was under Afghan and US official attention from April to September. The results on 5 April 2014, of the first round of the election required a 14 June runoff between Ghani and Dr Abdullah—increasing tensions between Ghani's Pashtun community, Afghanistan's largest ethnic group, and the Tajik community with which Dr Abdullah was identified, though he himself is a Pashtun. Following accusations by Dr Abdullah of widespread fraud in the runoff, (US) Secretary of State John Kerry brokered an agreement that led to a recount of all the 23,000 ballot boxes and the eventual formation of a post-election unity government in which Dr Abdullah, the losing candidate, became the Chief Executive Officer (CEO) of the government. The CEO was to function as a prime minister, pending a subsequent national deliberation over changing the constitution to create a formal prime ministerial post. The resolution of the election dispute paved the way for the long-delayed signing of formal agreements which would allow the US and NATO to deploy military personnel to train Afghan forces (Resolution Support Mission) and conduct counterterrorism operations (Operation Freedom Sentinel). This power-sharing agreement nearly paralyzed the Afghan central government. Dr Abdullah's role in government (was) limited and until early January 2015, the two top people in government were unable to agree on new cabinet appointments despite a constitutional requirement to form a cabinet within thirty days of taking office. The government (was) run in the interim by caretaker officials and bureaucrats lacking high-level policy direction. The cabinet choices reportedly represented a compromise between competence and ethnic representation. Government authority (remained) constrained not only by the power-structure but also by the exertion of influence by the long-standing internal power structure consisting of regional and ethnic leaders. Faction leaders often (maintained) groups of armed fighters who administered justice in an arbitrary fashion and were guilty of gross human rights abuses. These constraints slowed down Ghani's efforts to prioritize curbs on governmental corruption and promoting women's rights.[48]

The above authoritative analysis shows clearly how badly President Ashraf Ghani was placed when the demand was articulated for the dismissal of his government and fresh elections, a demand buttressed by pressure exerted by both the Americans and the Taliban. The United States had been pressing hard on Ghani to honour the agreement, which was brokered by a highly-placed US official, but the Afghan president stubbornly refused to honour his obligations. The Taliban Islamic Movement kept on saying that until the Afghan government honoured its own agreement to open up its institutions and drive corruption out of the system it would not agree to start negotiating for a peace deal. They of course knew very well that even if he tried honestly (which he was doing in truth) Ghani would not be able to do so for then his own supporters would revolt against him and his government would collapse. The Congressional report referred to above lends credence to Ghani's position that he was trying his utmost to cleanse his administration but was being deterred by his own men.

Ever since the war ceased, international human rights agencies and NGOs working in this field had been attempting to help ensure that the significant gains in civil society, women's rights and media freedom achieved since 2001 were

---

48 Congressional Research Service, *Afghanistan: Politics, The elections, and Government Performance*, Kenneth Katzman, Specialist in Middle Eastern Affairs, 12 January 2015.

preserved. Those gains had come despite the persistence of traditional attitudes and Islamic conservatism in many parts of Afghanistan—attitudes that caused the judicial and political system to tolerate child marriages and imprisonment of women who fled domestic violence. Islamist influence and tradition had also frequently led to persecution of converts from Islam to Christianity, and put curbs on the sale of alcohol and Western-oriented media programmes. Afghan civil society activists, particularly women's groups, asserted at the time that many of these gains were at risk as international forces departed. That these apprehensions were well-founded was proved by events subsequent to the withdrawal of Coalition forces in August 2021. Immediately after the Taliban took over control of the country, the first assault was mounted on women's rights. Girls' schools were shut down, women were once again prohibited from going out of homes alone unless accompanied by a male relative. The punishment for transgression of the sharia revisited Afghanistan with public caning, and imprisonment. Women's public baths were closed, and women workers were prevented from attending office. Only women healthcare workers were permitted to continue with their job. All existing facilities for boys and men were preserved.

Before we take up the topic of rampant corruption in the Taliban-freed Afghanistan, we would like to turn to the famous Indian treatise called the Arthasastra written by Kautilya in the 4th Century BC. This legendary practitioner of statecraft whose text taught kings, prime ministers and even common people how to lead their lives fruitfully while serving their interests. He cautioned his readers, 'All undertakings depend upon finance. Hence, foremost attention shall be paid to the treasury. Public prosperity, rewards for good conduct, capture of thieves, dispensing with (the services of too many) government servants, abundance of harvest, prosperity of commerce, absence of troubles and calamities, diminution of remission of taxes, and income in gold are all conducive to financial prosperity. Obstruction, loan, trading, fabrication of accounts, causes the loss of revenue. Self-enjoyment, barter, and defalcation are the causes that tend to deplete (the treasury).' Kautilya also provides the definitions of obstruction, and loan, trading. He also describes the varieties of punishment that any misconduct in the matter of state revenue shall attract. We easily realize the relevance of this treatise in guiding modern states in their most important activities such as setting up a kingdom, appointment of ministers, public servants, dealing with the public, etc.[49]

It was sheer misfortune that despite being taught at every step with the sanest advice on how to prevent corruption from affecting the state, Afghanistan failed to benefit and run the state efficiently. An illustration of how an independent body to regulate the appointment of provincial governors and the lower bureaucracy was corrupted to serve one individual's interests was provided by President Karzai who converted the Independent Directorate for Local Governance (IDLG) into his own fief. In terms of local governance institution-building, a key institution was empowered in August 2007 when the responsibility for selecting local leaders (provincial governors

---

49 R. Shamasastry, *Kautilya's Arthasastra*, Mysore Printing and Publishing House, Mysore, India, First Edition, 1915.

and below) was given to the IDLG. That function was taken out of the Interior Ministry. However, some international officials remarked later that the IDLG served primarily as an instrument for Karzai 'to mobilize voters'. It was headed by Abdul Khaliq Farahi, a former diplomat who was kidnapped in Peshawar, Pakistan, and held during 2008-2011 allegedly by militants linked to Al-Qaeda. To address the difficulty in recruiting staff to work in far-off areas, the 26 July 2012 Karzai administrative reform decree required the IDLG to fill open positions in provinces within six months, including in ministry offices in each provincial capital. It also required a review of provincial governors' performance in combating corruption and improving governance. The IDLG was an implementing partner for the District Delivery Programme (DDP), which was created to improve government presence and service delivery at the district level, and was funded by the United States, the UK, Denmark, and France. The programme was phased out in conjunction with a transition to Afghan leadership at the end of 2014. The IDLG also received assistance from the UN Development Programme's Afghanistan Subnational Governance Programme-II (ASGP-II). That programme provided $83.6 million to the IDLG from the European Community, Italy, Switzerland, and the UK.

Later, many came to believe that even more than institutional expansion, the key to effective local governance was the appointment of competent and incorruptible governors in all the 34 provinces. The United Nations, the US, and various international studies and reports all pointed to the beneficial effects (reduction in narcotic trafficking, economic growth, lower violence) of some of the strong Afghan appointments at the provincial level. There were numerous successful governors, such as, Mangal, Sherzai, Noor, and others mentioned in the CRS. But the successful governors were almost invariably accused of arbitrary administration of justice and excessive independence from central government authority. Despite the international and Afghan emphasis on expanding merit-based appointments, about half of the provincial governors continued to be political appointments. In September 2012, Karzai shuffled 10 out of the 34 governors (including Mangal), asserting that those taken out of their positions had fallen short of improving governance or combating corruption. However, many observers suspected the reshuffle was planned to place loyalists in key local positions ahead of the 2014 election. Some of the ousted governors were assigned to different provinces. Other than Helmand, the nine provinces where governors were changed included Wardak, Kabul, Takhar, Faryab, Baghlan, Nimruz, Laghman, Lowgar, and Baghdis. Since taking office, President Ashraf Ghani told IDLG officials to set clear benchmarks for provincial governor appointments as part of an effort to expand merit-based appointments and to improve the efficiency of provincial governors and mayors. One problem noted by governance experts was that the role of the elected provincial councils remained unclear. In most provinces, the provincial councils did not act as true local legislatures and were weak compared to provincial governors' offices. Legislation to expand the role of councils was under consideration by the National Assembly (Meshrano Jirga). But most recent versions of a provincial council law were stripped by the cabinet, of provisions to assign to the councils supervisory duties. Perhaps the most significant role the provincial councils played was in choosing the upper house of the National Assembly. In the absence of district councils (no elections held or scheduled), the provincial council elections 2007 chose two-thirds (68 seats) of the 102-seat body. Karzai appointed the remaining 34 seats in February 2011. The elections for the provincial councils in all 34 provinces were held on 20 August 2009, concurrent with the presidential elections....The first provincial council elections were held concurrent with the parliamentary elections in 2005. According to American officials, there had been 'measured progress' in developing effective district governance. District governors were appointed by the president, on the recommendation of the IDLG, and more than half of all district governors were appointed based on merit, as noted above. Some districts had no formal governance until the 2009 US troop surge. Some of the district governors in Helmand Province, including in Nawa and Now Zad districts, returned after the US–led expulsion of Taliban militants. The difficulty plaguing the expansion of district governance in addition to security issues was lack of resources. Many district governors had virtually no staff or vehicles. In about 40 districts, the United States and partner countries established District Support Teams (DSTs) to assist in district-level governance and service delivery. However, like the PRTs, the DSTs were turned over to Afghan control as the transition advanced. In essence, it was the long history of bad and corrupt governance which was seldom effective beyond districts adjoining Kabul, which led to the unending suffering of the people. The Koranic and sharia laws were interpreted by extremely orthodox clergy and foreign clerics to conclude that the country was ripe for taking up in earnest the concept and ideal of jihadism. Before the idea was implanted in Afghan minds, no Afghan had ever committed suicide as a means of punishing an individual or ruler and getting rid of him to usher in the 'just' life of a true Muslim living in an Islamic state.

CHAPTER 11

And Now On To Jihadism

HISTORICALLY AND chronologically speaking, Sayyid Qutb (1906-1966), born in Egypt, is the most well-known among the intellectual pioneers of radical political Islam, a movement that now stands for a radically reformulated notion of jihad, a doctrine shared by all Muslims. The debate around radical political Islam is thus increasingly a debate on the meaning of jihad. Concern for the umma, the global Muslim community, is part of the five pillars (rukn) of Islam and is binding on every Muslim. The Koran insists that a Muslim's first duty is to create a just and egalitarian society in which poor people are treated with respect (a fuller discussion of Qutb's version of political Islam follows shortly). The connection between state corruption and jihadism is but a short, necessary and preordained step which was established in many jihadism-afflicted Muslim states. Afghanistan reached this stage much later than the Arab states where jihadism first raised its powerful and hellish head.[50]

When Omar Abdal-Rahman, the leader of the Egyptian Islamic movement, imprisoned in the United States, denounced these 70 years without the Shari'a which he unequivocally denounced as being responsible for all the ills of his community, it appeared that he was trying to reconcile a profane norm with divine law which he valued above all else. But if the impact of this appeal was so clearly surpassed by the radical Islamist fringe, if much of the Arab world at the time was calling in unison and similarly for the 'application of the Shari'a,' and if the Islamist upsurge became, with all the repression, the focus for rebuilding the political scene in the region, it was because it had raised the stakes beyond 'the return of the sacred' to encompass the restoration of a symbolic order in its totality. The 'law of God' was there primarily endogenous rather than celestial. Of course, there were certain 'religious factions' whose acquaintance with the system of representation was less than smooth, but their philosophical, literary or political references—in fact all those ingredients that constituted an identity—though discredited by the intrusion of

---

50 A curious exception was Sri Lanka, by no means a Muslim nation, but where its extremists, the Liberation Tigers of Tamil Eelam (LTTE) entered the already-set confrontation zone between the northern Tamils (who had suffered especially since the advent of the 20th Century at the hands of the majority Sinhalese) and drew their inspiration and training from Northern Arabs in Tunisia, Algeria and Egypt, and brought together its combined strength to fight the remorseless and dangerously prejudiced Sri Lankan state for 26 years with its own version of jihadism. The first suicide jacket found outside the Arab world was discovered in Colombo harbour where a dead suicide bomber lay in the waters and media persons were invited to have a look at him one morning.

westernisation were no longer folkloric and their attraction and credibility were inexorably rediscovered. The upsurge, from the Iranian Revolution to the assassination of President Sadat and the double electoral victory for the Front Islamique du Salut, born in Algeria (FIS)—on 12 June 1990 and on 26 December 1991—was indicative of a political and economic rupture. However real the various catalysts might have been (especially the economic), however diverse its political expressions, it was essentially in the old dynamic of de-colonisation that Islamism took root. At first political, then economic, the distancing of the former coloniser through the rhetoric of adversarial Islam became ideological, symbolic and then more broadly cultural in the terrain where the shock of colonisation became more traumatic. In addition to endowing its own language, local culture and history with the dynamic of independence and with something that had been missing for a long time, ie, the special attributes of a sort of ideological 'autonomy,' that in turn recognised the right of those who propagated it to regain universality without denouncing the structural elements of their 'specificity.' Even if this chronology responded more to the demands of the didactic than of a manifestly less linear history, it was primarily the reaction to the cultural impact of the colonial irruption that later ignited what has been called the Islamist 'third stage' of the 'rocket of decolonisation'.[51]

---

51 Francois Burgat, *Face to Face with Political Islam*, IB. Tauris, Paris, 1996.

This cumulative rejection of and hatred for anything less than fundamentalist Islam eventually led to the sternest manifestation of jihad, and found its ultimate fulfilment in the 9/11 Al-Qaeda attacks on the United States of America which was regarded universally in the Arab world as the most evil of all evils. In the preliminary stages of this growing isolation of the United States and all Western civilizational claims that the country made, it was remarkable that jihadists and their civil supporters—especially among the young and educated Muslims—never gave up their ingrained faith in the inevitability of the eventual success of jihadism.

Within the Arab Muslim world, especially in those countries that were vital to regional stability and US interests, the radicals may have lost the war 'against the state but they won the theological debate.' In the Middle East and Pakistan, religious discourse dominated societies, the airways, and the thinking world. Radical mosques proliferated throughout Egypt. Bookstores were full of works on religious themes. In Saudi Arabia, one in five undergraduates majored in Islamic studies. In Jordan, a Salaafiya (an approach to Islam trying to emulate the way in which early Muslims practised their religion) form of Islam surged via informal social networks and eclipsed tamer forms of Islamism. In Pakistan, religious educated created a generation of zealots. The demand for shari'a, the belief that their governments were unfaithful to Islam and that Islam was the answer to all problems, and the certainty that the West had declared war on Islam: these were the themes that dominated public discussion. Islamists may not have controlled parliaments or government palaces, but they occupied popular imagination.[52]

Strengthening the appeal of political Islam was the illegitimacy of the governments that opposed it. Egypt was more authoritarian at the time of writing than it had been a decade ago. Saudi Arabia's government was casting about for ways to appear more legitimate without actually expanding political participation; Jordan delayed parliamentary elections and adopted newly repressive laws; Algeria was being run, behind the scenes, by its army; and Pakistan was ruled by a military dictator. The political oppression that had invited a violent reaction in the 1990s grew worse in some cases. There was liberalization only in a handful of countries, mostly small Persian Gulf states. The governments, of course, realised that some form of legitimacy was essential to their survival. They also realized that the wind was blowing towards Islam. Thus their quest led them to burnish their own Islamic credentials. Even Nasser appreciated this need. Sadat understood this need better still. He went to mosque, adopted the traditional dress, changed the Egyptian constitution to make shari'a a source for Egyptian law, and gave free rein to Islamist groups that ultimately gunned him down. Even as it threw Muslim brothers in jail, Mubarak's regime fought for control of religious discourse by strengthening its grip on the clerics of al-Azhar, licensing and staffing the mosques, and allowing family laws to be challenged in court, something that had so offended the Islamists. In Saudi Arabia the king's right to rule was solely

---

52 Daniel Benjamin, Steven Simon, *The Age of Sacred Terror Radical Islam's War Against America*, Random House Trade Paperbacks, Random House Inc., New York, 2002.

based on religious credentials. The regime used to imprison Islamists who questioned if the king was fulfilling his religious responsibilities, but the state also appropriated their language of piety and gave scope to employ their anti-Western rhetoric. As in Egypt, this deflected popular resentment from the regime and turned it towards the United States. The secular, British-educated General who ran Pakistan, used Islamic language to buttress his credibility in an increasingly strident religious environment. But his strategy of competing with the opposition on its issues could not be sustained indefinitely. Every flanking movement undertaken by these regimes validated the Islamist agenda. The state's claim to superior religious authority was not taken seriously and the official clergy were known to parrot government discourse. The game was played in the early 2000s by 'ibn Taymiyya rules': apostate regimes were illegitimate, and so were the ulema who defended them. In a race to show the people who was more Islamic, the Islamists would win every time. Sooner or later, these regimes discovered rather late and to their utter dismay that challenging the Islamists at their own game endangered their long-term survival. The most deleterious effect of this foolish course of action was that it pitted the ruler's role as patron and defender of Islam against his responsibilities as the leader of a modernising state. Today's relatively liberalized state came much later and after sustained struggles by civil society, especially the brave women of Saudi Arabia, and some Western-educated royals and bureaucrats.[53]

---

53 Daniel Benjamin , Steven Simon, Ibid.

The narrative of how the United States was manoeuvred into the trap of Islamism is available in a study of the growing relationship between Saudi Arabia and the US. The 9/11 massacres happened because of a decision taken by the first Bush administration in a bid to solidify its strategic position in the Middle East at a time when the zone was already witnessing the spread of the virus of jihadism and Islamism. Putting troops on the ground in Saudi Arabia, the Bush administration concluded, was the only solution to effectively defend the kingdom. Anything less drastic, such as a punishing round of air strikes, for example, was considered to be too feeble to deter President Saddam Hussein. But having resolved on direct intervention, the White House came up against an unexpected problem: Saudi reluctance to let sizeable numbers of American soldiers into the country. Since the days of Ibn Saud, the royal family had opposed any conspicuous foreign military presence in the kingdom—partly out of fear of colonial occupation (the fate of several neighbouring countries and the example of Afghanistan later in the 1970s too apparently worked powerfully on the Saudi government's mind) and partly out of fear of domestic protest. In 1945, Riyadh rejected an American proposal to station a small military training group in the kingdom, because, as William A. Eddy, the American ambassador explained to his superiors in Washington, according to King Ibn Saud it would provoke 'violent criticisms from reactionaries and fanatics'. Forty-five years later, the monarchy still dreaded such criticism, and so King Fahd resisted Washington's request for permission to deploy its forces there. In a desperate bid to change his mind, Bush sent Dick Cheney to Riyadh to try to convince the monarch of the urgent need for military action. This ingrained fear was well-founded: Osama bin Laden's hostility to the United States was primarily provoked by the deployment of American troops in Saudi Arabia and the continuing alliance between Washington and the Riyadh royal family. And though this alliance may have evolved over the years adapting to changing regional and international conditions, it remained, as before, a product of American thirst for imported oil and the royal family's hunger for protection. But the protection would not come to any happy conclusion either way. The local elections held in 2006 in Saudi Arabia led to the 'stunning' emergence of Islamist fundamentalism in the kingdom.[54]

No discussion on Afghanistan, the Afghan Taliban, and the various Muslim countries now permanently haunted by the spectre of terrorism can be complete without dealing with Pakistan. When one discusses the inter-relationship between the Muslim state and its various office-holders such as presidents, prime ministers and generals, it is imperative that sufficient notice be taken of the part that 'revenge' plays in settling scores among these stakeholders. The instinct of revenge figures very high in the 'national consensus' reflected in the anger of those who want generals offending against democracy 'punished as traitors'. But there are countless others who speak from rage of a personal nature: people affected directly or indirectly by the general's—we are speaking here mainly of Gen. Pervez Musharraf—decisions. The sceptics were convinced that as in

---

54 Michael T. Klare, *Blood And Oil The Dangers and Consequences of America's Growing Dependency on Imported Petroleum The American Empire Project*, Henry Hot and Company LLC, New York, 2004, pp. 50-5.

past cases, the general would be let off the hook and spirited abroad to live the high life in the Gulf on the basis of some deeply laid international plot which included America at worst and the Gulf Shaikhs at best. Musharraf's defenders were few, the most cogent of them surmising that an army facing terrorists in the Tribal Areas would not take the death of its ex-chief as a morale-booster. It could even encourage the troops to think, subconsciously, poorly of their seniors, who could be hanged by the civilians they pretended to defend. The political party which Musharraf had evicted from power hated him because he had deposed its Prime Minister Nawaz Sharif in October 1999 and put him in jail, charging him with treason, no less. In the Opposition, the Pakistan People's Party hated him because it believed that the 'deep state' under him had killed its leader Benazir Bhutto in December 2007. Less wise than his father Zardari, party chairman Bilawal Bhutto-Zardari uttered some harsh words about the ex-president.

Those in parliament, who should have had no complaints against him, joined the angry chorus because 'populism (was) the order of the day' thanks to the passionately anti-Musharaff media. After his trial was over, Musharaff said whatever he faced was not a 'fair' trial but a 'process of vendetta' through which a number of political parties sought revenge. He named the revenge-seekers: Mullah Fazlullah, then boss of Tehreek-e-Taliban Pakistan, the Balochistan Liberation Army, elements of Lal Masjid (Red Mosque), and Al-Qaeda, all of them banned as terrorist organizations in Pakistan. He avoided naming the party whose sense of grievance against him actually rendered the process of justice suspect. The judges of a special court hearing the treason case against him were party to the vendetta, his lawyers said. Justice, a process of 'closure' of the cycle of violence was said by experts to replace revenge, which was 'circular' in nature and therefore 'perpetual'. A TV anchor actually wondered whether the government in power and the judges in Pakistan would heed Nelson Mandela of South Africa who favoured reconciliation or prefer Sheikh Hasina Wajed of Bangladesh who favoured revenge.[55]

The reality for Muslims of the world in the first half of 2022, of all persons President Joe Biden of the United States pointed out while celebrating Eid-ul-Fitr on 3 May of the year, that around the world Muslims were being targeted with violence. Speaking at a White House reception for Muslims on the day, Biden said he appointed the first Muslim to serve as Ambassador-at-Large for International Religious Freedom. 'It's especially important because today, around the world we're seeing so many Muslims being targeted with violence. No one, no one should discriminate against or be oppressed for their religious beliefs,' he said. Arooj Aftab, a Pakistani vocalist and composer, was one of the speakers at the event along with First Lady Jill Biden and Dr Talib M. Shareef, Imam of Masjid Mohammed, known as the 'Nation's Mosque' in Washington DC. 'Today, we also remember all those who are not able to celebrate this holy day, including Uyghurs and Rohingyas and all those who are facing famine, violence, conflict, and disease', Biden said in his speech. 'And honour the signs of hope and

---

55 Khaled Ahmed, *Sleepwalking To Surrender Dealing With Terrorism in Pakistan*, Viking Penguin India Pvt. Ltd., 2016, pp. 365-383.

progress in the world we want to see, including the ceasefire which allowed the people in Yemen to honour Ramadan and celebrate in peace for the first time in six years', the president added.[56]

---

56   Lalit K. Jha, *Muslims being targeted with violence around the world, says Biden,* Press Trust of India, Washington, 3 May 2022.

CHAPTER 12

The Impact on Afghanistan

EACH OF these Muslim countries, right from Algeria, Tunisia, Egypt, Jordan, and Pakistan influenced Afghans in various ways, as they witnessed the spectacular rise of political Islam, and the birth of the legend of Al-Qaeda. The enormous impact of rampant corruption at the highest levels of the state, and the revolt of the pious fundamentalists and cultural isolationists, gave birth to widespread indignation and led to the rise of hardened Islamists in pockets of rural Southern Afghanistan. But there was a foreign intervention as well, the Soviet intervention and occupation of Afghanistan during 1978-89. This single development—this was by no means an isolated event in the history of Afghanistan—ie, the coup and takeover of government by the two factions of the communist party, prepared the country and its people, in more ways than one, for what was to come. Afghans were familiarised with the power of the barrel of a gun held by foreigners, and with a regime that gave abrupt orders and meted out instant punishment if disobeyed. Regimentation was creeping into the lives of ordinary Afghans who had so far only known and practised indiscipline. All these would help the Taliban to spread their fundamentalist tentacles all over the largely isolated, poor, and uneducated country. Perhaps the deepest damage was caused by the comprehensive manner in which the Soviet occupation hurt the Afghan citizen's independent spirit. Afghans were never comfortable with obeying their government without questioning and protesting. This was the reason why governance was always extraordinarily difficult in Afghanistan. As Khaled Hossaini wrote in his book '*The Kite Runner*', 'Long before the Roussi army marched into Afghanistan, long before villages were burned and schools destroyed, long before mines were planted like seeds of death and children buried in rock-piled graves, Kabul had become a city of ghosts for me. A city of hare-lipped ghosts…..Baba loved the idea of America…..At one point, Baba stood spilling his beer over the sawdust floor, and yelled, "Fuck the Russians." The bar's laughter, then in its full-throated echo, followed. Baba bought another round of pitchers for everyone.'[57] The hatred for Russians continued to reverberate through refugee Afghans former generals selling used commodities in flea markets, former rich businessmen working as gas station attendants, and doing all kinds of menial jobs, former university professors being employed as municipal workers, and ex-surgeons failing to get jobs in hospitals in foreign lands, in America. Their indignity knew no bounds which killed their minds and spirits every time they went out to work. That period seared the collective memory of Afghans

---

[57] Khaled Hossaini, *The Kite Runner*, Bloomsbury Publishing Plc., London, 2003, pp. 115-116.

even though years later Russia—no longer Soviet Russia—became one of Afghanistan's best friends.

On the societal level too, the overwhelming Soviet presence introduced and put into place firmly vital reforms: such as, girls' education was encouraged, many new schools were set up for them, women were given jobs in government departments, and more women, all wearing modern western dresses, were seen all over the streets and shops. In short, education and women's freedom spread all over the cities and urban areas. Women dressed in modern western clothes could be seen going all around. They were more visible in government and private offices than before. More Afghans and the clergy had to tolerate these 'abominations' but the resentment was smouldering in almost every heart. There could be little doubt that all these developments facilitated the emergence of radical Islam in a country whose culture had been hitherto suffused with the fine strains of Sufism. How could such a country accept Taliban rule? The answer lies in the developments which had meanwhile transformed the Arab world specifically, the birth and spread of Islamism, and the rise of jihadi politics.

As we have seen above, Afghanistan's transition from a subtler stratum of Islam to the extremity of jihadism owed its origin to the Arab countries which had already evolved into a crude form of fundamentalism via jihadism. But this evolution passed through several stages and over a period of time. It was the defeat of the Arab armies in 1948 and the subsequent creation of the state of Israel that convinced the Muslim society to expend its energies beyond welfare to armed politics. Hassan al-Banna (1906-1949), an Egyptian teacher and scholar, called for the formation of a battalion to fight in the Palestine. Said to be a state within a state, with its own 'armies, hospitals, schools, factories, and enterprises' the society was banned in Egypt on 6 December, 1948, and re-legalized in 1951. When young army officers led by Gamal Abdel Nasser came to power in 1952, the society gave them full support. But the society soon split with Nasser and sided with those who called on the military to recognize the freedom to form political parties and hand over power to a civilian government. Nasser moved to arrest those calling for civil disorder and more than 1,000 society members were arrested. In Nasser's prisons, some of them abandoned their vision of reform and created a new and potentially violent version of political Islam. If the reform vision was identified with the thought of Hassan al-Banna in the formative period of the society, the extremist turn came about through the pen of Sayyid Qutb (1906-1966), writing in prison. The experience of such brutal repression under secular government shaped the birth of a radical reorientation in Egyptian Islamic thought. The second experience, a more theoretical one, came from Marxism-Leninism, already the most important alternative to political Islam in intellectual debates on how best to confront a repressive secular state that had closed off all possibilities of democratic change.

Before we embark on a detailed narration of the Islamic concept of jihad and its several manifestations, a look at the standard Western perception of this unique concept may prove to be a standard and profitable exercise. Originally the doctrine against unbelievers catered to the expansion and protection of the Muslim community, and thus jihad is closely linked with hijra or emigration from non-Muslim society to a Muslim one. According to the doctrine, the sins of a person making jihad are remitted and death 'on the path of God is martyrdom which secures immediate entry to Paradise.' Scholars have also spoken of the 'greater jihad' as the internal struggle against one's own sinful tendencies and as a personal struggle for the good against what is forbidden. Jihad is a collective duty, but women, minors, and the sick are among categories which are legally excluded. It is also a personal duty, though not one of the five pillars of Islam. Shi'i teach that jihad can happen only under the leadership of the Imam, whereas the Sunnis accept the proclamation of an unjust ruler as the starting point. Most believe jihad cannot be declared against fellow Muslims, though Ayatollah Ruholla Khomenei did so against the rulers of Iraq in the Iran-Iraq War. In the colonial period, wars against external forces were often categorised as jihad. For example, in 1912, the Sanusi religious order proclaimed jihad against the Italians in Lybia, and in 1881 the self-styled Mahdi proclaimed jihad in the Sudan against the British and the Egyptians. Guerrillas fighting the Soviet occupation in Afghanistan in the 1980s saw themselves as mujahideen, as did several groups opposed to the Shah of Iran in the 1970s. Many authorities consider that if Muslims live in a society ruled by non-Muslims but not under threat and can perform their ritual duties, then jihad is not obligatory. States are not constantly at war, and good relations and treaties with non-Muslim powers are permissible. This is most relevant in the modern period when many Muslims in Africa, Asia and Europe live in nation-states that are neither under Muslim rulers nor where the ruler is a Muslim, under the shari'a. Modern reformers, facing a world dominated by non-Muslim powers in which Muslims live with members of other communities in many distinct nation-states with their own secular interests, have emphasized the moral nature of jihad. They see military jihad only as a defense against oppression. Nationalist movements most often stressed the homeland rather than the Muslim community as its beneficiary. Even where they made 'nationlism a quasi-sacred cause jihad was used rhetorically and opportunistically. Modernists such as President Bourguiba of Tunisia tried to appropriate the concept of jihad as meaning the struggle for national development. Radical Islamist movements scorn such interpretations and stress 'Islam as an expansionist world order'. Jihad is again a fundamental duty and active struggle for global application of the shari'a. They also seek to 'purify' Muslim societies from 'corrupt' and 'tyrannical' Muslim rulers. Thus President Anwar Sadat of Egypt was assassinated in 1981. The identification of sacred duty with violence or national wars is made in many political systems and states. Muslims qua Muslims are no more bellicose than followers of any creed, religious or otherwise. Jihad has been used in some Western writings to justify the view that all Muslims are aggressive fanatics, but this claim says more about Western views of others than about the behaviour of Muslims, and is false.[58] Sayyid Qutb is the most well-known among the intellectual pioneers of radical political Islam, a movement that now stands for a radically reformulated notion of jihad, a doctrine shared by all Muslims. The debate on radical political Islam is increasingly a debate on the meaning of the term 'jihad'. The concern for the umma, the Muslim community, is part of

---

58 Michael Gilsman, Jihad, in Joel Kreiger, ed. The Oxford Companion to Politics of the World, Oxford University Press, Oxford, 1993, pp. 490-491.

the five pillars (rukn) of Islam and is binding on every Muslim. The Koran insists that a Muslim's first duty is to create a just and egalitarian society in which poor people are treated with respect. This demands a jihad (literally, effort or struggle), on all fronts, spiritual and social, personal and political. Scholars of Islam distinguish between two broad traditions of jihad, al-jihad al-akbar (the greater jihad) and al-jihad al-asghar (the lesser jihad). The greater jihad, it is said, is a struggle against weaknesses of self; it is about how to live and attain piety in a contaminated world. Inwardly, it is about the effort of each Muslim to become a better human being. The lesser jihad, in contrast, is about self-preservation and self-defence directed outwardly. This latter jihad is what Christians call 'just war' rather than 'holy war'. Modern Christian thought, strongly influenced by Crusades-era ideas of 'holy war' has tended to portray jihad as an Islamic war against non-believers starting with the conquest of Spain in the 8th century. Tomaz Mastnak has insisted, 'Jihad cannot be properly defined as holy war: Jihad is a doctrine of spiritual effort of which military action is only one possible manifestation; crusade and jihad are, strictly speaking, not comparable.' At the same time, political action is not contradictory to jihad. Islam sanctions rebellions against an unjust ruler, whether Muslim or not, and the lesser jihad can involve a mobilization for that social and political struggle.

Historically, the practice of lesser jihad as being central to a 'just struggle' has only been occasional and isolated, marking points of a crisis in Islamic history. After the first centuries of the creation of Islamic states, the word jihad was used as marking a military mobilization only on four occasions. The first was when the Kurdish warrior Saladin in response to the conquest accompanied by slaughter of the first Crusade in the 11th century. The second widespread use was in the Senegambia region of West Africa in the late-17th century. In the second half of the 15th century Senegambia became the first African region to come into contact with the Atlantic trading system. By the second half of the 17th Century the slave trade had become the principal business of European powers on the African coast. One of its main effects was widespread violence in day-to-day life. Among those who sold slaves were Islamic rulers in the region. The crisis was felt most deeply in Berber society which was caught in a pincer movement between Arab armies closing in from the North and the expanding frontiers of the European slave trade in the South. Militant Islam began as a movement led by Sufi leaders (marabout) intent on unifying the region against the negative effects of the slave trade. The first War of the Marabout began in 1677 in the same area that had given rise to the 11th century Al-Moravid movement. The difference was that whereas the Al-Moravids had moved North, ultimately to conquer Spain, the marabout moved South. The second War of the Marabout culminated with the Muslim revolution in the plateau of Futa Jallon in 1690. Among the Berbers of the North and the peoples of the South, militant Islam found popular support for jihad against Muslim aristocracies who were selling their own subjects to European slave traders. The leaders of the revolution in Futa Jallon set up a federation of nine provinces, with the head of each appointed a general in the jihad. The third time jihad was widely waged as a 'just war' was in the middle of the 18th century in the Arabian peninsula. This was led by Muhammad Ibn Abdul Wahhab (1703-1792) who gave his name to a contemporary doctrine identified with the House of Saud, Wahhabism. Ibn Wahhab's jihad was declared in a colonial setting on an Arab peninsula that had been under Ottoman control from the 16th century. It was not a jihad against unbelievers. Its enemies included Sunni Muslim Ottoman colonisers and Shi'a 'heretics'. Its beneficiary was a newly forged alliance between the ambitious House of Saud and the new imperial power on the horizon, Great Britain. The fourth prominent example of jihad as an armed struggle was in Sudan when the anti-colonial leader Muhammad Ahmed (1884-1885) declared himself al-Mahdi (the Messiah) in 1881 and began to rally support against a Turko-Egyptian administration that was rapidly becoming absorbed into an expanding British empire.[59]

The battle for a jihad in this context was a battle against a colonial occupation that was both Muslim (Turko-Egyptian administration) and non-Muslim, (British). Al-Mahdi was spectacularly successful as the organiser of the revolt. Armed with no more than spears and swords, the Mahdists (followers of al-Mahdi) won battle after battle in 1885, reaching the capital, Khartoum where they killed Charles Gordon, the British general and hero of the second Opium War with China (1856-1860), and was the governor in the Turko-Egyptian administration. So long as they fought a hated external enemy, the Mahdists won widespread support in all regions. But once the victorious al-Mahdi moved to unite different regions and create a united Sudan under his sole authority, the anti-colonial coalition disintegrated into warring factions in the North—

---

59 Mahmood Mamdani, *Good Muslim Bad Muslim*, Pantheon, New York, 2004, pp. 49-56.

where Messianic interpretations of Islam fought it out against Sufi (mystical) ones—and a marauding army of Northern slavers in the South. As the war of liberation degenerated into slave raids, anarchy, famine and disease reign, it is estimated that the population of Sudan fell from around seven million before the Mahdist revolt to somewhere between two and three million after the fall of the Mahdist state. In 1898, as in Saudi Arabia and West Africa in previous centuries, the experience of Sudan also showed that the same jihad that had begun as the rallying cry of a popular movement could be turned around by those in power—against its supporters.

Whereas an armed jihad was not known in the nine decades preceding the Afghan jihad of the 1980s (against the Soviet occupation, see Khaled Husseini's novel, '*The Kite Runner*' quoted above) the call for one in radical Islamist thought can be traced to two key thinkers at the beginning of the Cold War: the Pakistani journalist and politician Abul A'la Mawdudi whose work began to be published in Egypt in 1951, and Sayyid Qutb. Mawdudi (1903-1979) appeared at a moment when the ulama, organised as the Jami'yat-i-Ulama-Hind (Society of the Ulama of India) were supporting a multi-religious, decentralized yet united India against demands by political intellectuals for the creation of Pakistan. As is known, Muhammad Iqbal, the renowned poet and political thinker, had envisioned Muslim political identity not in terms of a nation-state but as a borderless cultural community, the umma. The irony was that though the formation of Pakistan gave its Muslim inhabitants self-determination, this was as residents of a common territory and not as an umma. Instead of being a profound critique of territorial nationalism and the nation-state that Iqbal had intended his thinking to be, Pakistan was a territorial nation as banal as any other nation preoccupied with building its nation-state. Mawdudi seized upon this contradiction in his appeal to post-colonial Islamist intellectuals. He claimed that Pakistan ('the Land of the Pure') was still 'Na-Pakistan' (either 'not yet the land of the pure' or 'the land of the impure'). For Mawdudi, an Islamic state could not just be another territorial state of Muslims; it had to be an ideological state, an Islamic state. To realize that end, Mawdudi established Jamaat-i-Islami (the Islamic Community) in Karachi in 1941 and had himself confirmed as its emir.

Key to Mawdudi's thought was centralized power and jihad as the ultimate struggle for the seizure of state power. He defined the ultimate objective of Islam 'to abolish the lordship of man over man and bring him under the rule of the one God'. With jihad as its relentless pursuit: 'To stake everything you have—including your lives—to achieve this purpose called Jihad...So I say to you: if you really want to root out corruption now so widespread on God's earth, stand up and fight against corrupt rule; take power and use it on God's behalf. It is useless to think you change things by preaching alone.' With both eyes focussed on the struggle for power, Mawdudi redefined the meaning of Din (religion) in a clearly secular way: 'Acknowledging that someone is your ruler to whom you must submit means the same thing as state and government.' He also secularized Islam, equating it not with other religions but with other political ideologies that sought the conquest of the state, through popular sovereignty or monarchy or, above all, Communism. 'A total Din, whatever its nature, wants power for itself, the prospect of sharing power is unthinkable. Whether it is popular sovereignty or monarchy, Communism or Islam, or any other Din, it must govern to establish itself. A Din without power to govern is just like a building which exists only in the mind.' Mawdudi was the first to state the imperative of jihad for contemporary Muslims, the first to claim that armed struggle was central to jihad, and unlike any major Muslim thinker before him, the first to call for a universal jihad.

Before we return to our subject in focus, we may divert our attention a bit to examine the larger background of world history in order to understand the role of violence as a tool of social and political change. When Islamists call for jihad or universal jihad, one should expect violence on a very large scale—a perspective that has led to the world-wide campaign to fight jihad on a universal footing. What is fascinating is that violence in history—in European history and, to be precise, in British history—has also been a vessel for revolutionary changes leading eventually to freedom and even democracy. The question one has to ask is why the process of industrialization culminates in the establishment of a relatively free society? This question assumes more significance than it normally would in the context of a study of the Islamic world, especially the Arabic world, of a society which has lagged in industrialization and which has definitely balked at the idea of democratizing itself. That England has been a relatively free society for such a long time, perhaps more liberal than the United States in the crucial areas of freedom of speech and the tolerance of organised political opposition, seems plain enough.'[60]

---

60 Barrington Moore Jr., *Social Origins of Dictatorship and Democracy Lord and Peasant in the Making of the Modern World,* Beacon Press, Boston, USA, 1966, p.3.

Dazzled, as we are, by the lightning strike on and capture of Kabul and thereafter of Afghanistan, it is difficult for us to recall that the Taliban were similarly defeated and turned out of the country back in 2001. Any recapitulation and analysis of the fall of the dreaded terrorist group would be expected to answer the question, 'Why did the Taliban fall so easily?' The swift fall of the fundamentalist force obviously occurred due to a combination of several factors. The apparent cause was the drying-up of support from Pakistan, at the time being governed by army chief General Pervez Musharraf. Overnight, the Taliban became bereft of strength. Their military machine was significantly affected, as was the flow of resources that could have bolstered the regime. Even the clergy who were the mainstay of popular support for the Afghan terrorists, was no longer able to spend enough money to gather sizeable street and mosque demonstrations in support of the Taliban. To that extent, Musharraf was free of pressure from the population over whom he ruled. At the same time, the United States had pinned Pakistan down to a space where manoeuvrability for Islamabad was almost nil. In this adverse situation, the very legitimacy of the Taliban once again came to be examined and was found badly wanting. It was felt, at the time, that if the Taliban was 'home-grown' and not imported from Pakistan, they would in all probability survive; but that was not the case. The very 'foreignness' of the Taliban's ideology came to be highlighted every time their apparent rejection by the Afghan population came to the fore. The Afghan tradition of Sufi-infused Islam had remained so embedded in the people's psychology and intellect that the Arabian-origin jihadism could never take root in the soil of what was essentially a South Asian country. And finally, the tremendous pressure brought on the

Taliban by the American government and military were simply too strong and irresistible; and thus the surprisingly swift collapse of the regime.

One question, however, remained to be answered. Why did the Americans succeed where the Soviets could not? The answer lies in the fact that the circumstances surrounding the 1989 Soviet defeat and withdrawal and the 2001 Taliban defeat were dramatically different. In the case of the Soviet occupation force, it was seen as an alien invader but in November 2001 the Americans and their European allies were regarded as friends who had come to Afghanistan to save its people from the clutch of the fundamentalists. In the text above have been narrated instances of Afghan villagers secretly helping the mujahideen fighter in ensnaring Soviet troops. The Soviet officers and troops were seen as associated with the communists who had invited them to Afghanistan; and the Soviets on their part never made attempts to fraternise with Afghan civilians. The prevailing circumstances made the Soviet military and party officials look like cronies of the corrupt communist party and government officials who were universally hated and despised by commoners. Besides, the Soviet invasion suffered from a basic fallibility; communism was anti-religion and the hold of Islam was very strong upon Afghans. The Americans and their allies did not suffer from this particular black spot for they did not come to Afghanistan to destroy Islam but to, by their military onslaught on the Taliban, save Islam. Both Osama bin Laden who had actually sustained the Taliban fight back and Mullah Omar, the Taliban chief, managed to escape the international forces that had destroyed their dream of a khilafat and were destined to spend their last days in ignominy and hiding. They had become irrelevant in a way long before they were finally obliterated from current history.⁶¹

But bin Laden was made of sterner staff than he was given credit for. Within less than a year after its so-called 'eradication' from Afghan soil, the Al-Qaeda chief addressed an open letter to the American people, in which he wrote,

> The Islamic Nation that was able to dismiss and destroy the previous evil empires like yourself—the Nation that rejects your attacks—wishes to remove your evils and is prepared to fight you. You are well-aware that the Islamic Nation, from the very core of its being, despises your haughtiness and arrogance. If the Americans refuse to listen to our advice, and the goodness, guidance, and righteousness to which we call them, then be aware that you will lose this Crusade that Bush began, just like the other previous Crusades in which you were humiliated by the hands of the mujahideen, fleeing to your homes in great silence and disgrace. If the Americans do not respond, then their fate will be that of the Soviets who fled from Afghanistan to deal with their military defeat, political breakup, ideological downfall, and economic bankruptcy. This is our message to the Americans, as an answer to their questions. Do they now know why we fight them and over which form of ignorance, by the permission of Allah, we shall be victorious?⁶²

---

61 William Maley, *The Afghanistan Wars*, Palgrave MacMillan, UK and New York, 2002, pp.266-268.
62 Paul L. Williams, A Letter to America, Osama bin Laden, 24 November 2002, *in Osama's Revenge The Next 9/11 What the media and the government haven't told you*, Viva Books Private Limited, First Indian Edition 2005, Published by arrangement with Prometheus Books, Amherst, New York, US App.16-17.

This letter appears to be dipped in the sauce of religion, and pretends to be God and Allah's command. Whatever acts of outrage bin Laden and his jihadis had committed were first ordained by Allah the Merciful and that was to avenge a wrong committed on innocent Muslims by the West, especially by Americans. He said while beginning the letter that after Americans had raised certain questions about Muslim actions, he sought to answer two questions: Why are we fighting and opposing you? And, What are we calling you to, and what do we want from you? The answer for the first question is quite 'simple': Because you attacked us and continue to attack us. This is followed by some instances where Americans, according to him, attacked Muslims. These attacks occurred in Palestine 'which has sunk under military occupation for more than eighty years (by 2002).' This was followed by a short recapitulation of Middle Eastern history in the 20th century as perceived by Arab and Muslim political leaders, academics and clerics. 'Under your (American) supervision, consent and orders, the governments of these countries attack us on a daily basis'. The Kashmir case illustrates how carefully 'choosy' bin Laden became while addressing this point in his letter, for the truth is that the United States and its Western allies never supported the Indian government's actions in Kashmir, tried their best to get New Delhi condemned by the United Nations and it is only in recent years when the West has permanently 'lost' Pakistan to China's sphere of influence, have they begun to appreciate India's efforts to get the Kashmir valley free of foreign infiltrators. But for bin Laden no such truth can ever matter! After listing the 'tragedies and calamities' committed by Israel in Palestine, which are by and large, true accounts of what really happened, he explains that 'It is commanded by our religion and intellect that the oppressed have a right to return the aggression. Do not await anything from us except jihad, resistance and revenge. Is it in any way rational to expect that after America has attacked us for more than half a century, that we will then leave her to live in security and and peace???' As for targeting civilians, he argues that no American civilian can truthfully claim to be innocent of their government's actions because they and the American army come from the same stock and it is their tax money which goes to finance arms and other weapons with which 'innocent' Muslims are killed regularly.

The question that bin Laden raised in his letter to Americans regarding the continuing Israeli aggression against the Palestinians and Muslim-Arabs and Christian-Arabs in the Occupied Territories cannot be brushed aside by claiming that raising such a question helps buttress the jihadis' diatribe and incitement to violence. The history is there for all to see; and if the Muslim claims were untenable, why did Israel agree several times for participating in peace plans? It is another matter that all such plans were washed away in time by fresh floods of Israeli aggressions and Palestinians retaliation. Peace Now, a pro-peace organization, says Israel's policy spectrum with regard to the occupied territories can be examined with reference to the four peace plans between 1968 to 1992 by enquiring how many Palestinians would be included in the territories if the following plans were actually implemented: (1) The 1968 Allon Plan (Labour Party); (2) The 1976 Labour Party Settlement Plan (never officially adopted though 'it has informed practical decision-making and action'); (3) The Ariel Sharon Plan of 1992 (Likud Party) which created eleven isolated discontinuous 'cantons' for Palestinian autonomy; and (4) Defence Establishment Plan of 1992 (Labour Party), which dealt only with the West Bank. The plans together involved the fate of as many as 2,364,000 Palestinians (the 4th Plan did not mention the number of residents in Gaza at the time). Nearly four million Palestinians were involved in the process. Peace Now, however, showed at the time that another 150,000 Palestinians of East Jerusalem were to be brought under Israeli sovereignty in all the four plans. 'The Labour Party plan of 1976 would annex the greatest number of Palestinians from the West Bank and Gaza, while the Sharon Plan was the maximalist plan with regard to the West Bank, though ceding self-rule to more Gaza Palestinians than the Labour plans. As the analysis indicated, the policy spectrum was narrow and invariably rejectionist. The political blocks had differed on West Bank Palestinian population concentrations, Labour being more concerned about excluding them than Likud from areas scheduled for Israeli takeover. Washington had favoured Labour Party rejectionism, more rational than the Likud variety, which lacked any real provision for the population of the occupied territories except eventual 'transfer' (rejection). Israel thus successfully imported some artificial words the meanings of which differed dramatically from their original meanings. But each time, Israel won in its design, due to the powerful and unstinted backing it received from the United States government and the Jewish lobby in that country. Did the Palestinians ever have a chance of standing on their own feet and fighting back against the combined strength of such a powerful gang of powers? We can't do better than listen to the neoconservative intellectual Irving Kristol who stated in the aftermath of the Oslo II Agreement which was another way of establishing the triumph of firm and dedicated US-Israeli rejectionism, 'in isolation from world opinion but holding the guns and other levers of power'. Kristoll said, '...insignificant nations like insignificant people can quickly experience delusions of significance which must be driven from their primitive minds by force; in truth, the days of "gunboat diplomacy" are never over...Gunboats are as necessary for international order as police cars are for domestic order.' Fifty years earlier, British statesman Lloyd George while praising his government's undermining of the disarmament treaty declared, recognizing the importance of 'reserving the right to bomb niggers.' And Winston Churchill was quite enthusiastic about using poison gas against uncivilized tribes, specifically Kurds and Afghans, but also 'recalcitrant Arabs.' Theodor Roosevelt was another champion of the choice to keep uncivilized brutes under the control of their white masters.[63] Reviewing the extent to which the United States-Israel duo succeeded in reducing the rights and claims of the Palestinians to nothing, is a painful experience, as Edward W. Said remarks in his Foreword to Chomsky's book, 'Chomsky's major claim is that Israel and the United States—especially the latter—are rejectionists opposed to peace, whereas the Arabs, including the PLO, had for years been trying to accommodate themselves to the reality of Israel.' Chomsky supports his case by comparing the history

---

63 Noam Chomsky, *Fateful Triangle The United States, Israel and the Palestinians*, India Research Press, New Delhi, India, 2004, First published in the United States by South End Press, Cambridge MA.

of the Palestinian-Israeli conflict, 'so profoundly inhuman, cynical and deliberately cruel to the Palestinian people, with its systematically rewritten record', as kept by those whom Chomsky calls 'the supporters of Israel'. Bin Laden may have been hell-bent on taking 'God's revenge' on the Jews but he had plenty of ground to stand upon while dealing with the Palestinian question.

As shown in several analyses of how the Palestinian factor has contributed, perhaps most significantly, to the rise of radical Islam, it is absolutely true that the state of Israel is based on the immoral and illicit basis of might which in itself is a legacy of the old European imperialism. Most injustices committed during the centuries-old colonial period in history have been righted and stand removed; and new modern nation-states have replaced them. But the festering Palestine issue remains leading to a kind of permanent cauldron in which periodically scores of Arabs are sacrificed and a few Israeli soldiers and civilians occasionally lose their lives. The imbalance exists not only in the death toll but also in every aspect of civic, economic and political life of Palestinians. The other important contributor to the all-pervading sense of untreated injustice among Muslims all over is the manner in which the inhabitants of the area later known as Iraq were 'cheated'. What is Iraq today was Mesopotamia in ancient times, inhabited by various races such as Sumerians, Akkadians, Babylonians, and Assyrians. Mesopotamia came under Turkish suzerainty in 1638 and direct Turkish rule in 1831. Till the First world War (1914-1918) it was a province of the Ottoman Empire. With the break-up of the Ottoman Empire, and the victorious allies Great Britain and France found the opportunity to satisfy their long-held desire to exploit the oil-rich Arabian peninsula. 'During this period, the British and the French held secret negotiations on the modalities of carving Arab lands.'[64] By the secret Sykes-Picot Agreement they carved out the Arab lands into British and French areas of influence. They also decided at the time to divide the Arab lands into many small fragments so that the inhabitants keep fighting each other and are never able to unite and once again build up a powerful empire which would be Muslim by virtue of the vast majority of Muslims living there. 'Divide the vast Arab lands into smaller nation-states—which have no historical identity—and keep them under British subjugation as long as possible.'[65] With this nakedly colonial objective in mind, the Allied Powers sent agents provocateurs to Arabs and incited them to rise against the 'oppressive' Ottoman rule. The people of present-day Iraq, like other people, helped the Allied Powers in overthrowing the Ottomans. Contingents of forces from British India were also sent. Indian forces fought for the British. With their help, the Allied Powers occupied the area. After the war was over, the true intentions of the Allied Powers were revealed. In April 1920 the three wilayats of Mosul, Baghdad and Basra of the erstwhile Ottoman Empire were carved out and given as mandates to Britain, who called the 'new 'country' Iraq. The Iraqi administration was formed under High Commissioner Sir Percy Cox with Colonel Arnold Talbot Wilson as his deputy.

---

64   Albert Jurgen, *Iraq War*, Sparrow Publication, Kolkata, 2004, p.38.
65   Albert Jurgen, *ibid*, p.39.

The Arab inhabitants of Iraq were estranged as a consequence of a deliberate policy pursued by the British administration. They formed anti-colonial organizations and began to agitate against the new colonial power. Repression gradually grew in proportion to the agitation; within a short time, the Royal Air Force began to bomb civilians killing thousands of men, women and children. The British colonial repression soon united the entire country bringing in Sunnis, Shia's, tribals (Bedouins) and non-tribals. Later, the movement came to be popularly known as the Great Iraqi Revolution. In the face of stiff resistance, the British replaced the old administration with a provisional Arab government and installed Prince Faisal (the younger son of Sharif Hussein bin Ali, king of Al Hijaj) as monarch of Iraq in 1922. 'The British then held a plebiscite and cleverly manipulated it to give the British installed monarchy a neo-democratic standing. On the eve of the election, the monarch's chief rival Sayid Taleband was kidnapped and sent to Ceylon on a forced 'vacation'. Other such surreptitious arrangements ensured that Shah Faisal won the election.[66]

---

66 Nazrul Islam, *Islam 9/11 and Global Terrorism A Study of Perceptions and Solutions*, Viva Books Private Limited, Kolkata, 2005, pp. 60-70.

CHAPTER 13

Afghanistan Drawn Into the Cold War Vortex

IN APRIL 1978, a 'revolutionary' coup was engineered by a relatively small number of military men, members of the People's Democratic Party of Afghanistan (PDPA) raising Marxist-Leninist slogans. A post-mortem analysis done by the Central Committee of the CPSU after a decade of communist rule in the country wrote that these men were honestly trying to reform the country. They promoted a programme of radical socialist reforms for which there was neither a social nor an economic basis nor was there support from the masses. From the very beginning the situation was complicated by the sharp differences that prevailed in the two factions of the PDPA who were still feuding with one another in the period preceding the Revolution at one time, and fighting one another more than the forces opposing the Revolution...The most glaring mistakes and Leftist deviations were committed in the socio-economic sphere with regard to religion, alienating the people from the Revolution...

> Above all was the fact that the appearance of armed foreigners in Afghanistan was always met with arms in

the hands of the population. This is how it was in the past and this is how it happened when our troops entered Afghanistan, even though they came there with honest and noble goals...Moreover, the intensity of the internal Afghan conflict continued to grow and our military presence was associated with the forced imposition of customs alien to the national characteristics and feelings of the Afghan people which did not take into account the multiple forms of economic life, and other forms of life such as tribal and religious ones...However, often our people, acting out of their best intentions, tried to transplant the approaches we are accustomed to onto the Afghan soil, encouraging the Afghans to copy our ways. All this did not help our cause.[67]

All armed conflicts in the world today can be traced to the central role that one country, Afghanistan—one of the poorest and its people among the most ill-used pawns in power games—has played since the seventies of the twentieth century. To Afghans themselves, this unwelcome role was literally thrust

---

67 "CC CPSU Letter on Afghanistan" 10 May 1988, Appendix 8 from A. Lyakovsky, Tragedy and Valour of the Afghanistan Veteran (Moscow: Iskon, 1995), Translated by Gary Goldberg in "Toward an International History of the War in Afghanistan", 1979-89, Conference in Washington DC. 29-30 April 2002, Cold War International History Project in cooperation with the Asia Programme and the Kennan Institute for Advanced Russian Studies at the Woodrow Wilson Centre, the George Washington Cold War Group at the George Washington University, and the National Security Archive, Conference Reader, compiled by Christian F. Ostermann and Mircea Monteeanu, Washington DC., Woodrow Wilson Centre, 2002), www.woodrowwilsoncentre.org/topics/docs/toward_an_an_international_history-of_the_war_in_afghanistan_1979_1989_vol2_pubs_vol2pdf,409-423.

on them when the Leonid Brezhnev-led Soviet Union decided to send an occupation force to the strategically placed Southern country in order to help the rising communists capture and retain power. Through the two communist parties then fighting between themselves to ride roughshod over the other, the interests of the native population were ignored, and a fresh power game emerged in a country whose destiny was often decided by the mighty players in that power game.

The Leonid Brezhnev-led Soviet Union was looking for its own 'Inner Mongolia' to function as a buffer state between the USSR in the North and the traditionally turbulent Afghanistan and other Central Asian republics (CARs) in the South. In Moscow's reckoning, a buffer state is essentially a client state though in international diplomacy it is a neutral state and has to be built up to fulfil its specific functions. Therefore, Moscow under Brezhnev formulated two policies, one that was followed between 1980 and 1986 and the other adopted thereafter. The first policy has been described as the Sovietization of Afghan institutions and processes. However, the apparent failure of this policy left the Soviet Union with no other option but to replace the first policy with a policy of Afghanization of the nation's institutions and processes.

The entry of the Soviet army with Moscow's full backing immediately led to the United States of America's presence as well, though only in a covert manner. The Soviet invasion began on 25 December 1979 and the process was completed three days later on 28 December, immediately drawing in Saudi Arabia's royal house in its wake. At that time Saudi King Khalid and his brothers were fighting the rebel Juhaiman al-Otaibi (Wahhabi priest who led the Grand Mosque uprising in Mecca, and was executed) who was leading his followers holed up in the Grand Mosque. This was also the time when Ayatollah Ruhollah Khomeini was leading his countrymen and Shi'as around the world in a campaign against Iraq's Saddam Hossain. In short, the usually volatile West Asian region was more volatile than normal; and King Khalid was finding it difficult to maintain the royal family's hold on Saudi Arabia. The Soviet invasion happening in neighbouring Afghanistan came as a boon for him and his family.

At the time the Soviet Union invaded Afghanistan, Moscow sent a high-security cable to its ambassadors around the world instructing them to approach the respective heads of state or government and ministries to convey the message that the Soviet Union had sent a 'limited military contingent to Afghanistan to carry out missions requested by the Afghan government'. A small force had been sent to Afghanistan on the Afghan leadership's request to assist the authorities to maintain law and order. Moscow also sought to explain the change in leadership in Kabul by asserting that this was done at the request of the government. 'The leaders of the government of Afghanistan have turned to the Soviet Union for aid and assistance in the struggle against foreign aggression.' The USSR had responded to this request…with approval. The 'legitimacy' of the Soviet decision rested on the 1978 Treaty of Friendship with Afghanistan and the United Nations Charter's allowance for individual states grouping together in collective self-defence.[68]

---

68   Peter Tomsen, *ibid*, pp. 201-233.

The Communist Party of the Soviet Union (CPSU) was also marshalled to supplement the Kremlin's efforts to 'manage' reactions from world capitals. The communist party's task was to explain the invasion to 'friendly' communist parties across the world. A top-secret telegram sent from the CPSU's headquarters condemned the slain Afghan President Hafizullah Amin for 'violations of elementary norms of legality', 'widespread repression', 'impermissible acts', and 'terror against honest persons devoted to the cause of the revolution'. For good measure, the party telegram took pains to separately condemn the Central Intelligence Agency (which quite openly campaigned inside and outside Afghanistan to spread misinformation against the Amin government) and the Beijing leadership. For obvious reasons it did not touch upon the KGB's equally prominent role in controlling the entire gamut of Amin's overthrow.

The virtual Soviet takeover of Afghanistan, though a formal indigenous government remained in power, now being led by President Babrak Karmal (Friend of Labour) signalled the solidification of big power politics in the region. On 31 December 1979, the CPSU's Politburo's Afghan Commission praised Babrak Karmal's government in a post-invasion secret assessment:

> The situation in the country is normalizing... Babrak can be described as one of the more theoretically equipped leaders of (the) PDPA, who soberly and objectively evaluates the situation in Afghanistan; he was always distinguished by his sympathies for the Soviet Union and commanded respect within (the) party and the country at large. In this regard, the conviction can

be expressed that the new leadership of the (DRA) will find effective ways to stabilize completely the country's situation.

The report prematurely concluded that the Parcham-Khalq schism had been 'liquidated'. It complimented the Karmal regime's vow to fight for 'complete' victory of the revolution and to strengthen in every possible way the friendship and cooperation with the USSR'.[69]

The Soviet military was ubiquitous in Kabul and other Afghan cities in the months after the invasion.

There were a lot of reasons why I went to Hazarajat to find Hassan in 1988. The biggest one, Allah forgive me, was that I was lonely. By then, most of my friends and relatives had either been killed or had escaped the country or fled to Pakistan. Or Iran. I barely knew anyone in Kabul any more, the city where I lived my entire life. Everybody had fled. I would take a walk in the Karteh-Parwan section—where melon vendors used to hang out in the old days, you remember that spot?—and I wouldn't recognize anyone there. No one to greet, no one to sit down with for chai, no one to share stories with, just Roussi soldiers patrolling the streets.[70]

Soviet troops outnumbered the Afghan Army by four to one. Soviet soldiers directed traffic in the capital and guarded important government buildings. The Soviet Fortieth Army was headquartered and co-located with the Afghan Army's

---

69   P. Tomsen, *ibid*, pp. 208-209.
70   Khaled Hosseini, *The Kite Runner*, pp.178-179.

Central Corps headquarters at Darulaman. An Afghan military officer who defected, reported that Soviet military officers 'countersigned' all orders issued to Afghan units.[71] Even civilian life was being oriented towards total dependence on Soviet Russia. Articles being published in Afghan-language newspapers were actually being written in Moscow and then transmitted to Kabul for translation into Afghan languages. Afghan newspapers became carriers of Soviet views though they were meant for the consumption of Afghan readers. There was nothing innovative about such participation: merely, one state model (and not the best version at that) was forced onto another country. The Afghan First Secretary...couldn't take a single step without permission from the Soviet Central Committee advisor. The Afghan Minister of Defence could not issue an order without prior approval from the Soviet Ministry of Defense advisor.[72]

However, above the Soviet officers and advisors who reigned over the Afghan officers and the army as a whole, ruled supreme the ever-prying eyes of the dreaded KGB. Every Russian who worked in Afghanistan was shadowed day and night by KGB operatives in the familiar dreadfulness of a totalitarian state. Altogether, the accounts of those days are vivid and reading them seemed to bring alive those nightmarish experiences. The lives of Afghans including their President, Babrak Karmal, were spent in a surrealistic world. Babrak Karmal's life was never free of Soviet—and to be precise—KGB presence, right

---

71 Bruce J. Amstutz, Afghanistan: *The First Five Years of Soviet Occupation,* Washington DC., National Defense University Press, 1986, p.289
72 Bruce J. Amstutz, *ibid,* p. 289.

from his sleep to his food to his driving in a limousine to his everyday work in his office. He was guarded day and night solely by Soviet troops, and KGB operatives were present all the time in rooms, nooks and corners of the presidential palace. Three weeks after the invasion, Yury Andropov reiterated his satisfaction that 'Babrak's doing great work regarding the strengthening of unity.' The new Afghan President may have been less aggressive than Taraki or Amin but tribal values of badal (score-settling), personality politics and beating down rivals contesting the summit guided his actions. However, now that Karmal was in the presidential chair, his whole perspective of exercising power changed, and he set out to exact revenge on his enemies. Despite his total dependence on Soviet largesse and his commitment to Leonid Brezhnev to forge unity in the PDPA, he decided not to spare his Khalqi enemies. This set off an unequal struggle between the Parchamis and the Khalqis with the former gaining ground in the power struggle. The tussle soon spread to the national army and its divisions and at least one mutiny ensued. This in turn brought about disagreements between the Karmal-Soviet advisers, with the Khalqis telling their Soviet handlers that since they were the overwhelming majority in both the party and the army, they would not submit to the Parchamis who were in a hopeless minority. This placed the Soviets in further difficulty as the Afghan cabinet had been made in Moscow and not in Kabul; and the Karmal government was seeking dismissal of three Khalqi ministers, and the ministers were defiantly sticking to their posts. The discord in the PDPA burst out in street fights with the Indian ambassador Jitendranath Dixit recalling later that his sleep at night (in Kabul) was often interrupted by firefights between the Parchamis and Khalqis.[73]

After much further internal bickering, failing Soviet interventions, and killings, Babrak Karmal was eventually replaced by Dr Mohammed Najibullah. During Karmal's seven-year tenure which saw several booster doses administered from Moscow to help him survive the onslaught of the Khalqis, he had brought in several constitutional and governance procedural reforms. He managed to fulfil some of his promises: the release of some political prisoners, the promulgation of the Fundamental Principles of the Democratic Republic of Afghanistan, the change of the red Soviet-style national flag of the Khalq period to the more orthodox black, red and green, the granting of concessions to religious leaders, and the conditional restoration of confiscated property. Despite these progressive moves, Karmal was a much isolated man, not only in the country and in the international arena, but also within his own party. It was the solid presence of the Soviet Union behind him—which, while protecting him from his enemies also alienated him from other ambitious leaders—who could not openly conspire against him but bided their time to topple him. His selection by the party and the Revolutionary Council was not televised giving opportunity to his opponents to raise the issue of legitimacy.

His successor, Dr Mohammed Najibullah, would be the last communist and Soviet Union installed president in the period 1986-1992, and was promoted from the post of chief of the secret police. He was executed by the Taliban on 27 September 1996. His gory end played out a sordid drama of international confusion

---

73   JN. Dixit, An Afghan Diary: *From King Zahir Shah to Taliban*. Delhi: Konark 2000.

and one country's hesitation in helping or not helping him escape certain execution. Before we come to examine his death, we will have to take note of his role as a notorious chief of the KHAD, Government Information Agency. We, however, owe to Najib this evocative description of how KHAD—whose officers were chosen from Uzbek, Tajik and Turkmen origin—meetings were conducted in a colourful fashion: 'As the conference goes on, the debate gets higher and the (Soviet) advisors move closer, and the Afghans move away, and finally the Soviets are left to quarrel among themselves.'[74] Karmal's fall and Najib's rise occurred in the background of a situation growing in its own dynamics and which the Soviets were unable to control though they kept on trying in their own ineffective fashion. During this period, which included the latter part of Karmal's tenure and saw the rise of Najib, the overall political canvas was dominated by the growing friction and power struggle between the Parchams who were mostly in the saddle, and the Khalqis who were fighting to regain their lost power. It was said at the time that Afghanistan's last communist president died a horrible death because, being a Pashtun, he could never believe that the Taliban who were Pashtuns would kill another Pashtun. But in life such sentiments hardly matter; and they did not in Najib's case. There is, however, a fairly researched account of how Najib was let down by the United Nations which had guaranteed his safety in the last days of his life, and also by India which had previously come forward to protect him, in all likelihood by offering him asylum and spiriting him away from

---

74   Sandy Gall, *An interview with Commander Ahmed Shah Masud Former Minister of Defence at His Base in Jebal Seraj in North of Kabul on June 28, 1993*, Asian Affairs 25, No.2 (1994): 144-145.

Kabul to Delhi. The then Indian ambassador, Vijay K. Nambiar, was coordinating with the president, Sevan and various government agencies and the United Nations involved in the rescue act. The stage was set for the flight but first Dostum, and then the army chief Gen. Mohammad Nabi Azimi and foreign minister Abdul Wakil changed sides preferring self-preservation over fighting for Najib. Thus, on that fateful morning, the stakes had already changed and stacked heavily against Najib. When Najib left for the airport after the scene had already changed and when, after finding Dostum's men determined not to allow him to reach the plane, Najib turned back to take shelter in the UN compound.

The president was a lonely man in Kabul on the morning of 17 April 1992 after government forces had failed and mujahideen forces were at the gates. His wife and daughters had left for New Delhi, and Najibullah himself had planned to fly off to the Indian capital along with the United Nations humanitarian aid division chief Benon Sevan. The UN was not interested in associating itself with India in a plan which would surely aggravate India-Pakistan relations over the Afghan president. Sevan had already briefed Pakistani Prime Minister Nawaz Sharif about the plan to whisk Najib away to New Delhi. This was done before the UN had approached India for safe passage and asylum for Najib. Everything required diplomatically had been completed; and the plan should have been carried out without any hitch. But everything misfired. Why? This real-life drama would beat any pot-boiler in its intensity of excitement and uncertainty of fate. Najibullah had started for the Kabul airport where a plane was on the tarmac with a UN official sitting inside. But the unexpected occurred, and General Dostum, the firebrand Uzbek warlord, quarrelled with the president, and Uzbeki fighters stormed the airport and secured it against any force. Dostum himself was immune to any persuasion, and the president too had been foolish to try to browbeat the general. Wakil was so incensed with Najib that he sent out a message over Radio Kabul that 'Najibullah had tried to escape but was stopped by the armed forces…He must be held to answer certain questions of the Afghan people. The government had no intention of killing him. The soldiers at the checkpoint could have killed him but did not.' Najibullah's assertion to Nambiar that he could influence Afghan politics by staying abroad rather than staying at home indicated that he was quite hopeful of resolving the intense tussle between the advancing mujahideen forces led by Commander Ahmad Shah Massoud, bring about a coalition of these two groups, and save the nation from further turmoil. The mission to save Najibullah failed because the circumstances had changed, the Soviet Union had disintegrated, India was on a weak wicket, and chaos and gun-fighting reigned in the capital and in the country. Recalling the events, Nambiar later felt that Najibullah could perhaps have escaped alive had he left Kabul 'earlier.' Referring to the section in the Indian External Affairs ministry which advocated not helping the president, Nambiar said, 'Dixit and gang had the guilt of not saving Najibullah. We sent the plane (in which Sevan was waiting for Najibullah but which was not actually an Indian plane) to Kabul thinking that the Mujahideen would let him go. We told the world that we (were) taking Najib out but had no understanding with Dostum. We should not have waited that long to take him out.'[75]

---

[75] Excerpts from Avinash Paliwal, *My Enemy's Enemy: India in Afghanistan from the Soviet Invasion to the US Withdrawal*, Harper Collins, India, 2017.

CHAPTER 14

Mujahideen and the Civil War

THE AFGHAN mujahideen were solely a product of the 1979-1989 Soviet invasion and occupation of Afghanistan. But their impact on the politics of the country survived beyond that ill-fated foreign invasion and occupation. This narration will now seek to examine how the mujahideen fought and defeated a foe who was infinitely superior and who knew that he would win the war and continue to help rule a new colony in Asia. On 27 December 1979, Moscow ordered the Soviet army into Afghanistan. Organised, equipped, and trained for the execution of combined arms operations, that force embodied the concept of a blitzkrieg. Nine years later, it withdrew in defeat. At the time of the invasion, few experts would have believed that Afghans would defeat the invaders one day. But they did. How? We will have to recall that most knowledgeable people believed that resistance to the modern, mechanised, technologically advanced Soviet army would be utterly futile. It was also believed at the time that the Soviet Union had deliberately expanded their 'empire' to the South, creating a new buffer and client state to protect the Southern border of the country from the United States and its allies. Experts also compared the British experience with Afghan tribesmen and felt that this was no proper parallel as the Soviet army was infinitely stronger in all respects compared to the British Indian army which fought in Afghanistan and could never succeed and manage to stay and hold on to power in the mountainous country. Following the invasion, Saudi Arabia, other Arab countries and the United States began to help the mujahideen by supplying them with arms and materials with the idea that the fighters would be able to act as an ulcer which would bleed indefinitely. They never imagined it would force the Soviets to withdraw in defeat. What caused the Soviet withdrawal? The Soviets realised that they were trapped in an unwinnable war where they were being killed because it was the right thing to do. After failing to achieve military victory, the Soviet Union cut its losses and withdrew. Over 1.3 million Afghans died and over a third of the Afghan population became refugees, most of whom would return home only after the Taliban lost their regime in 2001 and a democratic state was formed and developed in the 2000s.[76]

Apart from being natives of the country and all too familiar with the terrain, the mujahideen enjoyed the added advantage of popular support. The Soviet occupiers and the ruling communists were both equally hated by ordinary citizens, and for that very reason the mujahideen being 'local boys' were fully

---

76 Ali Ahmad Jalali and Lester W. Grau, *Afghan Guerrilla Warfare In the Words of the Mujahideen Fighters*, Compendium Publishing Ltd., London, 2001.

backed by village populations. In an account of an ambush set by the mujahideen which went off successfully, a mujahid recalled the situation:

> 'We moved into the area the night before,' said Haji Sayed Mohammad Hanif, of Logar province, 'spent the night in a village and set up our ambush site the next morning North of Kolangar district headquarters. We were told that a column (of the Soviet army) was coming from Kabul to Gardez, and so we had time to set up the ambush during the daylight before the column arrived, since the convoys always left Kabul in the morning well after dawn. Kabul is about 50 kilometres North of the ambush site. We set up the ambush just South of the Tangi Waghjan Gorge. There, the river continues to run parallel to the road and restricts manoeuvre while providing better firing positions for the ambush force. We had a collapsed electric pylon that we stretched across the road as a road block...Then we set up the rest of our positions and we sent to some nearby houses for breakfast. At that time we were so popular with the population that we didn't have to worry about supplies. And the people were always feeding us in their homes or sending us prepared food. Mulla Latif left his RPG at the ambush position since the people were moving about freely and would keep an eye on things.[77]

---

77 78 Jalali et., *Afghan Guerrilla Warfare*, p. p.13.ibid.

In a commentary following this successful ambush, it was pointed out that the Soviet commander did not send scouts or reconnaissance teams ahead of the column so that the gorge—always a prime site for staging an ambush in a guerrilla warfare situation—would be secured. Nor did the column have helicopter cover. Thus, he moved his column in the fashion of a blind adventurer and as a result lost everybody and every equipment he was commanding.

However, every ambush, encirclement and combat did not turn out to be cakewalks for the mujahideen; and there were plenty of instances when adversity haunted and harmed the rebel Afghans. To begin with, the countryside always proved to be friendlier terrain than urban areas for the mujahideen. Afghans in the countryside lived relatively free of the constant presence of Soviet soldiers; but their urban counterparts were obliged to spend their days in the constant presence of foreign troops in the streets. Often there were surprise checks on homes suspected of hiding mujahideen. Fighting guerrilla warfare in such circumstances was proving to be quite bothersome for the mujahideen; and hence, there were mixed results with Soviet troops gaining the upper hand in many instances. Moreover, the Soviet Red Army men were quick to learn the Afghans' ambush and encirclement techniques and were able to employ them in many cases, thus winning over their adversaries. However, Soviet encirclements were not as foolproof as the mujahideen's; and thus the latter could ultimately get out of porous encirclements. In one such instance, exfiltration from Soviet and Democratic Republican Army encirclements became possible. In July 1986 when mujahideen Commander Haji Mohammad Seddiq took a detachment of 13 mujahideen to abduct a DRA officer from his house in the Kot-e Sangri section of Kabul:

> For several days we gathered information about the officer—his time of arrival and departure from his house and the road he took to and from his residence. We gathered the information from a contact at the Kot-e Sangri gas station. We discovered that the officer did not stay at his residence overnight but spent a few hours in the evening at home and then returned to his unit. We decided to abduct him at his residence during those hours. We spent the night in the nearby Deh-Bori section of Kabul. The next day at dusk we met with our gas station contact who reported that the officer was at his residence. I took three men who were dressed in army uniform with me. I had on traditional clothing. We went to the officer's home which was located between Qala-e-Shada security outpost and the Kot-e Sangri police station. When we reached the house, the uniformed mujahideen knocked on the door. The officer's daughter answered the door. One of the mujahideen told her that there was an urgent message from his unit. As he stepped out, I stepped around from behind the corner and told him to follow us. The officer made no attempt to escape. We escorted him through the streets to Qala-e-Shada and from there to the mujahideen base at Arghanday. At Arghanday, we turned the officer over to a Paghman commander named Zahed. The officer was supposed to have killed several mujahideen from Zahed's group. We spent the night at the residence/base of Shafeh, a local commander. Early the next morning, at about 0400

hours, we woke up to the noise of tanks approaching the village. At first, we thought the noise was from normal military traffic resupplying the security outposts along the Kabul-Ghazni highway. Then Shafeh's father climbed to the roof top and saw that the village was surrounded by tanks and other vehicles. Soviet soldiers and DRA men from Rashid Dostum's militia occupied the surrounding hills. We were trapped. Shafeh took us to a hideout near the house. It was a cave that they had dug to hide the mujahideen during the enemy's cordon and search operations. After a while, we heard and noticed movement of the Soviet/DRA search party and that they had posted a guard at the entrance of the cave. The guard called and asked if there was anyone inside. Then he asked for anyone inside to come out. Then he stooped over to check out the cave. At that point, Alam Gul whom we had nicknamed the Uzbek because he looked like an Uzbek, shot the soldier. The soldier's body fell into the cave. We pulled aside the soldier's body and rushed out of the cave. As we came out, we encountered soldiers on the streets. We fought our way to a natural ditch at the edge of the village. We jumped into the ditch and faced both directions. We all had AK-47s plus one RPG-7. We fought from this position until 1300 hours. At that time, some mujahideen units at Kot-e-Ashro, about 10 kilometres to the South-West, started shelling the area with BM-12 fire. The rockets' explosions forced the enemy away from the south side of the village. We took advantage of this and slipped out of the encirclement through the Southern gap and fled to Kot-e-Ashro through the mountains. One of my mujahideen was wounded.

'In a commentary, it was explained that the porous nature of the Soviet/DRA encirclement allowed the mujahideen to exfiltrate. It helped to have other distractions such as incoming artillery, sandstorms and nightfall to escape. The mujahideen were experienced exfiltrators and often small groups of Soviets or DRA guarding the cordon would allow the mujahideen to escape rather than risk a firefight against uneven odds. The Soviets resorted to scatterable mines, ground sensors, parachute flares, and other technology to prevent escape, but mujahideen groups would exfiltrate singly or in small groups, and regroup outside the encirclement.[78]

Carl von Clausewitz's definition of a country where 'a general uprising' against invaders could be staged contained the following preconditions: the war must be fought in the interior of the country in question; it must not be decided by a single stroke; the theatre of operations must be fairly large; the national character must be suited to that type of war; and the country must be rough and inaccessible because of mountains or forests, marshes, or the local methods of cultivation.[79] Afghan history makes it clear that throughout its existence, the country was prime land for resistance (in this case, guerrilla war); and the Afghan-Soviet war of 1979-1989 remains a prime example of why and how it happened, resulting in whatever results that

---

78 Jalili et. al, *ibid*, pp. 363-364.
79 Clausewitz as quoted in William Maley, *The Afghanistan Wars*, Palgrave MacMillan, New York, 2002, p.57.

war begot. As it emerges from the previous pages, Afghanistan was a ripe target for Soviet southern expansion in the 1970s when the Cold War was at its peak and the Soviet Union was feeling the pressure from the Western block. Moscow needed to create breathing space in the shape of a buffer state so that its Southern borders were not threatened directly by the aggressive West and its Asian allies.

As events turned out, if the Union of Soviet Socialist Republics (USSR) had to expand southward, then Afghanistan was also ripe for offering a stiff resistance. Why that resistance by an unevenly placed opposition ultimately triumphed over its mighty Northern neighbour also followed a predictable pattern, so well encapsulated in Clausewitz's definition of a popular resistance in a particularly hostile environment. We have seen above how the Afghan resistance developed from its initial deficiencies into a fine well-calibrated and well-resourced military machine with an admirable capability to absorb new tactics and strategies, learning from the superior Soviet army operating in Afghanistan. General Secretary Mikhail Gorbachev had developed serious differences over the continuation of the war and desired the Najibullah government to make a serious and honest effort in building a national reconciliation policy. In pushing for such a dramatic change in policy, Gorbachev clearly placed much importance on solving his country's internal problems. The economy had shrunk and the cost of the war in Afghanistan in terms of both men and materials and money was already proving to be unbearable. Besides, the satellite states around the USSR were rising in popular discontent, in opposition to Moscow's dictates, and even growing signs of separation from the mother country. By that time, Gorbachev's concepts of glasnost, perestroika and demokratizatsiia had taken root and began to be reflected in Soviet foreign policy. This process would very soon eat away at the very roots of Soviet power; and the world, particularly poor undeveloped and bleeding Afghanistan, saw that as a sure sign of weakness and decline. Events in Afghanistan developed in the way they did due to many factors as is evident from the history narrated in the above pages. However, an important turn came towards the end of the foreign occupation when the Gorbachev promoted national reconciliation policy came unstuck in the hands of the Karmal and Najibullah governments. While Karmal consolidated his personal and his faction's supremacy over the party as a whole, thus downgrading the rival Khalq faction, which was till then dominating the party, it was his successor Najibullah who promoted the concept of national reconciliation and also gave it an Islamic tinge to ensure that the majority of party members would be supportive. Besides, it was the time when communists had come to reconcile themselves to the prevalence of orthodox Islamic concepts and practices in the conservative and largely illiterate country. Najib did not differ much from his predecessor when it came to using power and pelf to win over dissidents. Thus, Najib was in office seeking to exert better control over both the party and the government as well as the Afghan army by injecting a mix of religion, nationalism and tribalism into the governing ethos; and the total package could be rolled and branded into a national reconciliation policy. The only thing he borrowed was the term 'national reconciliation' which was of Soviet origin and first came into public domain in the Pravda edition of 3 January 1986. This concept was adopted by the two presidents with ease as this was part of their overall approach to consolidate power in themselves though Gorbachev had conceptualized national reconciliation as an effective means of stopping fratricidal warfare among the mujahideen and ushering in stability in the country. This would have facilitated the Soviet Union's exit from Afghanistan in a smoothened fashion. The Soviet Union marketed it as a means of resolving 'regional problems', a code expression for the presence of Soviet troops in Afghanistan and Vietnamese forces in Cambodia. Gorbachev in an important speech delivered in Vladivostok on 28 July 1986 voiced 'support' for 'the line of the current Afghan leadership towards national reconciliation. Gorbachev persisted on selling this line to Karmal well before Najib became party leader. Interestingly, the concept was radically inconsistent with Marxism as it emphasised 'nations' rather than 'classes' as appropriate bases for solidarity, and 'cooperation' rather than 'struggle'. In this sense, it was both an aspect of 'new thinking' and part of the process of ideological dismantling that the Gorbachev era had inaugurated. It also reflected the failure of the military force to solve the regime's political problems. Najibullah stated this quite explicitly on 17 July 1987: 'I want to emphasize particularly that during the nine years of our fratricidal war we have not been able to resolve even one of the issues which caused the war, not one. Now, it has become clear that we cannot resolve these issues by military means.'[80] We have to take a detour of Afghan history at this point, and examine the role that former Prime Minister and President Mohammad Daoud Khan played to further the damaged economy when the foreign invasion

---

80 Maley, *ibid*, p. 121.

was about to take place. Until 1963, King Mohammad Zahir Shah appointed his relatives as prime ministers. He also had the power to dismiss or transfer the prime minister. From 1963 onwards, this changed. The head of the Afghan government was the prime minister and the government consisted of its ministers. It was the first time that the king did not play an important role in the government, leaving it to an elected authority. However, the changed rules also stated that the ministers could not engage in any other profession during their tenure in office. The 1964 Constitution also granted the prime minister the power to summon the Electoral College in case of the death of the king. The prime minister was only answerable to the Wolesi Jirga on the general policy of his government and individually for the ministers' prescribed duties. In April 1978, President Daoud was killed during a coup that started the Saur Revolution; and thereby the People's Democratic Party of Afghanistan (PDPA) revived the office of prime minister that year and it remained in place during the 1980s.

What did the concept of 'national reconciliation' consist of? In practice, it proved to be a mixture of symbolic and substantive measures. The former included steps such as the renaming of the 'National Fatherland Front' as a simpler 'National Front' on 15 January 1987 and of the 'Democratic Republic of Afghanistan' as the 'Republic of Afghanistan.' The renaming of the country was actually a restoration of the name that was applied in the period 1973-1978 when Mohammad Daoud, a powerful prime minister under King Zahir Shah (they were uncle and nephew), shifted the very character of the state from a self-reliant economy to a 49 per cent foreign aid-dependent economy for state revenue. Daoud was removed from power in 1963. He, however, staged a comeback in 1973 when he took over the reins of power and appointed himself president, a position he held till 1978 when he fell from power and was killed in the Saur Revolution. The renaming of the state under Najib was done on 13 July 1987.

With the detention of Najibullah, the mujahideen forces took over the governance of the country. Their seven factions, all sharply divided among themselves, remained as quarrelsome and divisive as possible with each trying to promote tribal interests. The Afghans continued to suffer though the Soviet/Roussi yoke was gone. However, this process took a fairly frustratingly long time to peter out. It involved several manoeuvrings and manipulations including a three-day wonder-coup in the Soviet Union to be accomplished.

By 1988, the military engagement in Afghanistan had become unsustainable for the blundering Soviet Union and the United States had grown fully impatient at the Kremlin's delay. During the summer months the Bush administration grew more frustrated over the impasse in the 'negative symmetry' negotiations. This particular term began to be used in American political parlance after the initial 'positive symmetry' which meant that the US would continue supplying arms to Afghanistan mujahideen as long as the Soviet Union continued supplying arms to the government and army in Kabul. The process of withdrawal would be lengthened as factions within the Soviet Politburo and government fought each other hard over the question of withdrawal. A 13 November 1986 Politburo meeting underscored the Soviet decision to pull out of Afghanistan. The Chief of General Staff Marshal Sergei Akhromeyev announced that, 'We control Kabul and the population centres but on occupied territory we cannot establish authority...We have lost the battle for the Afghan people.'[81] The discussion that followed reflected a no-blinkers analysis of the hopeless situation that Moscow found itself in, entailing an outgo between a minimum of $4 billion to $8 billion every year, mounting military casualties, and an uncomfortable international isolation, an unwinnable war and a growing anti-war sentiment within the Soviet population without any military progress to show for it. It was clearly time to leave! However, implementation of the decision to withdraw forces from Afghanistan proved to be much tougher than the taking of the decision itself. The following two years would be consumed in determining the exit strategy with the Politburo developing three intensely debating factions. One faction consisting of Prime Minister Ryzkhov, Deputy Foreign Minister Korniyenko, and Soviet Chief of Staff Sergei Akhromeyev (later military adviser to Gorbachev) advocated a liberal and rapid disengagement line. They emphasised that 'it was absolutely unrealistic to think that the PDPA would stay in power after the Soviet troop withdrawal.' To enable the party to survive it would be necessary to share major power by forming a coalition government representing the 'various sections of Afghan society.' This faction argued it would be essential to effect a 'quick disposal' of the Afghanistan 'albatross' so that the Soviet Union could turn its energy to developing strategic engagement with the West which would in turn facilitate Gorbachev's domestic economic liberalisation. The KGB

---

81 Document 18: 'Session of the CC CPSU Politburo November 13 1986' in 'The September 11th Sourcebooks, Volume 2', quoted in P. Tomsen, *ibid*, p. 756.

headed by Anatoly Chebrikov argued that the liberal option would expose the Soviet Union to international humiliation by abandoning Najib and the PDPA. It also argued that Ronald Reagan's bid for victory required the Soviet Union to keep Afghanistan in its sphere of influence. A decision by the Reagan administration to continue covert arms supplies to the mujahideen as long as the Soviets armed the regime in Kabul—even after a Soviet withdrawal—strenghened the conservatives' position. Otherwise known as 'positive symmetry.' Gorbachev and his Foreign Minister Eduard Shevardnadze made up the third stream of opinion which, ultimately, came out as the most influential of the three in the Politburo. They lent support to the second faction's contention of continuing weapons supplies and support to the regime in Kabul in the aftermath of the Soviet exit. Behind this decision lay the lesson learned at the time of the toppling of General Secretary Nikita Krushchev. Gorbachev, therefore, decided to postpone exit until 1988-89, the date when the Soviet occupation army left the soil of Afghanistan.

However, Gorbachev's decision to leave Afghanistan was linked to his domestic and military strategies. He followed his withdrawal proposal with the launching of the concept which had been floated earlier and rejected six years earlier of converting Afghanistan into a 'buffer' state. This occurred at the Politburo meeting of 13 November 1986. Foreign Minister Andrei Gromyko told the meeting, 'Our strategic goal is to make Afghanistan neutral...We have set a clear goal: help speed up the process so we have a friendly, neutral country and get out of there.'[82] A slightly hilarious note was added, no doubt unintentionally, when Najib, just installed as president, announced that his country had turned itself into a 'neutral, non-aligned' state. The Politburo, thereafter, approved an Afghanization strategy committed to rapidly turning over full military and political responsibility to a weak Afghan government. Afghan Commission Chairman Shevardnadze declared: 'We must regard Afghanistan as an independent country and entrust Najib to make decisions himself.' This quick handing-over process would entail hurrying and lack of training but somehow Moscow did not wish to be held back on this account. The weapons included hundreds of SCUD surface-to-surface missiles, with a Soviet team to fire them and MIG-27 aircrafts. However, judging by the accounts available of the aftermath of the exit policy implementation, the process did not go down well with the Soviet side. The account of a Politburo meeting held on 22 May 1987 talks about the grumbling of the commander of the Soviet Ground Forces in Afghanistan, Valentin Varennikov remarking, 'There is no sense of homeland there. There's kin, the tribe and the clan...We are agitating for socialism and imposing the idea of a national democratic revolution...but they don't understand any of that there.' Linked to this indifference was the mujahideen's spontaneous rejection of the idea of 'national reconciliation.' 'The leadership of the Afghan counter revolutionaries has unleashed a broad propaganda campaign to discredit and distort its substance and goals...As a result of

---

82 Document 18: 'Session of the CC CPSU Politburo, November 13 1986

threats and acts of terrorism many Afghan members of national reconciliation commissions have ceased work and even display obvious passivity,' a June 1987 analysis by 'Soviet military experts, remarked, indicating that the mujahideen interpreted the national reconciliation policy as a sign of weakness and that they only needed to press for the final victory.'

Today, it seems the Soviet exit policy and its implementation and the 'official' Afghan response to it, was implemented in its entirety by the Soviet side, with the Afghan President not being allowed to add to or subtract a word from it. It treated the other major Afghan players as if either they did not exist or they did not really amount to much. Yet, it was the latter and not the Afghan government who burnt the exit by the Soviet Union to cinders. A new light on this issue was thrown when the following analysis was made available: since the victory of the Khomeini Islamists in 1979, the Soviet KGB had waged war where they could against the Islamists, fearing contamination from Iran. In 1992, after the mujahideen veterans captured Kabul, the most violent of all civil wars in the former Soviet Union erupted in Tajikistan. It was apprehended that Uzbekistan could be the next 'domino' to fall. The Russian military feared that the Islamist movement could one day invade Russia itself, given its Muslim population of over 12 million, of whom 800,000 lived in Moscow itself.[83]

---

83 Astrid von Borcke, *Unforseen consequences of a Soviet, the Movement of the Afghans in Militant Islamism*, annotated monograph in English (Cologne: Bundesinstitut fuer Ostwissenschaftliche und internationale Studien, June 1996).

As the Soviets and then the Russians perceived it, once the last obstacle, the Ahmed Shah Massoud led Northern Alliance, to rabid Islamism taking over Afghanistan, was 'removed' thanks to the shortsightedness of the US administration, Moscow feared that nothing could now stop the Islamists from invading 'all' the Muslim republics of the erstwhile Soviet Union. However, this did not eventually come to pass though one or two of them briefly—very briefly—faltered. These republics were suffering from another affliction, drug addiction, which had penetrated the populations rather deeply. It was already known widely in the region that drugs were being smuggled across Afghanistan by Muslim extremist groups and the danger for Muslim republics increased manifold. There was also an anticipated threat from Islamists to the proposed joint venture between Shiite Iran and Russia to lay oil pipelines to export Caspian Sea oil to the West and to Asia. The threat would equally jeopardise its objective of beating the West in the race to explore and export oil, through pipelines to be laid across Afghanistan to the Indian Ocean ports. This SOCAL and other Western corporate plans had to be abandoned later in the face of the Islamist menace even though the American government and SOCAL held several meetings with the Taliban at the time who appeared to be gaining in their war of attrition against the other mujahideen groups including the Northern Alliance. By the way, the internal conditions of the Soviet Union at the time was reflected in Commander Ahmad Shah Massoud's comment that much of the military equipment that he received in his search for more arms and ammunition to fight the Taliban was made available not by the Russian army or by the Russian Defence Ministry but by the Russian arms mafia…intelligence officers admitted this at the time but also insisted that both the governments in Moscow and Tehran were involved in this illegal trade. The arsenal in use in 1998, from jet fighters to some fairly up-to-date tanks and armoured vehicles on both sides, could not be operated without foreign assistance. Both the Northern Alliance rebels (Massoud would say 'freedom fighters' which indeed they were) and the Taliban were using surplus weapons left over from the 1979-1989 war. The need for spare parts, regular maintenance, and training, forced both sides to solicit external help. The main rear supply and logistics base of the Northern Alliance in the late summer of 1998 appeared to be an air base in Tajikistan where 20,000 Russian troops were based and Moscow's political writ still ran.[84]

Russia had another reason to fear the threat of expanding Islamism, for its army (it was discovered much later) had exclusively Muslim soldiers—Central Asian 'castrated' soldiers—who were not only untrained in fighting but also were believed to be 'politically undependable'. They shared ethnicity and the same religious and cultural links with the Afghans they had to fight. Many spoke the same languages which was no surprise because ethnic Afghans were also Tajiks, Kazhaks and Uzbeks. The Russian army officers also found that as a result of this ethnic and religious affinity, Russian Muslims were passing on not only intelligence but also ammunition and even at times their personal weapons to the locals, and perhaps making their personal purchases in local bazaars. What may have caused some amount of mirth in the Soviet army camps was the discovery

---

84 James Risen, *New York News Service: Russia's New Role in Afghan Conflict*, in the International Herald Tribune, 27 Juky 1998, p. 3.

that some of the Korans printed by the CIA in Virginia, USA, were also on sale in these bazaars! By the end of March 1980 the Soviet Army realized that it had blundered and withdrew the Central Asians, replacing them with Russians, Ukrainians, and other non-Muslim non-Russian Slavs, all well-trained fighters and politically completely dependable. It was also found gradually that desertions from Central Asian units were not only rising but also increasing in numbers; initially efforts were made to trace, arrest and punish the deserters; but as their numbers expanded exponentially, even that attempt was given up, and a deserter would not be molested further. It was these deserters from the Soviet army who played an important role in the eventual break-up of the Soviet Union. By then, Afghanistan had been given up, and the Soviet Union was fighting a raging fire at home.

That raging fire gradually engulfed the whole world within a few years of the apocalyptic events of 9/11, and the gradual transition to superterrorism. How are we convinced that superterrorism is a reality? A number of incidents that took place in different locations between 1995 (when for the first time a prominent terror group, Palestinian Islamic Jihad (PIJ) hinted of its awareness about the devastating effects of biological weapons upon a population).

CHAPTER 15

The Exit of the Soviet Union

IN FEBRUARY 1988 Gorbachev stated publicly that the Soviet army would be leaving Afghanistan. The process of handing over army units to the Afghans had started; and the Afghan population had grown so weary of the Soviets that they could not visibly wait any more. The feeling in the country was that the Soviet Union was invited not by the people but by the Afghan communists; and that the people had never accepted their presence in the country. The feeling was also strong that the over-nine years occupation had harmed the country greatly. Over a million Afghans had been killed; the infrastructure had taken a terrible beating; and over a third of the population had fled to neighbouring countries such as Pakistan, Iran, and India and to the West. The best of Afghan civilians including retired army officers, leading businessmen, intellectuals, had all fled to safety and freedom. Irrespective of a consciously drawn exit policy, Soviet Russia would have no recourse other than acknowledge defeat and move over. This was the manner in which Afghans of those days looked at the end of the Soviet occupation. The dream of an 'ideal socialist state' in the heart of Central Asia had long faded.

But the worst damage to Afghanistan's modern age and its history, antiquity and ancient times, along with its culture, literature, music et al, and even its religion, which was based on the liberal tenets of Sufism, were left severely mangled by the Soviet occupation which created the conditions that eventually led to the birth, the rise into prominence and the re-emergence of the fundamentalist Taliban Islamic Movement in Afghanistan. The alien occupation, the sufferings of ordinary Afghans, and the Taliban's emergence were strung in a single thread; and for this supreme crime the communists would never be pardoned.

Each time Pakistan inserted itself in Afghanistan's political process, it has been perceived as yet another design to niggle the Western neighbour. Any government close to Pakistan, such as the Afghan Taliban government, will face automatic resistance by the Afghan people and will be opposed by the majority of Afghans including the Pashtuns. The outcome would be another cycle of warfare and chaos inside Afghanistan that would eventually spill over into Pakistan as well.[85] There are numerous instances to verify the truth in this statement. We can, for example, look at what former President Hamid Karzai was advising the Indian government in August 2019—when the peace negotiations were on—to be careful about Pakistan in the backdrop of the peace process. India should be 'wary' about a possible US-Pakistan 'deal', Karzai told Prime Minister Narendra Modi and External Affairs Minister S. Jaishankar when he met them in New Delhi. Right at that time, in Doha,

---

85   P. Tomsen, *ibid*, p.702.

Qatar, US Special Representative on Afghanistan, Zalmay Khalilzad, was set to begin another round of talks to try and reach a deal with the Taliban. Karzai told the media that he had conveyed his 'fears for Afghanistan' in case of a deal that involved Pakistan. 'We Afghans have suffered massively the consequences of American-Pakistan deals,' he said in an interview. 'Now too, this is very likely, and this is our fear and concern. We have been clear with Ambassador Khalilzad that we will fully back negotiations for peace in Afghanistan, but we draw a clear distinction between peace in Afghanistan and US-Pakistan deals in Afghanistan.'

Responding to then American President Donald Trump's comment where he framed the India-Pakistan problem over Kashmir as a religious issue, Karzai said that the US President was being 'too simplistic.' 'Hindus and Muslims have lived together for centuries in this part of the world and produced great achievements together. Any division on a Hindu-Muslim basis is very simplistic,' he said. Karzai also rejected Pakistan's threat that India's abolition of Article 370 (of the Indian Constitution which guaranteed certain exclusive powers to the state of Jammu and Kashmir) would have consequences for the Afghan peace process. 'Pakistan's desire to link the two [events] indicates that it still sees Afghanistan as a place for "strategic depth," to the detriment of Afghanistan. We don't see any link between events in Kashmir to the peace process in Afghanistan, and we would like that Pakistan doesn't try to hold the peace process hostage to its objections in Kashmir,' Karzai said.[86]

---

86 Suhasini Haidar, '*India should be wary of a US-Pak deal*, The Hindu, 22 August 2019.'

Well, writing in early 2022, Afghanistan was yet to come to this degree of grief, but the signs indicated that things had begun to go wrong and that the Taliban had been quick to detect the danger signals and was trying to take corrective measures. Two such steps can be mentioned at this stage. One was telling Islamabad and its army and the spy agency in clear terms, 'thus far and no farther.' The border skirmishes were preceded by that sharp rebuke at a time the ISI was going out of its way to stress to the world how well-behaved the Kabul rulers had been since they were brought in and installed in power. The Taliban in several succeeding steps, made it clear to Islamabad and the world that the Taliban were nobody's yes-boys. At the same time, in an obvious self-correction mode, they sought rapprochement with their arch-foe the Afghan National Resistance Force led by Amanullah Saleh and Ahmad Massoud. They had earlier in 2021 tried to defeat the NRF militarily, bombarded Panjsher Valley and district, stopped food and medicine for inhabitants in the valley and then went checking house-to-house in order to capture the resistance leadership, and then declared that the resistance had been finished. However, working from both home and abroad, the resistance leaders kept the world abreast of the actual developments which implied that the resistance was still alive. But the best confirmation of this claim was made available on 10 January 2022 when the Taliban announced officially that they had met NRF leader Ahmad Massoud in Tehran. However, the NRF immediately thereafter denied the Taliban claim emphasising that no such meeting had taken place. Further details were not available at the time but the impression gained ground that the Taliban were anxious to prove that they were trying to unite Afghan's factions. At the very least, the Taliban were trying to gain acceptability in the eyes of all Afghans and the world. This could well be just a manoeuvre, nothing sincere or well-motivated but at the very least the episode indicated a certain nervousness and a good deal of desire for gaining some amount of respectability.

Domestically also, the Taliban were responding to the actual demands of the Afghans in 2022, by not disrupting the good work that was being done by the Afghan National Statistics and Information Authority (NSIA). The Authority said on 3 January 2022 that it had distributed about 340,000 computerised national identity cards from September to December 2021. 'The nationwide distribution of the newly printed e-ID cards is now going on normally covering 13,000 to 15,000 applicants on a daily basis in 20 provinces of Afghanistan's 34 provinces,' the authority said. The ID card distribution process was resumed in fourteen provinces after assessment and evaluation of the administration's technical teams. The process of issuing e-ID cards and passports was halted after the Taliban's takeover of Afghanistan in August 2021.[87] This was a strong illustration of how the Taliban 2.0 had adapted itself to modernist requirements, compared to the medieval socio-economic condition of Afghanistan Taliban 1.0. In January 2022 occurred a stupendous defeat of the Netherlands cricket team by eleven Afghan cricketers, and the important event was justly celebrated in Afghanistan, with the Taliban fighters standing aside and creating no fresh trouble over 'un-Islamic sports activities'. Significantly, sportsmen were

---

87 Xinhua News Agency, 3 January 2022.

not being obstructed in their participation in international sports events, but their female counterparts who used to number in hundreds disappeared from the scene.

Generally speaking, we usually remain unmindful of the extent and nature of the impact that the Al-Qaeda-engineered aerial attacks on American soil, induced on American and international opinion after 11 September 2001. One of them impacted Pakistan's Afghanistan policy which simply 'collapsed' at the time. For much of Pakistan's independent history, relations with Afghanistan had been full of conflicts and tensions. The source of all these tensions lay in the great Pashtun divide marked by the British-created Durand Line. The Durand Line had been challenged by every Pashtun regime in Kabul. When Pakistan came into being on 14 August 1947, Afghanistan rejected the Durand Line which was the border between Afghanistan and Pakistan. Kabul reinforced its claim that the larger Pashtun-speaking areas that fell into Pakistan's North-West Frontier Province (NWFP) and Balochistan revert to it. To further reinforce this claim, Afghanistan went to the extent of opposing Pakistan's membership to the United Nations Organization (the original name of the world body, later shortened to United Nations). Kabul based its case on the presumption that the British mediator, Mortimer Durand, had 'arbitrarily' drawn the Durand Line and thus ignored the Pashtun-speaking areas in the NWFP and Balochistan, a historical wrong which should now be addressed and corrected. The Pashtun national movement, popularly known as the Pashtunistan movement, engendered tense relations between Pakistan and Afghanistan which received wide popular support on the Pakistan side and was mainly organised by the Khudai

Khidmadgars or the Red Shirts led by the legendary freedom fighter Khan Abdul Gaffar Khan. Tensions between the two neighbours rose occasionally to dangerous levels leading to the mobilization of forces on both sides as in 1955 and 1963. There were attacks on the Pakistani embassy in Kabul in 1955 and 2003. In the 1970s, President Daud Khan raised the Pashtunistan issue and moved the army to the Pakistan border. To counter the Afghan move, Pakistan's Prime Minister Zulfiqar Ali Bhutto supported the radical elements in Afghanistan who attempted a coup in that country. This involved people like Burhanuddin Rabbani, Gulbuddin Hekmatyar and Ahmad Shah Massoud. All these leaders later led the mujahideen forces against the Soviet occupation army.[88]

The 1973 coup which deposed King Zahir Shah also coincided with a rebellion in Balochistan and the NWFP, which was supported by the Afghan intelligence agency. At that time, several Baloch Sardars (hereditary local rulers) escaped to Southern Afghanistan seeking refuge. The Cold War came to the doorstep of the traditional Afghanistan-Pakistan conflict when the communist Khalq Party successfully staged a coup with full Soviet support, whereas, Pakistan, as an ally of the United States, jumped into the new area of confrontation. This Soviet occupation was also the spark that would quickly lead to world-wide Muslim unity and a common movement to fight the Soviet Union. For the United States it was a golden opportunity to humiliate its ideological enemy.

---

88 Kalim Bahadur, *Pakistan's Afghanistan Policy Post 9/11*, incl. In K. Warikoo-ed. Afghanistan The Challenge, ibid, pp. 128-136.

It was only when the Taliban came into power in Afghanistan in 1995-1996 with full and extensive Pakistani support, that Islamabad felt relief at last; otherwise, its relations with Kabul were never and could never be normalized. The same situation returned when the Taliban regained power in 2021. This time, Pakistan went a step further, and ensured that the Taliban government would consist of people recommended by it. But this time there was a difference in the attitude of the ruling Taliban. They apparently felt more self-assured and the historical dispute over the Durand Line continued. Incidents of shooting at each other's soldiers and civilians also occurred at intervals, indicating that the Pashtuns on both sides had remained as committed as before to a united identity.

However, it is a major characteristic of Pakistan's Afghanistan policy that it has been and will probably be essentially India-centric. Acknowledging that India was a far more powerful country than itself, Pakistan always sought the comfort of achieving a 'strategic depth' in its relations with Afghanistan. In other words, Islamabad preferred to see Kabul as a shield against New Delhi's 'designs'. From the Pakistani perspective, it was imperative that those who were in power in Kabul at a given time be pro-Pakistan so that in case of a serious dispute with India which might spark an armed conflict, Afghanistan would provide additional leverage for organizing better fighting with India. Judging by the initial conflicts between Pakistan and Afghanistan during 2021-2022, it may be said that the Taliban this time were a different kettle of fish altogether and would not be as obedient as during 1996-2001 period. As an analyst pointed out, Pakistan's defence planning is handicapped by the lack of territorial depth to absorb an attack by India and then to retaliate. This elusive search for 'strategic depth' guides Pakistan's ambitious involvement in Afghanistan despite its multidimensional implications for its own social fabric and political culture. This is one of the reasons why Pakistan's Afghan policy is kept beyond the civilian government's purview and scrutiny. Islamabad's or rather Rawalpindi's Afghan policy is closely linked to security considerations. This 'strategic depth' theory becomes the primary concern of the Army and the intelligence agencies. With such security parameters, Pakistan's Afghanistan policy was constructed with an objective to establish a subservient government that would be friendly to Pakistan, militarily too weak to question the Durand Line and unstable enough to be unable to raise the Pashtunistan issue. This 'grand' strategy determined the contours of the Afghan policy and continues till date to dominate the thinking of Pakistani defence policy makers.[89]

The concept of 'strategic depth' evolved during the Zarb-e-Momin military exercise. The idea envisaged in the model, however, was not totally a new one. In the earlier years, Pakistan's concerns were limited to having a friendly regime in Afghanistan that would not question the Durand Line, and thus a stabilized border could be maintained between the two countries. At that time, after the state of Pakistan was born and its chief ambition was not only to be recognized as a Muslim country but also as a leading country in the entire Muslim world. Therefore, the idea was not only to have friendly

---

89 Smriti S. Pattanaik, *In Pursuit of Strategic Depth: The Changing Dynamics of Pakistan's Afghan Policy*, incl. In K. Warikoo ed. Afghanistan The Challenge, ibid, pp. 137-162.

relations with Afghanistan but also with other Muslim nations in the region like Iran, Turkey and West Asian (essentially Arab) countries. In those early years, the flurry of diplomatic exchanges between Pakistan and its new Muslim interlocutors was a major point of study for the foreign office in New Delhi and other non-Muslim countries. Soon thereafter, Pakistan's geopolitical ambitions began to soar as the United States sucked it into its own vortex of anti-Soviet block of countries. Flush with lavish financial, military, and other strategic aids from the rich Western countries, the idea of a leadership role evolved in Pakistan's army and foreign office. This self-developed identity received a morale boost as India fast developed into a world leadership role under its first Prime Minister Jawaharlal Nehru who was soon acknowledged as one at par with the other world leaders. However, Pakistan's rising stature as a leading Muslim country did not help its search for so-called 'strategic depth' in Afghanistan as even the Taliban, during their first tenure in power, did not care to address Islamabad's concerns with regard to the twin issues of Pashtunistan and the Durand Line. Both issues remained in a limbo despite Islamabad's efforts to wrap them up once and for all.

Both issues of Pashtunistan and the Durand Line acquired considerable importance for the new state of Pakistan in the post-1947 period because the Soviet Union appeared on the scene to support the Afghan cause by calling the Durand Line a British imperialist ploy that should be resolved in favour of Afghanistan without further delay. The Soviet Union also supported Afghanistan in its demand that Pakistan not be accorded UNO membership before the settlement of the two issues. This was followed by the United Kingdom's clear stand that Pakistan had inherited the tribal areas of the NWFP as a successor state to the erstwhile British India.

However, this formal recognition of Pakistan as owning the NWFP and Balochistan did not diminish Afghanistan's Pashtun community's anguish at being separated from their natural kin on the wrong side of the Durand Line. This stand was shared by all Afghan governments including the Taliban who, being almost entirely Pashtun in ethnicity, had to adhere to the general line. The intensity of feeling for Pashtunistan for Afghans could be better appreciated if we compare the feelings of Germans for the reunification of the two Germanies on either side of the Iron Curtain. Pashtunistan, like the unification of Germany, was one of those causes that no national leader or politician dare renounce, however little faith he may himself have in it; the cause had its own logic.[90]

These two issues remain important but without any real possibility of a settlement for either Afghanistan or Pakistan. Given the thick bonds of ethnicity among tribal populations, as is the case with Pashtuns (or Pathans as they are known in India and Pakistan) it is but natural that Pakistan remain deeply concerned over this seemingly endless prolonged dispute.

---

90 John C. Griffith, *Afghanistan: Key to a Continent*, Andre Deutsch, London, 1981, p.57.

CHAPTER 16

The Rise of the Taliban

AN EXAMINATION and analysis of how the Taliban, thought to have been 'eradicated' from the soil of Afghanistan, could stage a comeback within a little over the first year after their defeat at the hands of American and international forces, deserves to begin with a quotation from Sir Olaf Caroe, the last British Governor of the North West Frontier Province in undivided India. He said: 'Unlike other wars, Afghan wars become serious only when they are over.'

Until recently, the campaigners of the 'War on Terror' were proof against palpable indications of a Taliban resurrection. It would not be wrong to say that after five years, the soldiers of the 'War on Terror' are caught in the midst of another war. If history is any guide, the typical characteristics of an Afghan war—which always goes round in a circle—have puzzled invading armies, and have remained rather incomprehensible to foreign military strategists. The emerging historical tendencies and the socio-political dynamics in the vast Pashtun tribal belt, which the US and its Western allies either failed to discern or simply overlooked, are unravelling once again. It may be said that in the course of these developments, the discourse on the Afghan civil war is changing.[91]

Vishal Chandra seems to have preferred classifying the American and Western policies for the Taliban and Afghanistan as instances of active ignorance, which he suggests could be very frightening indeed. This phrase was first used by the German polyglot Johann Wolfgang von Goethe (1749-1832) who wrote, 'There is nothing more frightening than active ignorance.' Did the US and Western policy for Afghanistan and the fundamentalist terrorists qualify as an instance of active ignorance? If not, then what could explain their utter failure to diagnose the disease and prescribe accurately the cure? As Chandra points out, it was way back in October 2003 when the United Nations Security Council was informed for the first time that 'In several border districts (near Kandahar and Paktika) the Taliban have been able to establish de facto control over district administration.' (See the report of the UN Under-Secretary General for Peacekeeping Operations Jean Marie Guehenno). Since then, from 2004 onward to the time they recaptured the national capital on 15 August 2021, people were regularly updated about the steady though slow advances that the Islamist force was making in the country, the main reason why their eventual victory caused little surprise among the people. But their progress was marked by tactical withdrawals, which were sometimes misinterpreted

---

91 Vishal Chandra, *The Taliban Resurrection and the Changing Course of Afghan Civil War, incl. In Afghanistan The Challenge*, ed. By Professor K. Warikoo, Pentagon Press, New Delhi, 2007,pp. 227-251.

as defeat-induced retreats. The Taliban used the retreats to melt away among the rural population, where sympathy and understanding were often available in plenty. This was the proper place to recall the words of the Taliban supreme leader Mullah Omar who told the Voice of America (VoA) in September 2001 (a few days before the 9/11 attacks by Al-Qaeda on the United States of America): 'I am considering two promises. One is the promise of God, the other is that of Bush. The promise of God is that my land is vast. If you start a journey on God's path, you can reside anywhere on this earth and will be protected…The promise of Bush is that there is no place on earth where you can hide that I cannot find you. We will see which one of these two promises is fulfilled.' Writing on Afghanistan in 2006, nearly five years since the Taliban and Al-Qaeda were ousted from Afghan soil, Chandra wrote that Afghanistan was at the time 'far more insecure'. As the Taliban stood resurrected, one was puzzled over the stated objectives of the 'war on terror'. It was difficult, then, to make out where it was heading. Perhaps the 'war on terror' throughout lacked in terms of scope and agenda as 'it consistently precluded Afghan realities'. From recalcitrant mujahideen leaders to drug-lords to anti-Kabul forces within Pakistan, all had remained outside the purview of the US 'war on terror'. It had been more focussed on Al-Qaeda elements active in areas along the Durand Line. The 'war on terror' was deliberately kept out of the purview of the Afghan political process. The 'war on terror' specifically remained a US agenda against the Al-Qaeda network in Afghanistan. The chasms between the broad objectives of the Bonn process and the narrow agenda of the US 'war on terror' were largely responsible for the resurrection of the Taliban and other problems in Afghanistan.[92]

The conclusions that Vishal Chandra reached at the end of his essay in 2006 accurately foresaw what actually came to pass in mid-2021. 'In a nutshell,' he wrote, 'it may be said that the world can afford to re-abandon Afghanistan only at its own peril.' Various Afghan factions, including the Taliban, were waiting for the West to withdraw from the region. It would have been prudent to realize that whether Mullah Omar or Osama bin Laden lived or perished, their legacy would live on until sustained international efforts were made to address the grievances of a nation which continued to bear the brunt of the last great battle of the Cold War era.

It was on 25 November 2001 that Kunduz, the last Taliban/Al-Qaeda-held city, fell to the advancing army of the United Front, effectively ending resistance in the North. The capture of the city, which continued to prove to be incomplete with pockets of resistance offering fight, followed the surrender of large numbers of Afghan and non-Afghan fighters, including the top Taliban commander Nooralla Noori. Doubts, however, persisted over the attitude of the Al-Qaeda fighters who were mostly Arabs, Chechens, and Pakistanis. The Afghan Taliban who had surrendered were segregated from the non-Afghans, and the United Front force under General Daoud Khan stayed ready for any eventuality, since the uprising of foreign fighters in Mazar-i-Sharif, leading to a bloody massacre after the surrender remained in memory. A PTI (Press Trust of India) story datelined Islamabad and dated 25 November portrayed

---

92 Vihal Chandra, *ibid*.

a visibly dismayed Pakistan at the surrender in Kunduz. A senior Pakistani official watched in dismay on Saturday as the television in his office showed Taliban fighters streaming out of Kunduz in Afghanistan to surrender to the (United Front). 'I am sorry to put it in this way,' he said switching off the television set, 'But Rumsfeld's been extremely callous.' Pakistan was mesmerized by the situation in Kunduz. There were reports that there were as many as 1,500 Pakistanis with the Taliban garrison in Kunduz and the extremists threatening to execute anyone trying to surrender. The Kunduz drama captured the frustration and anger of many Pakistani officials who entrusted their interests in Afghanistan to the United States after 11 September, when the Bush administration demanded that Pakistan join in the war against terrorism.[93]

By 1984, Peter Tomsen was writing that the number of Soviet civilian officers helping the PDPA to build Soviet-style socialism in tribal Afghanistan had risen to more than 10,000 and President Karmal later said the Afghans had 'stopped working' and decided to 'lay all the burden and responsibility for practical work on the shoulders of the advisers'.[94] The ruling PDPA grew so dependent on these Soviet officers that the latter were writing speeches and resolutions for the party's meetings, composing talking points for Afghan press conferences, formulating development plans, and even dictating the promotion policy for Afghan officers for various ministries.

---

93 Apratim Mukarji, *Afghanistan From Terrorism To Freedom*, Sterling Publishing Private Limitd, New Delhi, 2003, pp. 238-239, as quoted in Tomsen, ibid.
94 Artemy Kalinovsky, *The Blind Leading the Blind*, p. 12, citing Thomas J. Hammond, Red Flag over Afghanistan, The Communist Coup, the Soviet Invasion and the Consequences (Boulder: Westview Press, 1990), p.152.

The Soviets' encroachment into these spheres happened with the full consent of the president of the country. The people's discontentment and approaching revolt must have been ignored by party and government circles at their own peril.

At the end of November 2001 and during the beginning of a cold December, the mighty and fearsome Taliban regime was just blown into smithereens by the combined force of American troops and NATO soldiers, backed by a powerful air force and free-flowing financial resources and the goodwill of the peoples of the world. The Taliban and Al-Qaeda led by their terrorist leader Osama bin Laden first sought, desperately, shelters in inaccessible Afghan caves and then were driven out of Afghanistan altogether. The entire world heaved a cumulative sigh of relief at this momentous development and Islamist terrorists in Muslim and non-Muslim countries went into mourning with a vow of terrible vengeance upon the 'evil empire' of the United States of America. Since then, more than twenty-one years have elapsed but the citadel of America has remained steadfast.

However, the chink in the armour of the democratic world that remained was exploited with exemplary patience by the admirers and supporters of the Taliban, which included the state of Pakistan. Three nation-states played the principal role in the rise of the Taliban in Afghanistan: Saudi Arabia, United States of America and neighbour Pakistan. They played their roles in their own separate interests, but in the end the three sources of self-interest tended to merge into the single aim of facilitating the rise of the Taliban. All these perfectly matched the requirements of building such an Islamic force as defined by Mawdudi. They involved themselves in Afghan affairs when factional fights among the Afghan mujahideen grew intense and at one time it looked as if the Soviet occupation army could yet succeed in defeating them. It was then time for the United States' Central Investigation Agency (CIA) to meddle more closely with those mujahideen groups which favoured Americans. There were seven mujahideen groups in all. They reflected every kind of fissure, internal and external, to which the Afghan resistance was subject. The internal differences in the Afghan jihad were of two kinds. The first involved regional (North vs South), linguistic (Pashtun vs non-Pashtun) and ethnic (Pashtun vs non-Pashtun) differences. The lesson of history is clear: cultural differences need not translate into political differences. A different kind of internal division arose from doctrinal differences, such as, between Shi'a and Sunni. Doctrinal differences too did not need to translate into ideological and political differences. However, that this very thing still happened was a direct consequence of the political ideology that came to dominate Afghan politics and the state. The overriding ideological difference that came to be established among the seven mujahideen groups was between two political views: traditionalist-nationalists and Islamist ideologies. The traditionalisers came from religious leadership, whereas the ideologues came mainly from the ranks of political intellectuals. Traditionalists tended to treat doctrinal distinction—as those between Shi'a and Sunni—as non-political; in contrast, the tendency of ideologues was to turn doctrinal and cultural differences into political divisions.[95]

---

95 Mahmood Mamdani, see above, pp. 153-154.

CHAPTER 17

The Drug Connection

BEHIND THE Islamist terrorists' bravado lies a deep, traditional drug connection, their main source of revenue. I can recollect an experience which helps explain how every section of Afghan society has over the decades got intimately involved in the illicit drug trade. I was visiting the residence of a history professor at the Kabul University's sprawling campus dotted with a huge number of trees, giving the campus an impression of being inside a forest. As we sat and drank coffee, I asked how the professor was managing his finances since his salary of 40 Afghanis amount to nothing in terms of the US dollar, one US dollar being the equivalent of 45,000 Afghanis. This was a few months after the Al-Qaeda and the Taliban were 'eradicated' from Afghan soil. The university teacher smiled wryly and said, 'You will get your answer when you come down with me and we will take a round of this building.' The answer was there on the ground; every patch of land was rearing poppy plants, about two feet high at the time of my visit. 'Even a tiny patch of land can fetch a decent sum, around 10,000 dollars,' he said.

> We are making these drugs to kill Satan—America and the Jews. If we cannot kill them with guns we will kill them with drugs.
>
> —Fatwa of Hezbollah

> What better way to poison the West than through drugs. It's another weapon in their arsenal.
>
> —Donnie Marshall
> Former head of the US Drug Enforcement Administration

> The Afghans are selling 7 to 8 billion dollars of drugs in the West from Afghanistan. His people are involved in growing the crops, processing and shipping. When Americans buy drugs, they fund the jihad.
>
> —Yosef Bodansky,
> Director of the Congressional Task Force on Terrorism and Unconventional Warfare, 1998

At one time, the hottest-selling brand of heroin in the United States was named 'bin Laden'. Throughout the country, millions of Binny were sold on college campuses and street corners, in professional office buildings and public restrooms, at rock concerts and movie complexes by thousands of drug dealers. The cost fluctuated wildly, ranging from twenty dollars a bag in New York City to 200 dollars in Pittsburgh. Most customers preferred to make purchases by the bundle. Each bundle contained ten packs, enough for one month of 'recreational' use. The users weren't particularly concerned that they were funding the jihad. The Binnys remained the secret behind bin Laden's billions not his inheritance from his father's massive construction company nor the gifts from wealthy Saudis. The billions came not from investments in shipping lines, manufacturing plants, and Arabian oil companies, but rather from an alliance that bin Laden made in Afghanistan with a ragtag Pakistani army called the Taliban.

The Taliban first found itself in a position to oversee poppy cultivation when they seized Helmand province, a major production centre, in January 1995. In this manner, they chocked off drug revenue which was so long sustaining Gulbuddin Hekmatyar who had been the main rival of Commander Ahmad Shah Massoud. Hekmatyar, chief of Hezb-e-Islami, fled from his headquarters in Charasyab near Kabul, leaving behind his arsenal of sophisticated weapons, including stockpiles of rocket-propelled grenades (RPGs), machine guns, and Stinger surface-to-air missiles. At that point, the Taliban stood in control of much of Afghanistan, including the sole non-Iranian route between the Indian Ocean and Central Asia, 'the route that was to become the financial lifeline of Al-Qaeda'.

The new rulers of Afghanistan followed double standards in the governance of their country. While, on one hand, they imposed strict implementation of Shari'a banning overnight all forms of Western-inspired entertainment and banished women and girls to life inside the confines of their homes, at pain of the severest punishment imaginable. Even men were forced to grow long beards and compulsorily attend prayers at mosques five times a day, drug-selling continued to flourish with every drug dealer's street-corner shop being allowed to remain open and do business freely. Both selling and purchasing drugs remained legally permissible. Drug dealers grew rich overnight.

The drug connection in propagating jihad received a great fillip when Osama bin Laden, expatriated from Sudan at the insistence of the United States, landed in Jalalabad, South of Kabul, on a May 1996 day in his specially outfitted C-130 cargo plane along with his wives, his children, and 150 Al-Qaeda associates. Bin Laden lost no time in establishing an alliance with Taliban chief 'Emir' Mullah Omar in Kabul. The alliance was based on a variety of reasons. First, bin Laden was a great hero of the Afghan holy war. He had fought bloody hand-to-hand battles with Soviet soldiers at Jaji close to the Afghanistan-Pakistan border in 1986, and at Shaban in 1987. Two years later, he participated in the Jalalabad airport battle where he was hit by shrapnel and earned his rank as a mujaheed. He had fought under intense enemy fire and had earned his stripes, and was thus fully deserving of the respect of his peers who were all senior warriors by then, though still young in age. Moreover, his readiness to share his wealth with those who were pursuing the same goal, jihad against the West, consolidated his position as an equal partner of Mullah Omar. Thousands of recruits were imported, trained in camps built with his money. Fortifications along the border with Pakistan were built, and hundreds of miles of underground tunnels were constructed, to permit warriors to reach the rebel Northern Alliance's stronghold in the North. Scholars have also added a second reason why bin Laden was so quickly accepted and accorded his unique position in the Al-Qaeda-Taliban terror combine. He was a Sunni 'brother' who was seeking shelter under the Pashtun code of milmastia (hospitality), a code of conduct that called upon the Taliban to protect bin Laden and his associates 'even at the risk of their own lives'.[96]

However, the crux of the matter was that bin Laden's unlimited funds infused new life into the Taliban's jihad programme. The most vital task that lay before the Taliban at the time of bin Laden's arrival was the defeat of the Northern Alliance which had continued to deny the Taliban full control of Afghanistan. Herein also lay the supreme importance of funds generated by drug trafficking; and therefore, the drug connection via bin Laden became at this point of time, the most vital factor in Afghanistan's terror history. Drugs were first manufactured in Afghan factories which existed at the time in almost every home, and then transported out of Afghanistan through bin Laden's Al-Qaeda network with officials in Turkey and the mafia in Sicily coming into the picture later on. However, his fortune dwindled and almost tottered when he was living in Sudan and was under constant US surveillance and pressure. In 1995, US security sources reported bin Laden's net worth as being in excess of US $2,350 million. However, this estimate was described as part of America's disinformation campaign to put him under constant pressure, for it was simply untrue. American propaganda sought to portray him as an isolated millionaire mujaheed obsessed with waging his war against the Judeo-Christian world with his own financial resources. The reality of his financial position was quite the contrary to what was being given out by the US. In 1995, when Osama was living in Sudan he was going through a severe

---

96   Jack Kelley, *Tribal Leaders Giving 'Our Muslim Brothers' Safe Haven*, USA Today, 24 January 2002.

financial shortage. The situation reached a stage where his jihad was in danger of grinding to a halt. The proof of this contention was available in the 2001 trial of the Al-Qaeda activists who had been charged with the bombing of the US embassies in Tanzania and Kenya. L'Hussaine Kherchtou, a key Al-Qaeda operative, mentioned that bin Laden had admitted in 1994 that his financial resources were drained and that 'he had lost all his money'. As a result, the salaries and wages of all members of the Al-Qaeda group were cut to the bone; and his personal pilot could not renew his pilot's licence because money was 'too tight'. Bin Laden's affluence began to wane after the Saudi government revoked his citizenship and froze his assets. He had also been quite unwise in sinking vast amounts of money in Sudan by constructing an opulent headquarter for his family members and associates. While still living in Sudan, bin Laden also made large investments in his futile search for Weapons of Mass Destruction (WMD), the most important testimony in the pivotal case. The United States vs Osama bin Laden et alia came from a Sudanese national named Jamal Ahmed al-Fadl who apprised the court of his association with bin Laden and his terrorist group from 1992 to 1996. According to al-Fadl, he was singled out in 1994 to negotiate a deal for purchase of uranium from agents of the black market in Khartoum. The meeting was held in an office building on Jambouria Street. The money had to be paid 'outside Sudan'. Al-Fadl relayed the message to top officials of Al-Qaeda who, he said, found the terms 'acceptable' 'as long as the uranium was tested to be of weapons grade'. A second meeting followed in a different town outside Khartoum. In a small building there, al-Fadl was shown a small cylinder between two and three feet tall with specifications and engravings indicating that it was of South African origin. After making arrangements for a laboratory test to be conducted with machinery and technicians from Nairobi, the Sudanese witness was informed by Al-Qaeda officials that the emir would no longer require his services. He was then paid US $10,000, a sum that was obviously far below his expectations. He learned a little later that the test would be conducted in a Sudanese town, but he never learned if it was eventually conducted and, if so, what the result was.[97]

Before we leave the subject of the harmful effects of virtually legal production of drugs in Afghanistan under both the Taliban administration (1996-2001) and the democratic government (2001-2021), the second Taliban rule (2021 onward), marked a turn-back to the efforts that were made by the Hamid Karzai Interim Authority to curb the production and smuggling of drugs. It was felt at the time, when Afghanistan stood at the door of a new chance to make something of an honest attempt to build a modern state, that only a correct and adroit handling of the 'lubricant' (drugs) that had kept the wheels of jihad turning over the last few decades, would be necessary. And then in the post-Taliban period (2001 onward) drugs kept not only the wheels of terrorism but also that of the Afghan economy turning. It had to be kept in mind by all international interlocutors that more Afghans were immersed in the production and trade of narcotics than in any other trade. A United Nations report of the time said, 'A pre-assessment survey of opium poppy cultivation, conducted by the United Nations Drug Control Programme (UNDCP) from 1-10

---

97 *The United States vs Osama bin Laden et alia*, 14 February 2001, ibid.

February 2002, confirms earlier indications that cultivation has resumed (since the Taliban's defeat) at a relatively high level throughout the country after the considerable decline recorded in 2001'.[98]

How these nascent efforts at curbing illicit drug production faced stiff challenges from ground realities was evident in the UNDCP survey which reported that farmers being interviewed acknowledged that they were unsure of how the new ban imposed by the interim administration on further poppy cultivation could be effective because almost all their lands had already been harvested and that local traders were offering attractive prices. Thus, it was obvious even at that early stage that while the total cultivation could be brought down under law, a complete eradication would be out of the question. In a sense, at the very beginning of the new battle, defeat had already been conceded.

The picture three years later was something like this. In early February 2005, the Kabul government announced that the opium for the year 2005 would reduce significantly. The expected drop in opium production in 2005 would follow three years of production boom. Habibullah Qaderi, head of the newly established Counter-narcotics Ministry under President Hamid Karzai, estimated a 30 to 50 per cent reduction in opium cultivation in 2005. 'I want to see it with my own eyes', was the comment of Antonio Maria Costa, Executive Director of the Vienna (Austria)-based UN Office on Drug and Crime,

---

98 United Nations Information Service statement datelined Vienna, 28 February 2002, as quoted in Apratim Mukarji, *Afghanistan From Terror To Freedom*, 2003, Sterling Publishing Private Limited, New Delhi.

prior to his departure for Afghanistan on 13 February 2005.

The announcement of an anticipated drop in opium production in 2005 set off a spate of credit-mongering. First to claim credit was President Hamid Karzai. He pointed out that by slashing opium cultivation, the Afghan farmers had responded positively to his government's call for a jihad on the rampant drug trade. Among others who also claimed credit was Mohammed Daoud, a former militia commander and the government's 'anti-narcotics policeman'. Daoud, a deputy interior minister, had summoned the provincial police chiefs to Kabul and warned them to fire on those who did not halt poppy cultivation. Rejoicing in advance at the success of his 'strategy', he even claimed in an interview that he expected production to fall by 50 to 70 per cent. Some foreign diplomats claimed that the drop in poppy cultivation, if true, could very well be an initial response to President Karzai's US-sponsored campaign against the illicit narcotics industry in Afghanistan. In 2004, Afghanistan's farmlands supplied an estimated 87 per cent of the world's opium, the raw material for heroin.

It is important to note that after years of bumper harvests in the late 1990s, a sharp drop in opium production occurred in 2000 in Afghanistan. What had happened was that after taking control of the poppy fields sometime in 1996, the Taliban rapidly escalated opium production to generate cash for financing fresh recruits, training of militiamen, and buying of arms. Afghanistan had registered a record production of raw opium in 1999—estimated to have been 4,600 metric tonnes as by the United Nations International Drug Control Programme (UNDCP) Annual Opium Survey, which was more than twice the estimated amount of 2,100 metric tonnes recorded for 1998. Then in 2000, the Taliban government banned poppy cultivation and the United Nations and United States drug agencies determined that this decision led to an almost 96 per cent reduction in acreage devoted to the crop in the growing season of the year 2000. There were others who claimed that having reaped a huge financial bonanza from the increased opium production in 1999, the Taliban had imposed the ban primarily for two basic reasons. The first reason centred on the Taliban's strategy of establishing their credentials as an Islamic group by catering to the Muslims whose religion opposed the ingestion of all addictive substances. The second reason, perhaps, was to reduce fresh supplies of opiates in the already saturated market and thereby maintain the high level of prices in the European markets. In other words, the drug traffickers were acting on the dictum of the market forces which determined that if supply could be mantained considerably below demand, the price would definitely rise. Obviously, this was what happened. A bit of interesting history from that period is available in the fact that the day before 9/11 occurred, fresh opium was selling in the markets of Afghanistan at US $700 a kilogram, 'the highest level of price for almost a decade'. Two weeks later, apprehending an imminent US military attack on Afghanistan, prices on the streets of Jalalabad and Kandahar tumbled to as low as $100 a kilogram.[99] At the same time, the Taliban leaders imposed a virtual ban on poppy cultivation in the year 2000 in order to pursue a wider perspective. It was known that the Taliban had sent a high-level delegation

---

99   R. Maitra, ibid, pp.82-83.

to the United States in 1997 for talks with the UNOCAL, an international energy company that sought to construct a 1,300-kilometer-long gas pipeline bringing Turkmenistan's gas across Afghanistan to Pakistan. These delegates were made aware that in order to obtain a favourable response from UNOCAL and the United States government, it would be necessary to implement a drastic cut in opium production in Afghanistan. The Taliban delegates, who met Zalmay Khalilzad (who later became the American ambassador to Afghanistan) and Afghan President Karzai who had then self-exiled himself in the United States, were trying to evolve a response in Washington which could exert political pressure on the Clinton government. It was important for the Taliban to secure that recognition, and some felt at the time that Kabul had opted to impose a ban on poppy cultivation later in 2000 'as a necessary step to please the Americans'. The Taliban delegates did not know at the time that the Khalilzad-Karzai duo who were masquerading as UNOCAL representatives had probably charted out a set of measures for the delegates, which included a ban on poppy cultivation that Kabul must implement in order to get a favourable response from Washington and to lay the groundwork for the proposed pipeline.

However, all these manoeuvres were lost in history when Osama bin Laden's Al-Qaeda operatives highjacked two planes bound for the United States' Eastern coastline and smashed them into the Twin Towers of the World Trade Centre and into the Pentagon in Washington, killing nearly 3,000 Americans and others and wounding thousands of others. In fact, not only the United States but the whole world also changed abruptly and very deeply on that accursed day of 11 September 2001.

The cost of that single act proved to be too high for the Taliban who were already under severe American attack for robbing the Afghan people of their human rights and harbouring Al-Qaeda extremists and for practicing an obscurantist form of Islam but were now further identified as harbourers and protectors of the American people's Public Enemy No. 1, Osama bin Laden. Thereafter, the stage was set for a no holds barred war waged by the United States to punish both Al-Qaeda and the Taliban and 'eradicate' them from the soil of Afghanistan.

In a fine analysis of how drug money percolated down to the entire Afghan society and client markets in Europe at the time in scores of different ways is available. For instance, in 2005, almost US $600 billion in drug money got laundered annually through financial markets and international banks. Although the financial institutions would not admit it, the stock markets used all available money which also included the unaccounted drug money. CNN reported in 2003 that opium production in Afghanistan was 36 times higher—in an ironical twist—than it was at the end of the Taliban rule. Significantly, most of the Western financial markets, more specifically European markets, were passing through a deep recession when the Taliban rule collapsed in Afghanistan in 2001. Were their busy upward swings which lasted quite a few years even partially dependent on Afghan drug money? 'Naturally, this situation raised the question about the extent to which US and European banks had profited from the Afghan drug traffic. The high-end profits were of course realized in the countries of destination, not where the opium originated from. A scholar and former editor of the Geopolitical Drug Dispatch, Alain Labrousse, estimated that 80 per cent of the profits from drug-trafficking ended up at the time in the banks of wealthy nations and their branches in underdeveloped countries where control was not at the desired level.

Exactly after the first decade since former US Ambassador Peter Tomsen wrote his eponymous treatise on Afghanistan (quoted above)—containing his dire prediction about the US administration blundering into yet another major folly in its Afghanistan policy—that very thing happened. The Joe Biden administration did not consider the awful and avoidable consequences of a complete drawdown policy, but kept on pursuing this foolishness. As a result, not just his own country but Afghanistan and the rest of the world continue to suffer the terrible consequences. In a sense, Biden's decision left no other choice for the world but to make the best of a rather bad situation by laying down certain basic rules of international law concerning the recognition of governments, keeping in mind the manner in which the legality of the Taliban government in Afghanistan could be determined. Further, the options available to the states as they determine whether and how to.

Bin Laden's money woes began when the Saudi government revoked his citizenship and froze his assets. This happened simultaneously as bin Laden was sinking vast sums of money in Sudan, including into a headquarter for his family members and associates, training cells, road construction, agricultural projects, and an Islamic bank. All these were lost when he was exiled in 1995. A hunt for Weapons of Mass Destruction (WMD) was suspected as he sent agents to the international market to buy uranium. After all this, when one of his agents fixed an appointment, it was conveyed to the agent by bin Laden's negotiators that his services were no longer required.

The uranium's real worth never came to be revealed.

'The lure of Afghanistan,' Paul L. Williams writes in his colourful language, 'for the financially strapped bin Laden came not from the minarets but rather from the scent of the poppy fields. As his funds dried up, he turned to the bubas, the Turkish drug dealers, and the Sicilian mafia with a proposal for the production of choice Number Four heroin in laboratories that he was planning to set up outside Kabul. Prior to bin Laden's return, the Golden Crescent of Iran, Pakistan and Afghanistan, under the control of warlord Gulbuddin Hekmatyar, could only produce low-grade Number Three heroin that was acceptable merely for smoking and snorting. It was agreed among bin Laden and his co-investors in the venture that sophisticated laboratories would be set up near Kabul and that bin Laden would take over the poppy fields that Hekmatyar had been obliged to leave behind. He would also reopen the old trade route to the West. The bubas and the Sicilian mafia who knew that choice Number Four heroin was worth more than 100% of Number Three heroin, were too happy to help bin Laden; and as a result, the Arab terrorist's first recruits in Afghanistan were not more soldiers for his band of terrorists but highly qualified chemists from the now disintegrated Soviet Union who were unemployed at the time and were desperately looking for jobs and sustenance. Bin Laden also completed his negotiations with Afghan owners of large tracts of poppy fields. The agreement was that he would buy all the crops in their fields. It did not take more than a few months to set up the laboratories, already staffed with Russian recruits, and production of Number Four heroin began. The civil war among the various factions of the mujahideen continued to rage, as bin Laden's great venture began to hum. Soon, the labs were producing 5,000 metric tons of heroin a year, the world's largest production of heroin at the time, and bin Laden the largest producer of the deadly[100] drug. By 1997, the poppy fields were yielding a record 3,276 tons of raw opium; and as a result, revenues began to pour into the coffers of Al-Qaeda at a rate estimated between US $5 billion and US $16 billion a year. By the following year, it was estimated by America's National Household Survey that 148,000 new households had joined the bourgeoning army of heroin users, who in turn required treatment for their addiction. Not surprisingly, 80% of new addicts were under the age of 26 years. The new addict was spending on an average between US $150 and US $200 a day. While the illicit drug trade began to rise sharply in the United States, it flourished exponentially in Europe. From 1996 to 2001, corresponding to the Taliban 1.0 rule in Afghanistan, Europeans consumed in excess of 15 tons of heroin a year—double the amount that was sold in the United States. There was no secret behind this phenomenal experience. 'Terrorism, organised crime, and the illegal trade are one interrelated problem,' a deputy interior minister of Tajikistan Abdurakhim Kakharov told a congressional committee on 6 September 2001, five days before Al-Qaeda terrorists carried out the unprecedented attacks on the United States. 'The terrorist groups and the drugs are exported from the same source, Afghanistan.'

The drug, now manufactured, packaged and ready to be exported, was sent on to the next round of countries which

---

100 Jason Burke, *Afghanistan: Heroin in the Holy War*. Observer, New Delhi, 6 December 1998 and Williams, ibid, pp. 33-35.

were Afghanistan (the place of manufacture), Northern Iran (bin Laden's contacts with Hezbullah helped the Shiite terrorist group), and through Turkey to Sofia (entering Europe) in Bulgaria where the 'wheelers and dealers' of the global drug trade—and the bubas and mafiosi resided in well-equipped villas or, of all places, government guest houses. A US congressional committee was informed in 1998 by a former director of the Drug Enforcement Administration, John Lawn that 'their presence is so obvious and their deals so flagrant that it is impossible to conclude they are enjoying official protection. Sicilian dons were the main benefactors of this openly traded drug consignments, and both the Turkish and Bulgarian governments kept the uninterrupted flow of the drug trade adequately protected.[101] However, Al-Qaeda had higher ambitions than procuring raw uranium and manufacturing a WMD. They dreamed of making nuclear explosives. Exploiting their close relations with the then Sudanese government, bin Laden's men started work on producing nerve gas. Sudan was at the time fighting Christian rebels in the South of the country, but it could not achieve much progress—they were aiming for a decisive victory so the rebellion that had gone on since 1983 through a succession of governments in Khartoum could be brought to a satisfactory conclusion. A huge number of civilians and soldiers had lost their lives in the prolonged fighting. An influential section of officials still believed that chemical

---

101 Paul L. Williams, *Al-Qaeda: The Brotherhood of Terror*, Alpha Books, New York, 2002, p.165. A fine expose on the Sicilian mafia in this trade is available in Claire Sterling's Octopus: How the long Reach of the Sicilian Mafia Controls the Global Narcotics Trade (Simon and Schuster), New York, 1996, p.162.

weapons would do the trick, and bin Laden obligingly invested large sums of money in a project run by the government's Military Industrial Corporation to manufacture WMD. This project was followed up to the next stage which was nuclear weapons. It was in respect of this rolling programme that al-Fadl's testimony in the New York court became crucial because the American government could now fathom the width and depth of Osama bin Laden's jihad against the Americans and the Jews.[102]

Osama bin Laden and Al-Qaeda would like to have pursued a long-term plan to punish the Americans for their 'intransigence' in black African Muslim countries, and had struck elaborate roots in Sudan and previously in Somalia for the purpose. They appeared to have analysed the situation in a graded manner, since preparations to gain sufficient expertise and strategic capabilities were made before striking at the 'foreign Devil.' They were also exploring and weighing the situation for the same purpose in the African country of Kenya where they would finally stage massive attacks against the Americans, British and Israeli interests. The gory history of terrorist assaults on its proclaimed enemies, the US, the UK and Israel that Osama bin Laden and his killing-machine Al-Qaeda had notched up in the span of 17 years between 1993 and 2010 covering a wide spectrum of the world from the World Trade Center, Manhattan, to Aden in Yemen showed the length and breadth of Al-Qaeda's violent operations.[103]

---

102 Daniel Benjamin and Steven Simon, *The Age of Sacred Terror*, ibid, pp. 128-129.
103 *Wikipedia*.

The close and profitable relationship between Osama bin Laden and his financial backers, however, was based on the exploitation of another channel, Pakistan, which helped him and his organisation to gain an easy and excellent access to nuclear weapons technology. Since the massacre of 11 September 2001, many unknown facts which were till then kept hidden from American eyes, became accessible to Washington. Some of them were: credible intelligence including declassified intelligence reports 'about continuous trilateral interaction' between the ISI, ISI cutouts, and bin Laden during the late 1990s up to the day of 'Devil's Death'. These were found to have been voluminous. 'Private sector' cutouts Hamid Gul, former ISI officer Khalid Kharaja, who also knew bin Laden well, Khalid Sheikh Mohammed and Ahmed Omar Saeed Sheikh routinely circulated between the ISI and Al-Qaeda representatives in Afghanistan and Pakistan. Two Pakistani nuclear scientists, one reportedly previously involved in Pakistan's secret nuclear weapons programme, visited bin Laden in Kabul two weeks before 9/11. Retired ISI chief Hamid Gul was the 'honorary patron' of their NGO, known by its acronym UTN. An active duty Pakistani army brigadier was a UTN director.[104]

As the Soviet occupation wound down to a prolonged, painful, and quite willing departure—strikingly similar to the Biden administration's inglorious escape from the accursed country in 2021—the turbulent process of ethnic disintegration of the Soviet Union itself began to churn furiously starting

---

104 Robert Anson, *The Journalist and the Terrorist*, Vanity Fair, August 2002.

with Afghanistan. Much happened during the Afghan civil wars climaxing with the fall of the communist Najibullah government—a government chosen by Gorbachev himself, one of the latter's last ill-conceived acts. With the entry of various mujahideen groups into Kabul in April 1992, the factions started cooperating with their ethnic cousins from across the border. At this time, in February 1994, it was reported that Pakistan was hosting a conference in Davos, Switzerland, to find a common platform to bring about stability in South and Central Asia. Talks between Pakistan's then Prime Minister Benazir Bhutto and the presidents of Turkey, Uzbekistan, Kazakhstan and Turkmenistan emphasized that the three Central Asian republics shared a common language between themselves, the Turkish language, bonding them with Turkey itself. The Uzbeki President Islam A. Karimov disagreed with Bhutto that the situation of growing disunity and internal disturbances that helped spread political Islam or Islamism of the jehadi variety was not a regional problem that would be hard to crack. Karimov advocated a line that clashed directly with Pakistan's indirect and covert support for Islamism as he continued to demand more stringent action from Pakistan and not secretly extend help to Islamists in Afghanistan which was further destabilizing Afghanistan and the entire Central Asia region. Uzbekistan, however, was itself in touch with the Uzbek warlord General Rashid Dostum who was fighting the Afghan extremists along with Russian troops in Afghanistan and who was also in touch with Pakistani Pashtun warlord and—a complete creation of Pakistan—Gulbuddin Hekmatyar, who was fighting the Tajik-origin mujahideen President Burhanuddin Rabbani. The president's defence minister was

Tajik Commander Ahmad Shah Massoud whose biggest enemy was perforce the same Pakistani proxy Gulbuddin Hekmatyar. Around this time Uzbek troops were also fighting with Russian troops to save the former communist president of Tajikistan. It was officially but informally announced that Pakistani and also Saudi money was still buying 'fuel for Islamist fires' in the former Soviet republics and 'even inside the Russian Federation itself'. This trend lasted till 1998 forcing the United States to confront a major dilemma. Its Pakistani and Saudi allies were still financing the Taliban who sheltered its proclaimed enemy Osama bin Laden. In a quirk of fate, the Americans found themselves in sympathy with their old rivals Russia and Iran who were also looking for ways to stop the advance of the Taliban.[105]

At this point, we will have to pick up the thread of drug connection with our narration because just like the American troops fighting in Afghanistan returned home with drugs in their baggage, their Russian counterparts too, on return home, were found to be steeped in the drug culture. In any case, both American and Russian demobilised soldiers found that heroin was in abundant supply in their home countries. The world's most dreaded terrorist Osama bin Laden and the Taliban were clearly winning the war against Western power and civilisation. For long now, drugs have been recognised as a vital weapon to fight enemies, especially when the state and its army are rogues. Of course, in the 21st century, cyber attacks have turned out to be equally dangerous weapons in the hands of states and all

---

105 John K, Cooley, *Unholy Wars ibid*, pp.168-170.

states appear to be deft in applying it.

Lastly, drugs and their abundant supplies have also led to the generation of a new global threat—the rapid propagation of communicable diseases, particularly HIV-AIDS, along the heroin routes. Intravenous heroin abuse is rapidly increasing across most of Eurasia and HIV-AIDS is infecting numerous populations that extend well beyond drug user communities. This is probably the greatest threat resulting from heroin trafficking as it can, in the short term, lead to 'devastating consequences' for development, demographics, and social cohesion. According to eyewitness reports, increased drug trafficking through Central Asia and opium/heroin production in Afghanistan has encouraged heroin consumption along the drug trafficking routes. Intravenous heroin consumption has surged both in Central Asia and Russia, as far as Novosibirsk and Irkutsk in Siberia, where heroin first appeared in 1999.[106]

While the Taliban never banned poppy/opium cultivation and heroin production in Afghanistan during their first rule (1996-2001), they banned these activities on 4 April 2022 surprising both Afghan farmers and producers of the opiates (opium, morphine and heroin) and the external world. The ban was imposed just when Afghan farmers were preparing to harvest the standing crop. The Taliban said that 'under Islamic Sharia Law consumption of non-medicinal drugs for pleasure is haram (illicit). 'The poppy fields will be burned and destroyed; and offenders (who defy the ban) will be punished under sharia

---

106 R. Maitra, *ibid*, p.94.

law and jailed, or publicly flogged and even executed.'[107]

The Afghanistan Opium Survey 2021 Cultivation and Production, said that the production of opiates was Afghanistan's 'largest illegal economic activity. The gross output of Afghanistan's illegal economy was estimated to be US $1.2 to US $2.7 billion in 2021, accounting for up to 9 to 14 per cent of Afghanistan's GDP. The total cultivation acreage in Afghanistan in 2021 was 177,000 hectares. This had come down by 47,000 hectares in 2020. This was a significant reduction given that the total opium production was increasing by an average of 4,000 hectares per year during the last two decades since the collapse of the first Taliban regime.[108] For all its complaints, the international community failed to halt, or even substantially curtail, the growth of the drug economy. The British took the lead in the counter-narcotics effort in 2002 but their 'hastily conceived' idea of compensating farmers for each acre of poppy 'eradicated' led to the perverse effect of raising the price of poppy while in reality convincing more farmers to plant the crop. The United Kingdom subsequently trained an Afghan drug Interdiction Force and doubled its support for counter-narcotics to US $100 million. But the implementation of a separate American programme in May 2004 signalled the failure of the British to make any significant inroads in the sector. The US Congress appropriated US $220 million for counter-narcotics in 2004 , and US $780 million in 2005.

As for terrorism, the evidence leaves us with no option but

---

[107] Amrutha Pagad,.2022. April 04,. *Taliban bans opium in Afghanistan,* the drug that brought them to power: 5 points. DailyO. https://www.dailyo.in/politics/taliban-bans-opium-afghanistan-35680

[108] Afghanistan Opium Survey 2021 https:reliefweb.int/report/afghanistan/afghanistan-opium-survey-2021…

to conclude that between 1998 and 2001, Pakistan at the level of the ISI, perhaps also the army, and finally the government knew at least one or two of the several deadly strikes that Al-Qaeda took at harming the United States; and did not inform the US government at any level. And yet, all this time Pakistan was one of America's closest allies. At the very least, this was no ally-like behaviour. But a more damning information came in 2004 when a member of the British Parliament hinted in a newspaper article that the Pakistani government was no passive observer of what was going on between the ISI and Al-Qaeda and the information about the 9/11 strike may also have been known to Islamabad![109]

Just as the absence of a functional criminal justice system undermined reconstruction efforts in Afghanistan, so did the drug trade. In 2005, poppy was being cultivated for drug trade in all of Afghanistan's provinces with 10 per cent of the population involved in production.[110] For all its complaints, the international community failed to halt, even substantially curtail, the growth of the drug economy.[111]

The comfort of knowing that Afghanistan's drug economy was proving to be the most significant contributory factor in sending the world economy into a tailspin with the huge inflow of illicit drug money into world markets would, however, soon enough prove to be a double-edged sword. For,

---

109 Michael Meacher, *The Pakistan Connection*, The Guardian, 22 July 2004.
110 2005 World Drug Report, p.180.
111 Marvin G. Weinbaum and Andrew Finkelman, *Rebuilding the Afghan State: The International Dimension*, incl. In K. Warikoo ed. Afghanistan The Challenge, ibid, pp. 18-21.

the Frankenstein that Pakistan had let loose on the Western world, had now begun to haunt its creator as early as 1998 but a return to a more innocent past was no longer an option. As long as Al-Qaeda and other terrorist groups were based on Pakistani soil, Islamabad could comfortably monitor their activities. The Taliban mullah had also listened to and observed the advise that their ISI handlers handed over to them while there were still Pakistani camps and also when the ISI was helping the Taliban conquer other parts of Afghanistan. But after the mullahs returned to Afghanistan and settled down in Kandahar and Kabul, they grew less tolerant of ISI instructions. The mullahs perhaps could be faulted for believing they were far more qualified than Pakistanis in organizing an Islamic state; and therefore they felt it was a waste of time to listen to their handlers. Osama bin Laden was always painstaking in showing his subservience to Pakistani President Zia ul-Haq and the ISI during the 1980s. He changed subtly after his return to Afghanistan when he began to move and act more freely, i.e., independently of the ISI and Pakistan. He and Mullah Omar established a symbiotic relationship, personally, spiritually and politically. There could only be an outsider's role for Islamabad in this scenario. It was only after 9/11 that Pakistan's deeper and nefarious nexus with the Al-Qaeda and other terror groups became known and many still-undisclosed encrypted intelligence about Islamabad's actual involvement in promoting terrorism became exposed. These new reports laid bare Islamabad's dangerous double-game of playing with terrorism of the most vicious kind on the one hand and standing with the United States as the leader of the terror-fighting world on the other hand. Playing this unscrupulous double-game was easy for Pakistan as long as Osama bin Laden, Al-Qaeda, the Taliban and sundry other terror groups with varying nuisance capabilities were residing on Pakistani soil and therefore, under Pakistani patronage and surveillance. But, when the Taliban, Osama, Al-Qaeda, and the other terror groups moved West to Afghanistan and settled down around Kabul (while the popularly elected government was ruling in Kabul and Eastern provinces were becoming increasingly intransigent), the behaviour pattern of all these players changed from a touching docility to quiet defiance. The Taliban mullahs were a powerful class of former allies who also defected as they accompanied the Taliban to Afghanistan. While they listened to the advice their ISI handlers gave them, they stopped following it once they were back in their country. Thus, in one go, the former allies became completely inattentive to their ISI handlers in the changed circumstances.

One of the strangest aspects of the deep connection between global terrorism (which embraced Al-Qaeda, the Taliban, and all other major terrorist groups active in different nations) and the governments of Afghanistan, Pakistan and the United States, is that this connection stayed alive and working even when the horrors of 9/11 had come to pass, and the all-out War on Terror had begun with all guns blazing. Let us consider the following inputs from the United Nations: 'A pre-assessment survey of opium poppy cultivation conducted by the United Nations Drug Control Programme (UNDCP) from 1-10 February 2002, confirms earlier indications that cultivation has resumed 'at a relatively high level' throughout the country after the considerable decline recorded in 2001.[112]

The UNDCP said that its country office for Afghanistan and the Illicit Crop Monitoring Programme (ICMP) conducted a pre-assessment survey in 208 villages in 42 districts in the traditional opium poppy growing areas of Southern and Eastern Afghanistan in the provinces of Helmand, Kandahar, Oruzgun, Nangarhar and Kunar. Those five provinces accounted for 84 per cent of the total poppy cultivation area in Afghanistan in 2000. The Northern region of Afghanistan was not included in the survey because the colder climate in that area usually delays the poppy planting season and cultivation cannot be observed clearly in February. 'Based on the findings of this limited survey and assuming that poppy cultivation (was) also resumed in the provinces and not covered by the pre-assessment, it is estimated that opium poppy cultivation in Afghanistan could cover an area between 45,000 hectares and 65,000 hectares in 2002,' the survey said. 'This range of estimates compares to the levels of cultivation reached during the mid-1990s, but remains lower than those recorded in 1999 (about 95,000 hectares) and 2000 (about 82,000 hectares).' The UNDCP pointed out that the interim administration (installed on 22 December 2001) banned poppy cultivation on 17 January 2002. 'At that time, however, most opium poppy fields had already been sown. Although most farmers interviewed during the pre-assessment survey said (that) they were uncertain about being able to

---

112 United Nations Information Service statement, datelined Vienna, 28 February 2002.

harvest opium this spring because of the ban, the high prices offered by local traders create a powerful incentive'.[113]

The results of the survey were confirmed by the time the Second Annual European Conference on Drug Trafficking and Law Enforcement opened in Paris on 26 September 2002. Drugscope, a British charity and organiser of the conference, estimated a staggering 1,400 per cent jump in Afghanistan's production of poppy since the fall of the Taliban government in November 2001. Chief Executive of Drugscope, Roger Howard said, 'If we are to stop the return to full-scale opium production, the international community must fulfil its commitment to help rebuild Afghan society, giving communities and individuals another option. Enforcement on its own is not the solution.' (emphasis added)[114]

Drugscope said on that occasion that 'The total likely yield for 2002 will be between 1,900 and 2,700 tons which amounts to a rise between 900 per cent and 1,400 per cent, in the space of only one year.' It pointed out that although this figure was still lower than the level of production in 1999 or 2000, cultivation is back to a very significant level. It would also come as a blow to the countries which, in April 2002, agreed to take the international lead in assisting the Afghans develop their counter-narcotic capacity. The charity invoked then British Prime Minister Tony Blair's words uttered in October 2001, 'We act also because the Al-Qaeda network and the Taliban regime are funded by the drugs trade. Ninety per cent of all heroin sold in Britain originates from Afghanistan

---

113 Posted on http://www.unis.unvienna.org.
114 Apratim Mukarji, *ibid*, pp. 17-19.

and (stopping this) is again directly in our interests.' The Paris conference identified the problems facing the Afghan government in tackling the drugs trade as follows: poorly trained and ill-equipped staff, damaged buildings in poor conditions, gaping holes in walls and ceilings, no furniture and no glass on the windows, no operational police equipment, and lack of communication equipment, lack of transportation facilities, absence of scientific support capacity or a basic narcotic test, and lack of systems for use of intelligence. Interestingly, while the British foreign secretary Jack Straw announced in July 2002 that almost a third of Afghanistan's poppy fields had been destroyed, an investigation by the BBC found that there was little evidence to establish that the crops were being eradicated. And the authoritative survey conducted since then confirmed that far from being eradicated, the crops were actually much larger than the previous year's. The BBC also quoted a military commander to the effect that better eradication of poppy crops would require an agreed plan, with alternative job opportunities offered to encourage farmers away from the lucrative cultivation of poppy. Farmers, on the other hand, took the stand that though they realized the dangers posed by heroin, the economic situation left them with no choice.

Has the situation changed for the better since then and especially, during the long two decades that intervened between the two Taliban regimes?

CHAPTER 18

The World in a Dilemma: To recognise or not to recognise?

THE ROOTS of the problem of international recognition to be accorded to the Taliban government that forced its way to power in Afghanistan in August 2021 lay in its very illegality and ambiguity. States began to face difficulties regarding the question of recognizing the Taliban and providing guidance to assist in the interpretation of ambiguous statements and actions of states, including with regard to their engagements with the Taliban. Ordinarily, the government of a state is easily identifiable: it is normally the entity with stable and uncontested power over that state's territory, usually with a constitutionally legal base. Changes to a state's government take place smoothly, such that identification of the government is unlikely to be contentious. Identifying a state's government is not always so simple, especially where power changes hands unconstitutionally, and as often happens in these cases, there arise competing claims to being the government of a state. Especially where the identity of a state's government is contested or otherwise in doubt, recognition of government is important. In addition to providing evidence that an entity enjoys governmental status under international law, recognition as a government involves the acceptance that an entity is entitled to represent the state in its international relations, including in foreign municipal legal systems, and to exercise the state's rights under international law.[115]

The uneasy question of legitimacy arose as the government dogged the first Taliban, and the terrorists faced much more intractable circumstances in 1996-2001. The whole world was actively and resourcefully anti-Taliban at the time, and there was no scope for moderation on either side. The phenomenon was unique to both Afghanistan and the international community; and neither party was willing to give in whatsoever little way they could. The terrorists were maddened by their untested entry into the world of absolute power, and were entirely contemptuous of the opposition, both inside and outside the country.

An incisive analysis of the difficulties in granting recognition to a government which seizes power by force—which, plainly speaking, boils down to forcing the majority of people in a country to bow down to diktats of a tiny minority which possesses military strength and lacks moral power—shows that such instances require cautious handling and the establishment of an international consensus. Recognition for a new government which is already marked as 'forced' and 'hence illegitimate until recognized' presents unforeseen and complex challenges to individual governments. Yet, recognition must be acquired or granted. When the change of government is constitutional and hence legal and there is no rival claim,

---

115 Justsecurity.org 7 September 2021.

recognition is virtually taken for granted and approved without difficulty. This is why recognition matters for a host of reasons. The government of a state has the sovereign right to control its territory, but the exercise of that right is subject to its other international obligations. For example, a government has the responsibility to protect and respect the human rights of all its citizens, to uphold Security Council resolutions that are binding on all member-states of the UN and to protect diplomatic missions within its territory. And it has the prerogative to request that other states provide humanitarian, military and/or economic assistance. One way to think about the key issue is: To whom do you look to carry out the obligations of the state?

Nine months since they regained the power to lord over Afghanistan, the Taliban appeared to exhibit an air of near indifference to world opinion, warning, advice, and threat by the international community. This was reflected once again when the 4th Regional Security Dialogue on Afghanistan—a functioning group of nine neighbouring countries comprising Russia, China, India, Turkey, Pakistan, Iran, Kyrgyzstan, Tajikistan, and Kazhakstan, took place in Dushanbe, the Tajik capital, on 27 May 2022. India's National Security Adviser Ajit Doval and his counterparts reiterated the Taliban government's obligation to maintain internal and external peace, secure the Afghan people, give back the people's fundamental rights, including school education for girls, and jobs for qualified women. However, the exercise did not appear to have been successful in the sense that the fundamentalist rulers did not react publicly. There was not even a press statement to place their views on the matter. No doubt, the preceding three dialogues had met with the same kind of fate, which could not be better described than 'indifference'. Thus, the advantage stayed with the new rulers of Afghanistan. And the task of making Afghanistan fall in line with international laws and conventions had also become 'utterly frustrating' for the international community.

Conditions for Recognition

By December, four months after the seizure of power in Kabul, a few aspects of the political changes were clear. Since no constitution was in force and because the suspended democratic constitution did not fulfil the requirements by itself, the Taliban government was illegitimate and this fact cannot be shouted down. The terrorist regime continues to be acutely conscious of this deficiency and looks unable to figure out an honourable exit strategy. Unfortunately, it is also placed in acutely untenable conditions at the same time. It is virtually bereft of funds; international humanitarian aid and financial assistance to the government of the day—which used to be the mainstay of a wobbly economy till the Ashraf Ghani government came into being—is not forthcoming and the Taliban government is caught in a trap made by itself. The regime's extremely shameful record in the fields of human rights, women's rights, the right to education and the right to information, equal treatment of all citizens and of aliens, all represent a frighteningly bleak future for ordinary Afghans. The Taliban burnt all the bridges behind it and tried to bash on regardless, a policy which could only backfire under the circumstances. And that was what was occurring in December 2021. Its pitch was further queered by the astonishing self-sustaining capacities and stamina of the opposition National

Resistance Front (NRF) and its army. The Taliban appeared to be incapable of wiping them out from the soil of Afghanistan. Worse still and a major source of diplomatic embarrassment for the Taliban, was the united diplomatic staffers of the previous government. The ambassadors and their staff remained determined to stick together and help the representatives of the previous regime to fight the usurpers on the diplomatic stage. And surprisingly, Taliban diplomacy failed (as of the end of 2021) to get the upper hand. The diplomats remained fighting despite not receiving their salaries since 15 August and having lost their diplomatic entitlements. Providentially, however, the host governments refrained from taking subsequent actions, such as, derecognizing the personnel, since they were yet to recognize the incumbent government in Kabul. Thus, what could have been a blessing for the Taliban government became a veritable curse. In a sense, the much-maligned former President Ashraf Ghani appeared to have had the last word in emphasising in his resignation letter that, 'The Taliban won victory in the judgment of the sword and gun and they have a responsibility to protect the honour, or prosperity and self-respect of our compatriots.' He followed this up by appearing to suggest that the Taliban did not currently have the legitimacy to govern but must earn it. 'Didn't they win the legitimacy of hearts. Never in history has dry power given legitimacy to anyone and won't give it to them. It is necessary for (the) Taliban to assure all the people, nations, different sectors, sisters and women of Afghanistan to win the legitimacy and the hearts of the people.' Besides, the position taken by the former Vice-President Amrullah Saleh back in August 2021 that he was the legitimate caretaker president of Afghanistan could not be countered by the Taliban government because the very issue of the latter's legitimacy remained in limbo. By all respects, this was a unique situation in the history of world diplomacy.

Looking back, it seems that the Taliban were in a far more comfortable situation in the 1990s when they first conquered Afghanistan. At that time, the terrorist force was in denial and cared a fig for anybody's recognition. The three countries that recognized the regime—Saudi Arabia, United Arab Republic and Pakistan—were in any case, expected to do so and nobody was surprised. The United States, though, did admonish them for their wrongful action. But the Taliban proved to be a hardened lot and did not pursue the matter. Also, the terrorists felt secure in the knowledge that it was they who were in control of the territory of Afghanistan and that its people were beholden to them for their lives. It was the supreme weapon of fear and loss of life that was being exploited to rule the country. Saleh's stand was followed by the previous legitimate government's claim to the country's seat in the United Nations. The fight over this crucial diplomatic position continued for many days till the Taliban regime virtually left the UN with no alternative but to leave the position unfilled.

It may help if we take a look at the provisions of the recognition of a new government as enshrined in Article 4 of the United Nations Charter. Since the question of how existing states recognise a new state is an intra-state matter, and given the state's central role in international law and international relations, it would seem as though a clear and codified definition of a state exists in international law. However, such was not the case. Since 1945, several attempts have been made to arrive at such a definition. During the negotiations over the draft text on the Declaration on the Rights and Duties of States (1949), the Vienna Convention on the Law of Treaties (1956 and 1966) and the articles concerning Succession of States in respect of Treaties (1974), attempts had been made to define the concept of the state. However, none of these efforts succeeded as a codification of the definition of a state turned out to be 'too politically sensitive'. Despite the lack of a clear definition of what constitutes a state, international law provides some guidelines on how to approach the issue of statehood. For instance, the existence of effective control is widely regarded as an important, perhaps crucial, consideration in assessing the emergence of new states. A codification of Jellink's 'Drei Elementen Lehre', which affirms that a state consists of three essential elements can be found in the Montevideo Convention on the Rights and Duties of States of 1933 (Montevideo Convention). Article 1, of the Montevideo Convention provides a description of the state as a subject of international law: 'The State as a person of international law should possess the following qualifications: (a) A permanent population; (b) A defined territory; (c) A government, and (d) Capacity to enter into relations with the other States.' The Montevideo Convention is a relatively old, inter-American convention with few ramifications. Its description of the (modern) state, however, is almost without exception considered the starting-point for any discussion about the state as an international legal personality. Article 1 of the Montevideo Convention is regarded by many as the 'most widely accepted formulation of the criteria of statehood in international law. Eventually, the following six criteria have been settled upon by the international community as the only basis for extending recognition to a state, and there is none else. They are: defined territory; permanent population; government; effectiveness; independence; and capacity to enter into relations with other states.[116]

It would be profitable in the context of the Taliban government in Afghanistan that we delve a bit more into the intricacies of the sixth criterion for qualifying to be a state recognized by all. The capacity 'to enter into relations with other states' is not the exclusive entitlement of states: autonomous national authorities, liberation movements and insurgents are all capable of maintaining relations with states and other subjects of international law. While states do possess that capacity, it is not a requirement but a consequence of statehood. In the case of Afghanistan, the stalemate over the question of recognition was primarily caused by the Taliban's desire to be accorded membership to the international community. Unlike during Taliban 1.0, this time the insurgents were bent upon being counted as a respected member of the world order with the full capacity to participate in international relations. This was where the resistance by the other states proved too strong to break, and the Taliban foundered. The Taliban leadership, that kept on knocking on the door of the world order for entry into the 'exclusive' club of recognised states, would not accept defeat, but at the same time they would not play by the rules. Therefore, the stalemate continued.

---

116 Tilburg University Faculty of Law Department of International Law and European Law, LL.M. Thesis Public International Law https://arno.uvt.nl/.showcgi?fid=121942. PDF file

The crucial point at which recognition of the Taliban by 'other states' failed was the Taliban's conscious policy of not giving in to pressures to step back and permit 'concessions' which, in the language of international diplomacy were deemed as 'absolutely necessary adjustments'. The efforts at reaching an understanding failed at the very beginning when the Taliban refused to heed the advice of other states, not excluding Pakistan, not to name the new country an Islamic Emirate. Besides, the Taliban Islamic Movement's various forces continued with their deliberate suppression of every expression of democratic freedoms, such as, human rights, women's rights, trade unions, free media, a liberal education curriculum, etc. Ever since the Taliban's return to power it has become impossible to air one's opinion freely in Afghanistan. It was the deliberate policies of the Afghanistan government that blocked all avenues of granting recognition by the international community. The group's rank and file suppressed demonstrations across the country, demonstrators and journalists are being detained and beaten up. (The) Taliban leadership have effectively banned girls' education, discouraged women from returning to work in a number of sectors and disbanded the Ministry of Women's Affairs replacing it with its historically notorious Ministry for the Propagation of Virtue and the Prevention of Vice. At least some elements of the group have begun enforcing brutal law enforcement policies, including public execution.[117]

---

117 Kate Batman, Asfandyar Mir, Ph.D., Ambassador Richard Olson, Andrew Watkins, *Taliban Seek Recognition But Offer Few Concessions to International Concerns Economic and humanitarian needs are key drivers of Taliban's overtures,* https://www.usip.org/publications/2021/09/taliban-seek-recognition-offer-few-concessions-international-concerns 28 September 2021.

Reminiscent of the 1990s, Pakistan once again took the lead in trying to persuade the international community to come closer to the Taliban regime and concede recognition to the new Afghanistan. Following Islamabad's persistent campaign, it was able to gather some support on the issue when 17 Shanghai Cooperation Organization (SCO), reached an agreement and declared on 28 September 2021 to the effect that Pakistan would only grant recognition to the Taliban-controlled country if the following criteria were met: 1) Afghanistan would be run by an 'inclusive' government representing all ethnic and minority groups and women; 2) Assurance of human rights; and 3) Adherence to the principle that Afghanistan's territory would not be used for terrorism against others. The other SCO members on the panel were Iran, Uzbekistan and Tajikistan. However, despite repeated pleas, the Taliban government remained exclusive till December-end. On the contrary, the Taliban deliberately defied the international community by bringing into the cabinet as many as 14 top-level international terrorists and giving them important portfolios. When the world community expressed its shock and dismay and demanded immediate retrenchment of the terrorists, even the combined might of the international community failed in its mission. Recognition was stalled but the Kabul authorities did not appear to have lost any sleep over the stalemate. It continued its efforts to persuade individual states to reconsider their positions and to think 'sympathetically' on the plight of poor, deprived Afghans who were somehow eking out a miserable existence without adequate nourishment or money. Drugs were in short supply; and food scarcities became the order of the day. Malnutrition became rampant, diseases spread forcing people to continuously migrate from villages to cities and towns, with the capital city taking the bulk of these internally displaced persons. Altogether, Afghanistan was in an extremely pathetic situation; and the Taliban apparently kept on hoping that this grim situation would eventually persuade the international community to show its humanitarian face and help the country and its people. But, even here, difficulties appeared as donor countries insisted on a total absence of government personnel and agencies in transferring humanitarian aid to ordinary Afghan recipients. After a long tussle with its conscience and duty, the Indian government agreed to gift wheat to Afghanistan but only after the Afghan government came into the picture. New Delhi described the first agreement as 'professionally satisfactory.'[118]

Another obstacle to taking the Taliban capture of Afghanistan in a normal manner was the fear—quite justified in the light of past experience—that other terrorist groups would be encouraged by the success of the Taliban in Afghanistan. The Tehreek-e-Taliban Pakistan (TTP) was not slow to jump in the fray by resorting to armed attacks, arson, kidnapping and torture, etc. It also benefited substantially when its leaders and fighters imprisoned by the former Afghan government were released by the regime in Kabul. Conversely, Pakistan was endangered to a certain extent by the strengthening of the anti-state terrorist group. But, not surprisingly, Pakistan continued to lend strong support to the Afghan Taliban in order to

---

118 Kate Bateman and others., as quoted above.

preserve its self-interests. The Imran Khan government was very careful not to seek the Kabul authorities' assistance in restraining the TTP. The government appeared to have kept the two issues—despite their close inter-relationship—separate. However, there were reliable reports available at the time that Islamabad had sought the Afghan Taliban's help in restraining the TTP and that the latter had responded positively in the matter. Generically speaking though, Kabul declared that it would not permit its territory to export terrorism to other countries. But it could be that this was meant to be applied to the Islamic State-Khorasan (IS-K) rather than to the Afghan Taliban. All in all, the Taliban government's dubious fashion of carrying on the state's international obligations—which in the most emphatic manner demanded that terrorism must not spread from Afghanistan—created its own contradiction and thereby strengthened the unreliability of the regime in the eyes of the international community. And what would be the result? Further uncertainty of Afghanistan being granted recognition by other states![119]

The rigours of international law and practices regarding granting recognition to a new state or a usurper government came close to a necessary amendment when the United States Treasury sent a clear signal that humanitarian assistance should not be held hostage to certain policy decisions and actions by the Taliban Islamic Movement. Almost all countries faced this hard choice by the end of 2020-21 when the plight of the

---

119 Kate Bateman and Others, quoted above.

people of Afghanistan began to prick the world's conscience. Yet, the world community could not make a clear choice because of its own contradictions. Thus, the stalemate over recognition of the new Afghan regime could not be resolved because of persistent contradictions on both sides. Analysts were urging Washington to separate the two issues: let the rigorous international law and practice be adhered to as far as the question of other states' recognition was concerned; and let humanitarian aid flow to the affected people even though this required direct negotiations with the government in Kabul. The example of India—preceded by China, United Arab Emirates, Pakistan, and Turkey—was much discussed in international circles, particularly in diplomatic and academic circles.

If one were to go by the harsh treatment meted out to women by the Taliban from early May 2022 onwards then it would seem as though the Taliban had finally given up on any hope of international recognition anytime soon. Otherwise, there could be no sensible explanation why the Taliban issued a decree on 7 May 2022 ordering women who were permitted to go out of home only on urgent and necessary work, to wear the head-to-toe burqa, the dress which honoured Afghan culture and sense of honour. The order has been mentioned and discussed above.

While the Taliban culture of unbelievable torture of women continued in 2023, a particularly chilling example was set when the fanatic rulers finally killed a woman lawmaker in January. The parliamentarian, Marisa Naiade, who was elected to Parliament in 2019 to represent Kabul, had stayed after the Taliban takeover in 2021, and while the legislature had been abolished, she continued to work for an NGO she was long engaged with, and had defied the new rulers ignoring the various warnings issued to her. This was the first time a lawmaker had been killed, as almost all the female parliamentarians had escaped abroad in the immediate aftermath of the return of the Taliban. The Kabul police said Naiade and one of her bodyguards were killed at 3 am when they were sleeping on the first floor of her home, which she was using as her office. A second security guard and her brother were injured, while a third guard fled with money. The police did not answer when it was asked if they were aware of any motive and who could be possibly involved. The imprint of the Taliban on the murder was obvious, and there were condemnations, including by another woman lawmaker, even within the country.[120]

It was no surprise in the Taliban-ruled Afghanistan that a fresh prohibition was imposed on women athletes in January 2023. Nuora's determination to play sports was so great, reports say, that she defied her family's opposition for years. Beatings from her mother and jeers from her neighbours never stopped her from playing the sports she loved. But the 20-year-old Afghan woman could not defy her country's Taliban rulers. They had not just banned all sports for girls and women they had also actively intimidated and harassed those who once played, often scaring them even from practice, Nuora and other athletes, said. Nuora was left shattered. 'I am not the same person any more,' she said. 'Since the Taliban came, I feel like I'm dead.' A number of girls and women who once played a variety of sports told reporters

---

120 Associated Press, *Afghanistan: Former lawmaker, her guard, killed at Kabul home*, Kabul, 15 January 2023.

they were intimidated by the Taliban with visits and phone calls warning them not to engage in the sports they had played. The women spoke on the condition of anonymity, fearing reprisals which might at times include death.

However, some of the women's sense of defiance of their tormentors was so high that they deliberately posed for photographs establishing that they were practising fencing, with the helmets, lances and armour after taking care that they were fully covered in burqas so that their identity could not be established. While the girls continued to defy the Taliban diktat, they gradually lost steam as repeated vigilante acts by the rulers eventually made it impossible for them to continue to play their sports. A 20-year-old girl was participating in a competition with other girls in a stadium hall in Kabul in August 2022 when news came that Taliban fighters were approaching the outskirts of the city.

A 20-year-old girl who had grown up playing football with neighbourhood boys was warned repeatedly after the return of the Taliban, but continued to play till the Taliban caught up with her after a cousin betrayed her to the authorities. This girl had become a star footballer before the Taliban came and her coach had taken up her training and she had been chosen to represent the country. Even before the change in the power equation, it had become clear that the democratic government would not last long, and foreigners and Afghans were escaping abroad.

The girl's coach called up her mother and advised immediate escape abroad. 'Ask her to come to the airport and go abroad by the very first plane available.' But, instead, the girl was taken by her family to their native town, and then her football career came to an end. Another girl, who was continuing to practise with friends, was warned repeatedly but she defied the ban and was still doing so. 'I'm determined to fight back because I am a fighter. I shall never give up my fighting,' she told reporters.[121]

---

121 Associated Press, *Barred by Taliban, Afghan women athletes: 'Not the same anymore,'* https://apnews.com/article/sports-soccer-youth-taliban-college-875079d49a1c8c7063da7c14f317a8b3 11 January 2023.

CHAPTER 19

Tortuous Negotiations

THE NARRATIVE of long, uncertain, and at times even indefinite process of peace negotiations between the established world order, including the neighbouring countries of Afghanistan, the United States of America, and regional blocks, proved to be frustratingly unsatisfactory. The process came in time to engulf almost every aspect of statecraft in which the Taliban Islamic Movement and the Afghanistan of 2020s were involved, and as a result shades of frustration could be read in every move and comment. A prime example was the long-delayed announcement of the winner of the presidential election, Ashraf Ghani, in February 2020. It took no less than five months since the election was held. Instead of exhaling a collective sigh of relief, Afghans and foreigners interested in the fate of the country felt they were facing an 'infinite crisis'. The conclusion they reached was that Afghanistan was 'no closer to peace' after the declaration by the Afghan Independent Election Commission that President Ashraf Ghani was the winner of the 28th presidential election held on 28 September 2019. Instead, the continuation of Ghani at the presidential post was expected to 'deepen the political crisis'.

That it took almost five months to declare the official results—Ghani secured a widely discredited victory with 50.64 per cent votes against his main opponent Dr Abdullah Abdullah's 39.54 per cent—itself pointed to the seriousness of the crisis. Abdullah called the results 'fraudulent' and vowed to form a parallel government. Had he done so, the already feeble Afghanistan administration 'whose writ did not reach beyond the main urban centres,' would have been further undermined. For the Afghan voter, this was a déjà vu moment. In 2014 Ghani was declared winner of the election but Dr Abdullah, who opposed him then too, refused to accept the result. Then US Secretary of State John Kerry brokered a power-sharing agreement which allowed Ghani to take over the presidency and made Abdullah the government's Chief Executive. Thereafter, throughout the five years of tenure, they were at odds with each other while the Taliban expanded their hold across the hinterland and stepped up attacks on its city centres. Unsurprisingly, only less than a fourth of registered voters turned up in September, raising questions about faith in the democratic process.[122] It is probable that the voters were responding to the call of the Taliban, who were not participating in the election but were assuredly the most interested party in the exercise. On 7 August 2019, the insurgents warned that the registered voters better keep themselves away from polling booths. The statement said, 'Our fighters should stand against this theatrical and sham of a process to their full capabilities, to prevent losses, God forbid,

---

122 The Hindu, *Infinite crisis*, The Hindu, editorial, 20 Feb 2020.

from being incurred by our fellow compatriots, they must stay away from gatherings and rallies that could become potential targets. Afghan elections do not hold any value.' In the light of the 2014 election experiences, in an election that was mired in fraud allegations, the United States brokered a power-sharing deal between Ashraf Ghani and Abdullah Abdullah to rescue the process of government formation.[123] However, this particular saga of mutual recrimination and muscle-flexing continued over the following months till matters once again came to a head with both contenders announcing that they had decided to hold separate swearing-in ceremonies to register their disagreement over the last agreement. On 7 March 2020 Dr Abdullah Abdullah issued invitations to all national and international organisations to the swearing-in ceremony and said all necessary precautions had been taken. This development followed the election commission's declaration of result in February of the year, announcing Ghani as the winner and the next president. Abdullah had immediately challenged the verdict and claimed that he and his supporters had won the poll. He announced that his separate swearing-in would take place at the same time as Ghani's official ceremony. This piquant situation further ate away at the feeble democratic process that was still surviving in the country. The United States asked for a breather so that it could have a chance of persuading the old rivals to reach a compromise. The compromise finally came on 17 May 2020 when a power-sharing agreement was signed by

---

123   The Hindu, *Taliban asks voters to stay away: Electoral rallies and gatherings could become potential targets, warn insurgents*, 7 August 2019, Taliban asks voters to stay away Electoral rallies and gatherings could become potential targets, warn insurgents

Ghani and Abdullah Abdullah. While in 2014 the latter had agreed to be the chief executive officer of the government—a prime minister of sorts—this time his designation became the head of the National Reconciliation High Council. As a further concession to Abdullah agreeing to take the post, some of his team-members were taken into Ghani's new cabinet of ministers. For Abdullah Abdullah, this post offered a unique challenge to establish his prominence in the country. The Reconciliation High Council was vested with the authority of handling and approving all affairs related to Afghanistan's peace process, meaning that he would be directly dealing with the Taliban who had been growing in strength all the time. The agreement and the subsequent government formation was welcomed by all countries wishing to see an end to the incessant bickering among the top political leaders of Afghanistan.[124]

The bizarrely tortuous wrangle, as reflected in the tragicomic reality of two men taking the oath of office as president, reached a resolution on 17 May 2020 when President Ashraf Ghani gave his chief rival Abdullah Abdullah the leading role in the country's peace process with the Taliban and a 50 percent share in the new cabinet. The deal drew to a close a political crisis that had cast a major shadow over efforts to end the war with the Islamic terrorists. All but one of Afghanistan's presidential elections since the 2001 American invasion ended in dispute. Then after Abdullah disputed Ghani's victory for a second term in September 2019's election, both the sides dug their heels in, indicating that the fight would not end soon.

---

124 Associated Press, *Afghan President rival sign power sharing deal*, 17 May 2020.

As international pressure grew, and the Taliban appeared to be benefitting from the continuing political disarray, the two sides began talks to find a way out. The new deal which was mediated by political leaders including former President Hamid Karzai, stripped Abdullah of an executive role but gave his coalition half the cabinet appointments. The deal also promoted General Abdul Rashid Dostum, a controversial figure and a former vice-president to Ghani, who was also a backer of Abdullah, to the highest military rank, that of marshal. At the time of his promotion, Dostum was facing an open court case against him. The case was based on accusations made in 2016 by a political rival who accused the then vice-president of abducting him from a crowded sports arena, torturing him and ordering his rape.[125]

This intense in-fighting occurring at a time when the Americans were nearing finalization of an agreement with the insurgents, exposed the weakest side of the Afghan administration. For, even though the government was not a participant in the peace negotiations, its interests were very much in the reckoning of both the Trump administration and the Taliban. To that extent, the latter knew well that Kabul was scarcely in a position to bargain for anything. As a matter of fact, Trump had to exclude the Ghani government from the talks because the Taliban had said they did not consider it as an Afghan entity and viewed it only as a puppet of America, and therefore it was not a 'legitimate' Afghan government.

---

125 Mujib Mashal, *Afghan rivals sign power-sharing deal as political crisis subsides*, The New York Times, 17 March 2020.

They also knew that an American withdrawal would weaken the Ghani regime dangerously which could collapse soon after. And that was what exactly happened after another year!

All through the period when the (unofficially) disinterested Americans were seeking a way out of their Afghan predicament, the supreme irony lay in how the ordinary Afghan civilians felt at the time about their eventual fate. One report should be sufficient to illustrate this point. In one of Afghanistan's most insecure provinces, government forces said they made 'key' territorial gains over the previous year (2019), retaking three districts that had been contested by Taliban fighters for 'years'. 'But for many civilians in the area, the military victories upended their lives and brought ongoing clashes.'

Taliban fighters had converted an old fort along the main road in the small village of Say Qala into a checkpoint, forbidding women from appearing in public without male escorts. They were also engaged in attacking nearby government troops. Despite the restrictions on movement by the public, residents later said they had found a way to bypass the restrictions in order to live out the insurgents' rule while leading a normal life to the extent possible. Muhammad Naseem, a teacher in the village, said that for months Taliban fighters allowed his then-pregnant wife to travel with a male guardian to a hospital in the government-controlled Ghazni for medical checkups. But when Afghan government forces began a push to retake the territory in September, the road was no longer accessible for civilian use. By October when the wife went into labour pain, it was no longer possible to travel beyond the village and she was forced to give birth to a baby at home and died soon thereafter.

Depending on the results of localized battles and the identity of the winning side, life used to be determined by changing power equations and live somehow. More than 2,500 civilians were killed and 5,600 injured during the first nine months of 2019 according to the UN report of the time, making the year 'one of the deadliest' years of the decade. Ghazni turned out to be the fourth most dangerous place for civilians in 2019. Amid frequent government claims of retaking district after district, the Taliban in effect were controlling nearly half of Afghanistan around this time. Ironically, while American and Afghan government sources hailed the 'steady' run of victories for the government forces, local government circles and human rights groups said the 'ramped-up military campaign by the army was making civilian life far worse than otherwise'.[126]

Ever since President Biden stuck to his decision, which was an extension of his predecessor's decision, debates have raged both in the United States and elsewhere about the correctness of the decision to withdraw troops and support staff altogether. Naturally, opinions supporting the withdrawal decision and criticizing it are both available. But, interestingly, there is a highly provocative view as well, which depicts the entire American military bureaucracy, the diplomatic corps, and left and liberal intellectuals as the main and only engine that has been driving American foreign policy of unwarranted interference all over the world wherever 'democracy' is at stake. But of that later. Presently, we will see how the US decision

---

126 Susannah George, *Dangers for civilians in Afghan-Taliban conflict*, The Washington Post, Ocala.com, 9 February 2020.

to exit Afghanistan was analysed, particularly at a time when the internationally backed government could not have survived without American and NATO military support.

The critical view holds that the American government should not have negotiated with the Taliban on the issue of fixing a timeline but on the issue of determining the conditions that would have allowed a logically desirable transition of power in the country. By treading on the path of negotiating a fixed date of withdrawal, the United States allowed the Taliban to successfully pursue their own agenda. Their tactic of waiting out American troops' presence bore fruit following the announcement that by 15 January 2020 the total number of US troops would be reduced to 2,500. The Trump administration successfully created leverage by engaging directly to meet the paramount goal of a US withdrawal in exchange for genuine peace talks and counterterrorism guarantees. This strategy brought about unprecedented negotiations between Afghan government representatives and the Taliban in Doha. Thus began a walk down a conditions-based long and winding path to peace. But at each step along the way, the US government made concessions in the form of accelerated troop reductions with seemingly little of value in return. As the Trump administration's term was approaching its end, plans for a troop withdrawal were accelerated and the Taliban's dream of biding their time until the Americans left moved closer to reality. As the future unfolded, it was seen that the Taliban did not really have to exert themselves too much in defeating the government forces; and the ignoble abdication by the Ashraf Ghani government crowned the terrorist force with an unexpected success. It was found later that several conditions which should have been met in the agreement were not included in the deal at all. The agreement made clear that four elements within it were inter-related, ie, the US troop withdrawal timeline, Taliban counterterrorism commitments, the start of direct talks including the Afghan government, and reductions in violence. The agreement left the question of how the third and fourth conditions would affect the troop timeline. An assessment of the negotiations made in November 2020 raised questions over whether the agreement would protect the rights of the Afghan people and the integrity of the Afghan state. What the world witnessed a year later was the collapse of both these conditions. In early 2022, the Afghan people remained at the mercy of the Taliban Islamic Force and the Afghan state stood condemned to a state of non-recognition by the world community, with all the attendant consequences—no international humanitarian aid, a severe shortage of funds, shortage of food and medicine.[127]

So whatever happened to the overall promise of arriving at a political solution to the underlying causes of war that would at the same time, preserve the rights of the Afghan people and the integrity of the Afghan state? Examining the prospects, it was felt that 'a rapid, unconditional withdrawal' would put that outcome in serious jeopardy. And that was what happened when the Ashraf Ghani government abdicated its responsibility of leading the country, the Afghan national army threw aside its military assets and ran away from the battlefield, and the

---

127 Scott Worden, *Afghanistan Withdrawal Should Be Based on Conditions, Not Timelines*, 19 November 2020, https://www.usip.org/publications/2020/11/afghanistan-withdrawal-...

Taliban fighters entered the gates of Kabul with a triumphant cry of victory. But all this came much later. If we go back to the Doha talks, all the positive signs of a probable signing of a peace deal were discernible. The Taliban were willingly talking to a delegation that consisted of representatives of the Ghani government, other political and civil society leaders, including four women. This was too good an opportunity to lose in a play of negativity. The Americans were feeling happy because, honouring their commitment, the Taliban had refrained from attacking their troops. Simultaneously, however, negativity too prevailed. The Taliban had intensified attacks on government forces without breaking off officially and visibly their ties with the Al-Qaeda and other dangerous terrorist groups. Suspicions of undisclosed motives on the part of the Taliban gripped the nation and the government. In the United States, President Trump's appreciation of the 'progress' made in the 2019 talks led to worries in his administration whether the optimism was misplaced and if the Taliban were getting the better of the United States. It was clear to all that the war in Afghanistan had become simply 'intolerable' to Americans, and that the president would not dare do anything to destabilize the talks. His own administration was feeling worried about the appropriateness of the announcement of a US intention to 'quickly withdraw' from Afghanistan, giving a long rope to the terrorist force. David Petraeus, a retired general who had served in Afghanistan, warned the American president on 17 August 2019 that 'Under no circumstances should the Trump administration repeat the mistake its predecessor [under Barack Obama] made in Iraq and agree to a total withdrawal of forces from Afghanistan.' (article in The Wall Street Journal). A former State Department official, Laurel Miller pointed out that a lot 'will depend on the details (of the agreement). For instance, it seems that the Taliban were prepared to call a ceasefire but with US troops not with the Afghan army.' Months later, when a new government led jointly by President Ashraf Ghani and Chairman of the High Council for Peace and National Reconciliation, Dr Abdullah Abdullah, renewed their pledge to lead the country, there prevailed an atmosphere of hope and doubt about the future for peace negotiations. An Afghan analyst, Hekmatullah Azami, said, 'Being the go-to guy for peace talks, Abdullah will have to deliver by starting the talks. However, there are times like these when Ghani will push for military operations. There will be a difference of opinion between the President and Abdullah on this very matter. I anticipate in the coming days that there will be certain blame-gaming between the two when Abdullah will ask to move forward on the peace talks but Ghani might want to focus on the military approach.' Zalmay Nishat, a close aide to Dr Abdullah, said, 'There is the war rhetoric and the peace rhetoric within the administration in Afghanistan. If the war rhetoric is stronger, its implications will block efforts of prisoner release initiating talks, which could translate to an increase in violence. It will create friction between the two. That is my worry.'[128]

All these developments tended to help the Taliban strengthen their position at the negotiations and tighten their

---

128   Ruchi Kumar, *Settlement without peace Abdullah's new job is to lead talks with Taliban at a time when president Ghani is going for war*, The Hindu, 24 May 2020.

hold over the other side. As the talks resumed and advanced, with encouragement from the United States and most other countries barring sceptics like India (which had come to take a stiff position on joining any peace effort as long as the terrorists held the upper hand). Russia was another strong supporter of continuing with the negotiations and its position was elucidated by Zamir Kabulov, Russia's special presidential envoy for Afghanistan and head of the second Asia Department in the Russian Foreign Ministry. Speaking after the Americans and the Taliban signed an agreement to carry forward the peace process, he said,

> There are grounds for optimism about the future for sure. We commend the signing of an agreement between the US and the Taliban movement that took place in Doha on 29 February 2020 and are convinced that it paves the way for finding a lasting settlement of the situation in Afghanistan. We see that both sides, the US and the Taliban, are interested in fulfilling this agreement and launching intra-Afghan peace talks as soon as possible. Much will depend on Kabul, namely, on how quickly the authorities of the Islamic Republic of Afghanistan will be able to complete the prisoner exchange with the Taliban by swapping 5,000 Taliban detainees for 1,000 soldiers and establishing a negotiating team that the Taliban will be willing to engage in a dialogue with. The Taliban movement has changed. There are multiple reasons for that. First and foremost, the Taliban (have) had enough time to learn from (their) mistakes. As we can see, (they have) abandoned some radical and jihadist principles. For instance, the Taliban now (underline) that (they

are) interested in maintaining constructive and good neighbourly relations with all regional countries. The recent statement by the Taliban spokesperson about non-interference in the internal affairs of other states issued with respect to the fake publications about the Taliban supporting Pakistan's position on Kashmir is a good example.[129]

---

129   Atul Aneja, '*The Taliban movement has changed*', The Hindu, 6 June 2020.

CHAPTER 20

Internationalising Terrorism

A UNITED Nations report made available in late-May 2022 was more revealing and, consequently, more alarming than many other UN. reports concerning Afghanistan. The report said that Pakistan-based terror groups Lashkar-e-Toiba (LeT) and Jaish-e-Mohammad (JeM) were present in the Taliban-controlled parts of Afghanistan where they were running training camps and had deep links with the reigning regime which included holding meetings with top-level Taliban leaders. The United Nations Monitoring Team on Afghanistan further informed that Al-Qaeda in Indian Subcontinet (AQIS) had between 180 and 400 fighters including 'nationals from Bangladesh, India, Myanmar and Pakistan— located in Ghazni, Helmand, Kandahar, Nimruz, Paktika, and Zabul Provinces'. However, the report pointed out that even though Al-Qaeda 'enjoys greater freedom under the new Afghan regime', it was unlikely to mount or direct attacks outside Afghanistan for the next year or two owing both to a lack of military capability and Taliban restraint'. The UN report quoted a member-state as saying that the JeM was maintaining eight training camps at the time in Nangarhar province three of which were under direct Taliban control. The LeT was said to be maintaining three training camps in Kunar and Nangarhar provinces and had 'provided finance and training expertise to Taliban operations'. 'The same member-state reported that in January 2022, a Taliban delegation visited a training camp used by the LeT in the Haska Mena district of Nangarhar.' 'In October 2021, according to one member-state…LeT leader Mawlavi Assadullah, met with Taliban Deputy Interior Minister Noor Jalil'..

The UN report referred to the JeM as a Deobandi group that was ideologically closer to the Taliban. 'The leader of the group is Masood Azhar, and Qari Ramazan is the newly appointed head of (the) JeM in Afghanistan,' it stated. On (the) LeT, the report noted, 'Within Afghanistan, according to one member-state, it is led by Mawlawi Yousuf.' The monitoring team assists the UN. Security Council's Sanctions Committee and this May 2022 report was the first since the fall of Kabul in August 2021. Circulated among the United Nations Security Council (UNSC), the report sought to provide guidance for the United Nations' future strategy for Afghanistan. At the time this report was presented to the Security Council, India was the chair of the Sanctions Committee, with Russia and the United Arab Emirates as the vice-chairs. All the 15 member-states of the UNSC were represented in the committee.

The report also noted that 'the Taliban appear confident in their ability to control the country' and 'wait out' the international community to obtain eventual recognition of their government.

According to the report, the strength of groups like the ISIL-K had declined and they were not believed to be 'capable of mounting international attacks before 2023 at the earliest'. The report also detailed for the first time the internal power struggle within the Taliban, the emerging power structure in the regime and the arms and weapons left behind by the US and NATO forces. The report informed that about 180 senior Taliban travelled for deliberations with the Taliban's supreme leader Hibatullah Akhundzada for a three-day jirga during 22-24 March 2022 to Kandahar. 'The gathering revealed some divisions within the movement as consultations on key policy decisions ended with Hibatullah backing the decision to ban girls' education. It exposed Kandahari versus Haqqani, Kandahari versus the de facto cabinet, and military versus ulema rivalries. There was no Tajik or Uzbek representation, and key figures such as [Foreign Minister] Amir Khan Mottaqi...were absent', the report said. The report said the foremost division within the Taliban was defined by opposing views between moderate and hardline blocks. The moderate block consisted of senior Taliban, including Mullah Baradar Sher Mohammad Abbas Stanekzai who believed the Taliban must engage in a working relationship with foreign partners and be integrated into the international system, especially where global finance was concerned. On the other hand, the hardline block consisted of senior Taliban centralized around Haibatullah Akhundzada such as Mohammad Hassan Akhund, and several other senior Taliban from Kandahar. This block had taken a more ideological approach with less emphasis on relations with the international community. [Perhaps the hardliners were mentally inclined toward establishing a perfect Islamic state without bothering about the Afghans as long as they remained faithful to the demands of a true Islamic state under *Shari'a* law. Similarly, the moderates could be perceived to be more concerned about the common people's plight and were eager to provide a normal life with the world as a legitimate and necessary ground for interaction and exchange of ideas and the necessities of life. There was a third block, though the report did not name it as such, it may pass under the nomenclature of 'independent'. This block was led by Sirajuddin Haqqani of the Pakistan-based and fully ISI-controlled group Haqqani network, who were seen to be more closely aligned with the hardliners but preferred to adopt a pragmatic approach to securing Taliban interests.

The UN sponsored Regional Security Dialogue on Afghanistan report, which recorded all known facts about developments within the Taliban leadership on the issue of international recognition came up with an important piece of information that the Kandahari (Durrani) Taliban were assessed to be the ascending bloc within the Taliban leadership at the end of the ninth month of their rule in Afghanistan. It came to the fore immediately after the Taliban came into power and began the ministry-making exercise, and when the Taliban were busy selecting interim ministers and apportioning ministries to them, the Haqqani network moved into the picture and mounted pressure tactics to advance claims for its own members to be allotted key portfolios such as interior, intelligence, passports and migration. Sirajuddin Haqqani became the interim interior minister and Khalil Ahmed Haqqani the refugees minister. However, the other two blocks, especially the moderates, sought to push back Haqqanis' pressure tactics. The report said it was known during the March jirga that the Haqqanis had expected an endorsement of Sirajuddin's elevation to the deputy prime minister's post but this did not materialize. A decision to conduct house-to-house searches in Kabul was made without Sirajuddin being consulted and without Haqqani commanders being exempted from the searches, actions seen as challenging (the) Haqqanis' authority.

An important finding of the report was that a few member-states had reported the Taliban claimed to possess 40 operational aircraft. It was believed the aircraft included two Mi-17 helicopters confirmed as operational along with two UH 60 Black Hawks, two MD-530 Cayuse light helicopters, two Mi-24 helicopter gunships, and one fixed-wing transport aircraft, all of which were observed flying. 'Flying these aircraft has propaganda value for the Taliban but little military utility,' the report noted. For the few aircraft in service, the Taliban lacked parts, trained mechanics to maintain them, and most importantly, pilots to fly them, it added.

This identification of a time-defining stage in the annals of Taliban governance in Afghanistan also urges us to pause and ponder over and determine the character, characteristics, and goals of such a unique regime-entity. In the entire world in 2022, perhaps the Taliban-governed Afghanistan remained the only country being ruled by a group of sanctioned terrorists whom the world and certain countries would like to have arrested, prosecuted and jailed. But they were ruling a country of over 40 million people. Though the government and the state were not recognized by the international community, they were in constant contact with a large number of countries on humanitarian grounds and international aid including finance. Altogether, this was a unique moment in world history.

And surprises began to appear on the scene from mid-

2022. On 2 June 2022, the Taliban announced that they had launched a massive all-out programme to eradicate poppy cultivation from Afghan soil. Even though thousands of farmers and farm labourers were reduced overnight from affluence to poverty, the fundamentalist rulers did not pause in their sudden turn to rule-based governance. On a recent day in Washir district in Southern Helmand province, one of the biggest centres of poppy cultivation, armed Taliban fighters stood guard as a tractor tore up a field of poppies. The field's owner stood by, watching. The Taliban had issued an edict in early April banning poppy cultivation throughout the country. Those violating the ban 'will be arrested and tried according to *shari'a* laws in relevant courts', the Taliban deputy interior minister for counternarcotics Mullah Abdul Haq Akhund said in Helmand province's capital city Lashkar Gah.

Afghanistan, as we have noted several times above, is the world's largest producer of opium and a major source for heroin in Europe and in Asia. Production of heroin kept on spiralling over the past twenty years (from 2001-2022) rendering infructuous the billions of dollars going downhill in campaign after campaign to stop poppy cultivation. As a matter of fact, one big reason for this failure was the fact that poppy cultivation and production of heroin had become a part of ordinary Afghan life and culture which could not be suppressed by campaigns run on democratic lines. Now that the Taliban had chosen to appear on the scene with the same mission as the Americans and the rest of the world, it would be educative to find out if Afghan intimacy with illegal drugs would still prevail or perish, and it might be feasible to imagine a world with fewer drugs to destroy lives and families. There was also the question financing of terrorism through drug smuggling money. If Afghanistan produced less poppy and heroin in 2022-2023 and the world received considerably less drugs over a significant period of time, and society as a whole benefitted, the Taliban would be entitled to be a beneficial factor for Afghanistan in the international community as well.

However, the grim reality of real-time Afghanistan promised a different end to the story. The ban would strike a heavy blow to millions of impoverished farmers and day labourers who were totally dependent on proceeds from the poppy crops to survive. And what was the state of Afghan economy when the ban was pronounced? At a most inopportune moment, one would say. The Afghan economy had been in doldrums even before the Taliban came to power, and since August 2021, with international humanitarian and financial aids being closed the economy had touched rock-bottom. The country was bankrupt, and the government and the central bank had no purchasing power. Trade and commerce was almost at a standstill. Even government employees were often not paid their salaries. A food crisis had gripped the nation, and despite food supplies from India and several other countries, most rural people kept on going to sleep with empty stomachs. On top of all these nightmares, successive bouts of severe drought had clawed their way into Afghan lives all over the provinces.

An important connection exists in Afghanistan between drought or lack of adequate water for farming and poppy cultivation. For example, a media report quoted Noor Mohammed, a farmer in Washir district of Helmand province whose poppy field was destroyed by the Taliban, 'If we are not allowed to cultivate this crop, we will not earn anything.' His field was small and lacked water and could survive only on cultivating poppy. This was the reality in Afghanistan. The Taliban also ignored the fact that the village economy revolved around poppy cultivation. Farmers would borrow money to purchase food items like wheat, flour, sugar, and cooking and heating oils on the understanding that the coming poppy crop would bring them enough funds to repay the loans. Even day labourers could earn upwards of US $300 a month harvesting opium from the poppies. Throughout the twenty years of international campaign to rebuild Afghan economy, a major programme was to educate Afghan farmers on the cultivation of high-yielding profitable crops other than poppy; and they failed disastrously because the programme never covered a sizeable portion of Afghan farmers, and as the Taliban forces advanced into the programme, the foreign experts and funds dried up.

However, this time the eradication campaign was said to have been directed against those farmers who had proceeded to cultivate the opiate after the ban in April 2022. Besides, a Taliban minister declared that his government was in touch with other governments to introduce other commercial crops instead of poppy, in a re-run of the earlier programme that had failed.

One characteristic of Afghanistan's poppy cultivation was that while it remained the largest in the world, it also kept on rising in volume year by year. In 2021, the total poppy crop was estimated to have been planted on 177,000 hectares yielding 650 tons of heroin, according to the United Nations Office on Drugs and Crime. This represented an increase from 590 tons in 2020. The total value of Afghanistan's opiates in 2021 stood at US $1.8-US $2.7 billion, accounting for 14 per cent of the country's GDP. Afghanistan remained the world's top-ranking heroin producer and supplier, accounting for as much as 80 per cent of the world's total heroin production.[130]

This episode suggests a tendency on the part of the governing Islamists to shift their style of governance from the illogical to the logical, perhaps to attract the sympathy and understanding of the world for the extremists ruling Afghanistan. As the first year of their rule came to an end without any change for the better in the international community's attitude, the Taliban appeared to be indecisive about the right policy that could answer all questions of the world community.

Right when the devastating earthquake had struck Paktika province, and the Taliban government was preoccupied with rescue and relief operations, the Taliban leadership called an all-male jirga of 3,000 Islamic scholars and priests to proclaim to the world that it was time for them to recognize the government in Kabul. The incongruity of this call was too palpable to be missed. An eleven-point resolution passed at the end of the conference calling for recognition of the Taliban government in Kabul and for unlocking foreign aid in return for a pledge to take 'valuable steps in the direction of realizing national interests and people's welfare and preventing poverty and unemployment'.

This high-sounding resolution failed to fool the international community, for the simple reason that the policies being pursued would not be conducive to a restoration of

---

130 Free Press Journal, Afghanistan: *Taliban launch campaign to eradicate poppy crop, leaving farmers ruined*, 2 June 2022, https://www.freepressjournal.in/world/afghanistan-taliban-launch-campaign-to-eradicate-poppy-crop-leaving-farmers-ruined

normal relations with global society. Women have faced more restrictions than before in 2023; cultivation of opium poppy has risen by 37 per cent in just one year, between 2021 and 2022. The Taliban administration has been actively supporting farmers switching over from other traditional crops to opium poppy because the authorities cannot provide better monetary benefits to the farming community and because the marketing of opium and its by-products is infinitely easier with marketing channels actively engaged both at home and abroad.[131]

In that year, Afghanistan accounted for 85 per cent of the total world opium production. Despite the steady improvement in the efficacy of the country's specialised intelligence and policing units over the years when the democratic government ran the country, seizures of drugs and arrests of people involved in the smuggling of drugs had declined, implying active encouragement from the authorities. Besides, the more drugs were produced and smuggled out, the more the revenues flowed in than before. But as a direct result of this policy of the Taliban government, drug consumption in the global society increased phenomenally and, as the UNODC found it, a total 275 million people consumed drugs in the world in 2022.

Meanwhile, as we have already noted in the preceding pages, torture on women increased by leaps and bounds. Najiba's case particularly drew the word's attention when she was murdered on 17 August 2021, just three days after the return of the

---

[131] United Nations Office of Drugs and Crime: UNODC.
Afghanistan addresses impact of crises on communities while celebrating the International World Drug Day 2022, November 2022.

Taliban. They had earlier warned the family and when they were approaching the house, Najiba's mother yelled at them to stop. They paused for a moment and then threw a grenade in the next room and fled. Many women in Najiba's village were the widows of Afghan soldiers. They were now earning money by selling milk but the 'Taliban won't allow that...we don't have men in our houses so what shall we do? We want schools, clinics, and we want freedom like other women, men—other people.'[132]

For some reason, the Taliban denied having killed Najiba and her daughter but their word was contradicted by witnesses and local officials who confirmed the death of a 45-year-old woman whose home was set ablaze. However, the fearless women of Afghanistan have not cowered down under the weight of the Taliban's assault on their minds and bodies; and they are fighting back in equal measure. Dozens of Afghan women risked their lives by demonstrating on the streets against their oppressors. Many of them held banners which read 'No government is stable without the support of women' and 'Freedom is our motto/It makes us proud.' In order to drive renewed fear into the demonstrators, a member of the Taliban ascended into the crowd but witnesses told the media present at the demonstration that the man was angry at those who had stopped to watch rather than the protesters themselves.

Meanwhile, there ensued a windfall profit for burqa-sellers the demand for which has only soared. The Taliban takeover was so swift that many women suddenly found themselves

---

132 CNN, *The Taliban knocked on her door three times. The fourth time they killed her* 18 August 2021, https://edition.cnn.com/2021/08/17/asia/afghanistan-women-taliban-intl-hnk-dst/index.html

without the requisite female uniform which became mandatory overnight in the terrorist-ruled state.

The Taliban had long realized that their quest for international recognition would not fructify as long as their policies remained unchanged and unsuited for world opinion. With unbending tenacity they wreaked their vengeance upon their opponents. They seem to have hit upon a symbol of their enemies, the American flag. The following story sums up their rigid mentality. 'Scattered across central Kabul are the ruins of another empire. Tattered sandbags and discarded redbed tank traps unused sit on the sides of the road. Red and white check points manned 24X7 point towards the sky. Not long ago the neighbourhood, however, known as the Green Zone, was a diplomatic enclave—buzzing with the sounds of the multibillion dollar war effort in Afghanistan. Armoured vehicles rumbled down the streets shuttling diplomats and high Afghan officials, while the thud-thud-thud of American helicopters echoed in the sky. The most striking example was painted on a wall that buttressed the former US embassy. The wall depicts a vertical American flag with columns of red stripes and white and blue stars. Beside the flag a dozen hands are pointing down the red columns as if toppling a series of dominoes. 'Our nation with the help of God', is scrawled on it.[133]

---

133 Christina Goldbaum, *As Taliban settle in, Kabul's green zone comes back to life*, New York Times, 16 February 2023.

CHAPTER 21

In Afghanistan, there cannot be any conclusion

JUST AS this book was reaching its conclusion, there came a clarification from the highest quarters in the Taliban group. The supreme leader of the Taliban, Sheikh Haibatullah Akhundzada had served notice on the international community in July 2022 that his government would not pursue any negotiation with any other country if the ruling group's demands were not accepted. Since then, the United States, the United Nations and the Taliban have met several times and have announced that the release of impounded Afghan assets has been agreed upon in principle and that actual steps would be taken soon. However, as has been clarified earlier, none of the released funds would go to the Taliban but their release would be decided upon by an international board of trustees.

The narration that fills up the pages of this book on Afghanistan may have induced a sense of bewilderment and helplessness among readers who are non-Afghans. The long queue of events probably gives rise to a feeling that this one country may well continue to suffer from fiercely competing streams of national consciousness: on one side, the majority of urban, educated and freedom-loving Afghans, majority of them being women and girls, and on the other hand, the fundamentalist Islamists and their supporters who still dominate the rural South and Eastern Afghanistan. What is truly unfortunate is the complete absence of connection between the two competing sides. Right now, the Taliban and their supporters, inside and outside the country, are the stronger and hopeful side as they wield power. The other side is made up of ordinary citizens, living and fighting from both inside the country and from abroad, a clutch of daring escapees who are fighting and risking their lives.

It is clear from the activities and statements of the ruling terrorists that the Taliban are pretty confident of their continuation in governance. But they are not satisfied with what they have achieved so far. The issue of international recognition is hanging fire, and the ruling party does not like this. They want a settlement of the question on their own terms, but that too does not appear to be feasible. Circumstances, meanwhile, are influencing events towards benefitting the Taliban. We can take the example of the decision by the United States government to release the impounded Afghan assets previously placed under United States and United Nations sanctions, as an indication of this recent trend.

The supreme leader of the Taliban, Mullah Akhundzada told a meeting of 3,000 tribal leaders, officials and religious scholars at the Southern city of Kandahar that 'We will deal with the International community as per Islamic *Shari'a*...if it doesn't allow it, we will not deal with any other country.' Akhundzada told the large and representative gathering of pro-Taliban elements that, 'This meeting is called to think about the freedom we received by the blessings of *Allah*, which we achieved from the blood of our mujahideen (fighters).'[134]

Meanwhile, the ISIS (Khorasan) continued its mayhem targeting the Taliban rule. In a huge explosion, at least twenty worshippers were killed and scores injured at a mosque in Kabul on 17 August, two days after the Taliban terror group celebrated the first anniversary of their victory in Afghanistan. The police said there were multiple casualties but did not say how many. One Taliban intelligence official told *Reuters* that as many as 35 people may have been wounded or killed and the toll could rise further. *Al Jazeera* quoted an unidentified official saying 20 people had been killed. Kabul's Emergency Hospital said on *Twitter* that they had received 27 patients wounded in the blast, including a seven-year-old child. A witness told *Reuters* that a powerful explosion was heard in a Northern Kabul neighbourhood, shattering windows in nearby buildings. Ambulanes rushed to the spot. 'A blast happened inside a mosque... The blast has casualties, but the numbers are not clear yet,' Kabul police spokesperson Khalid Zadran said. A Taliban intelligence official speaking on condition of anonymity, said the explosion occurred in a mosque among worshippers in Khair Khana area of the capital city. The Imam of the mosque was among those killed and the death toll could still rise. Intelligence teams were at the site of the blast with the probe continuing. On the same day, 17 August, the Taliban were also found indulging in killing a former leader and a Shia Hazara Afghan. The assassinated man was known as the

---

134 https://www.al-jazeera.com/news/2011/7/1-taliban-supreme-leader-...

first commander of the group hailing from the minority Shia Hazara community, officials confirmed on 17 August, adding that he had rebelled against the de facto government. Mawlawi Mahdi was shot dead by Taliban forces near the border with Iran as he attempted to flee the country, the defence ministry said in a statement. Mahdi's appointment as a commander some years back was touted as an example of the Taliban's improved position on the inclusion of minority communities in administration and forces. The origins of the schism between Mahdi and the governing force has not been made public, but as far back as June, the defence ministry had spoken of a clearance operation against rebels in Northern Afghanistan. The defence ministry identified the dead leader as a rebel. The ministry described Mahdi on 17 August as the 'leader of the rebels in a district North of Sar-a-Pol.[135]

The international community has known for quite some time that terrorism and its main conveyer, the Taliban Islamic Force, continues to live and cause untold misery in different countries because of one safe haven, Pakistan, which has actively facilitated terrorism for several decades. Pakistan has continued to defy world opinion and sanctions and its economy is now in doldrums, all due to the inexplicable attraction of terrorism in the shape of Islamic fundamentalism. The latest reiteration of the international community to eradicate terrorism was declared in Moscow in February 2023 when the fifth Regional meeting of the Secretaries of the Security Council/National Security

---

135 Reuters, *Taliban kill ex-leader from minority Hazara community*, Kabul, 17 August 2022

Advisers on Afghanistan in Moscow. The Indian representative NSA Ajit Doval said that 'terrorism has become a major threat in the region, and (that India was) dealing with *Da'esh* (Islamic State) and Lashkar-e-Toiba and Jaish-e-Mohammad in the Indian sub-continent'. He urged the international community to ensure that terrorism is effectively tackled and destroyed by a constant exchange of relevant intelligence among the affected nations. He also spoke about the importance of the United Nations Security Council Resolution No. 2593 that called for terror outfits and those designated as such by the top United Nations body to be denied sanctuary in the region. The Moscow conference, Multilateral Security Dialogue on Afghanistan was attended by Russia, China, India, Iran, Kazakhstan, Turkmenistan, Uzbekistan and Kyrgyzstan. Pakistan was not present at the conference.[136]

As this book goes into print, events in Afghanistan will continue to happen, giving rise to the feeling that there is really no conclusion to the developments in Afghanistan.

The Taliban are here to stay

The bare truth about today's Afghanistan is that the Taliban are here to stay, that their government—however pariah it be in the eyes of the international community—is running the administration, that its authority is imposed and unchallenged by their political opponents, that even the international

---

136 Financial Times, *No country should be allowed to use Afghan territory to export terrorism*, National Security Adviser Ajit Doval at Moscow meet, New Delhi, 9 February 2023.

community is being forced to negotiate with them on diverse issues, and that their humour has to be tolerated from time to time.

Yet, this picture is far from perfect. The Taliban authorities are oppressing the Afghan people, and the international community is keeping a close watch over their activities. Despite their defiance, the Taliban authorities are running counter to international public opinion on its policies and activities.

For example, in early May 2023, when China and Pakistan invited the Afghan Taliban to hold a dialogue in Islamabad, an Afghan delegation led by Foreign Minister Amir Khan Muttaqi was prevented from crossing the border into Pakistan due to the UN prohibition against designated terrorists from leaving Afghanistan. Muttaqi could proceed to Islamabad only after the United Nations waived this travel restriction. The global apex body did this not in sympathy with the Taliban but to facilitate the holding of a trilateral dialogue between China, Pakistan and Afghanistan.

The UN decided to help out China and Pakistan because the main agenda of those two countries in having a dialogue with the Taliban government was to bring home to the latter that it was time the Afghan government exercise restraint on those elements who were interested in spreading terrorism to 'neighbouring countries', a reference to China and Pakistan. India was not being mentioned in this respect because China and Pakistan did not want New Delhi to be included in the dialogue. Pakistan hosted the trilateral dialogue that sought 'to promote regional security, trade and counter-terrorism collaboration'. China's Foreign Minister Qin Gang and his Pakistani counterpart Bilawal Bhutto Zardari led their delegations' presentations sharing with the Taliban representatives the security concerns stemming from a growing threat of terrorism in Afghanistan and the challenges it posed to neighbouring countries. They also exchanged views about how to support the de facto Afghanistan authorities in the economic reconstruction of the abysmally poor country. Qin said before the delegation-level talks began that China and Pakistan were ready to support 'actively' the Afghan reconstruction efforts but he pressed the Taliban authorities 'to deliver on their regional and international commitments'.

The statement that was issued in Islamabad indicated at least one commitment that had to be made by the Taliban government, namely, that 'The three sides (agreed) to advance political engagement, counter-terrorism cooperation, and enhance trade, investments and connectivity under the trilateral framework. No further details were disclosed at the time.

Howsoever much the Taliban government in Afghanistan wanted to ignore their international commitments and rule the country as they wished, regional and global interference could not obviously be avoided. The United Nations was forced to 'reiterate its commitment to the people of Afghanistan, men, women and children'. The report said that in a review of its operations in Afghanistan in the light of Taliban's ban on women working for the international organization, the United Nations Mission in Afghanistan (UNMA) reiterated its 'commitment to stay in Afghanistan on behalf of the men, women and children of Afghanistan'.

It is yet another indicator of the utter confusion that the terrorist organisation suffers from in administering Afghanistan that while its government does not hesitate to apply for a waiver of the travel ban on one of its functionaries but at the same time makes sure that the United Nations and its sister-organisations cannot function properly due to the enforced absence of local employees.

But the utter confusion—or, perhaps, a better word would be an astonishing lack of coordination between various wings of the group—was reflected more specifically on the major issue of women's education. One of the first prohibitions that the first Taliban government and the second Taliban government introduced was a total ban on the education of girls and women, this leading to an immediate shut-down of girls' primary and secondary schools, and universities in Afghanistan.

In a stark contrast to the experiences during the first Taliban reign, there was, however, considerable criticism and outright opposition to the move from the Taliban group's own circles.

The government effectively banned female students from attending university in the edict cracking down on women's rights and freedoms in late-February 2022. Despite initially promising a more moderate rule respecting rights for women and minorities, the Taliban proved that irrespective of any promise they made, they would be steadfast in observing *Shari'a* laws in the country. The difference between the Taliban rule and Afghanistan under other rulers was that the former's implementation was based on an extremely narrow and fundamentalist interpretation of the laws.

The decision was announced after a government meeting. A letter shared by the spokesman for the Ministry of Higher Education, Ziaullah Hashmi told private and public universities to implement the ban as soon as possible and to inform the Ministry once the ban was in place.

Now, why did the government reintroduce the prohibition, knowing well that this step would be considered as renegade in international quarters and would further damage any prospect of recognition that might be possible in future? United Nations Secretary-General Antonio Guterres described it as another 'broken promise' and a 'very troubling' move.

They had already banned girls from middle schools and high schools, restricted women from most job opportunities, and ordered them to wear head-to-toe clothing. Women also remained banned from public parks and gyms.

The inner-contradictions that had earlier surfaced resumed with a new vigour, perhaps indicating that the group was no longer able to control the thought process of its members, and that members were beginning to publicly express their notes of dissent.

On 30 June 2022, at least one participant at a gathering organised by the Taliban of 3,000 male religious and ethnic leaders from across Afghanistan called for reopening of high schools for girls. It was the first such gathering to take place at the time since the Taliban took over power in August 2021. It was not clear at the time how much support this sentiment would receive or how a decision on the issue would be reached.

However, in April 2023, Afghan religious scholars criticized the continuing ban on female education even as a key Taliban minister warned clerics not to rebel against the government on the controversial issue.[137] Reports from the country

---

137 AP, *Afghan religious scholars criticize girls' education ban*, 8 April 2023, https://apnews.com/article/afghanistan-taliban-girls-education-ef86d548a6f6d736557000943f49d323

indicate that there is widespread resentment over the women's education policy not only among the women and the general public but also among clerics who are officially siding with the government and the Taliban group as far as state administration under Islamic law is concerned. The level at which opposition has grown was illustrated by reports that a senior minister had to warn the clerics at the gathering not to push too hard their point of view. The government resorted to subterfuge by presenting the ban on women's education as a temporary measure which it was certainly not at the time. Was it because the government was careful not to antagonize too many people at one time by following its hard policy on women? If so, could this be yet another chink in the Taliban's armour? The *AP* report mentioned two eminent religious scholars who said (on 8 April 2023) that the authorities should reconsider their decision. One of them, Abdul Rahman Abid, said that the institutions should be permitted to re-admit girls and women through separate classes, hiring female teachers, staggering timetables, and even building new facilities. 'Knowledge is obligatory in Islam for men and women,' he said, adding that Islam 'allows women to study.' 'My daughter is absent from school,' he said, 'I am ashamed. I have no answer for her. (She) asks why girls are not allowed to learn in the Islamic system. I have no answer for her.' Another scholar who was a member of the Taliban, said that there was still time for ministries to solve the problem of girls' education. He cited ministries comprising the inner circle of the supreme leader, Mulla Hibatullah Aknundzada who was based in Kandahar. It was on his orders that the government banned girls from classrooms. 'Islam has allowed both men and women to learn, but hijab and curriculum should be considered,' he said. Acting Higher Education Minister Nida Mohammad Nadim said on 30 April that clerics should not speak against government policy. He made his remarks after another scholar, Abdul Sami Al Ghaznawi, told students at a religious school that there was no conflict over girls' education and that the Islamic scripture was clear that girls' education was acceptable. While a regular dialogue seemed to be brewing in Afghanistan, the United Nations reported that an Afghan rights activist who had campaigned for girls' education had been arrested. The UN Mission in Afghanistan reported that Matiullah Wesa, founder and president of *Pen Path*, was arrested in the Afghan capital on 26 March (2023). He was reportedly picked up after his return from a trip to Europe. The UN urged the Taliban authorities to clarify Wesa's whereabouts, the reasons for his arrest, and ensure his access to legal representation and to his family. His brother said that earlier the Taliban police had surrounded their house and beat up his two brothers and insulted their mother.[138] But bad news for Afghan girls' education came from other directions as well. Realizing that any hope for school reopening was distant, the girls decided to make use of virtual classroom facilities but a poor internet connectivity spoiled or at the least reduced the benefits of the online facility. By the way, the Taliban administration had allowed individual girls and women to study from their homes and use the internet for that purpose. The administration itself and the Taliban Islamic Force group use the internet to get onto social media to make announcements of

---

138   AP, *Activist for girls' education held in Kabul*: UN, 28 March 2023, https://apnews.com/article/afghanistan-taliban-girls-education-activist-arrested-a72718f4ca796460db667677af97afd5

various kinds. The global internet tracker Ookla puts Afghanistan as the slowest mobile internet-performing country among 137 countries. As far as fixed internet is concerned, the country ranks 179 among 180 countries.

Meanwhile, the other inhuman features of the fundamentalist government continued without any signs of moderation. A former female lawmaker and her body guard were shot dead in central Kabul in mid-January 2023 by 'unknown assailants'. Mursal Nabizada was among the few female parliamentarians who had stayed back in Kabul after the Taliban returned to power. But her killing also marked the first occasion when a parliamentarian from the previous regime was murdered.

Meanwhile, the Taliban government continued to be as brutal as before. A UN report released on 8 May 2023 said that in the past six months alone, 274 men, 58 women and two boys were publicly flogged in Afghanistan. 'Corporal punishment is a violation of the Convention against Torture and must cease,' the report quoted Fiona Frazer, the agency's human rights chief. In response, the Taliban foreign ministry said that Afghanistan's laws were determined in accordance with Islamic rules and guidelines, and that an overwhelming majority of Afghans followed those rules. Zabiullah Mujahid, the top government spokesman, said that the decision to carry out the punishments was made 'very carefully' following the approval by three of the country's highest courts and the Taliban supreme leader Mullah Hibatullah Akhundzada.

If we take a close look at the pattern of Taliban governance and its handling of international relations, it indicates self-contradictions, confusion or self-doubt traversing its mind. As the Taliban Islamic Force and its state are hurtling towards the completion of two years of rule in a hostile world, the urgency for a settlement is rising as far as the fundamentalist rulers are concerned.

The Taliban have also been feeling an equal urgency to explain to the Afghans why their government has adopted a certain policy vis-a-vis the international community. Such an occasion occurred in July 2022 when the supreme leader of the Taliban, Sheikh Haibatullah Akhundzada, served notice on the international community saying that if the ruling group's demands were not accepted, his government would not pursue any negotiation with any other country.

However, exceptions to this dictum were soon available. The United States, the United Nations and the Taliban government met several times, in negotiations over the frozen assets of the Afghanistan government (from the previous years). Was this any sign of malleability on the part of the United States and the United Nations? An answer was also available at the same time. It was held firmly by the Western world (as represented by the United States) that no matter what, no funds were to be released to the ruling fundamentalist group, and that funds would be controlled by an international board of trustees.

Are the Taliban then indulging in theatrics to hide their weaknesses vis-a-vis the international community? However, this should not engage our attention so much as what the continuing stalemate over Afghanistan has brought for millions of Afghan women and girls whose lives are on the verge of being destroyed as a final and irrevocable settlement escapes the world's attention. Meanwhile, inside the country two separate groups of Afghans have gathered together to look after their own interests, one group identifying itself with the Taliban enjoying far more resources and power and the other the deprived men, women and minority communities all of whom are under constant attack from the ruling fundamentalists. Women and girls are the worst sufferers among them.

It is pretty clear from recent statements and activities that the Taliban are sure of their continuation in governance but they are not satisfied with what they have achieved so far. The issue of international recognition continues to hang fire, and this they don't like. They want a settlement on their own terms, as was stated in July 2022 by Akhundzada, but this in particular does not appear to be feasible in the near future.

The international community has known for quite sometime that terrorism and its main conveyor, the Taliban Islamic Force continues to live and cause untold misery in many countries because of one safe haven, Pakistan, which has actively facilitated internationalization of terrorism for several decades. Islamabad and, more specifically, the army and the Inter-Services Intelligence Directorate in Rawalpindi and Islamabad, has defied world opinion. As we said before, in early May 2023, China and Pakistan invited Afghanistan to join a trilateral dialogue on security and regional cooperation. In the first stage, the host Pakistan and the organiser China emphasized the Taliban government's responsibility in ensuring that terrorism was not exported to regional countries, harming their interests. The two countries, whose foreign ministers met with the de facto Afghan foreign minister in Islamabad on 7 and 8 May 2023, insisted and drew a sworn statement from Kabul's representative that the Taliban government would be careful to stop this practice. In return, China and Pakistan presented a sop to Kabul by way of promising funds and technical assistance for economic reconstruction.

China and Pakistan also offered a considerable benefit to Afghanistan by proposing to include the latter within the ambit of the ambitious China Pakistan Economic Corridor project. Kabul obviously agreed to regularize its relations with the two regional powers in the hope of beating the international boycott that the world at large has pursued since August 2021. It was not difficult to appreciate why India, an equally involved country in the matter of the Taliban-ruled Afghanistan, was ignored in the confabulations; but reports indicated that New Delhi did not take kindly to the sops offered to Kabul without keeping New Delhi informed.

However, May 2023 also witnessed the latest Taliban depravity in harassing both the United Nations and Afghan women who worked for the international body. The idea obviously was to prevent the UN from gathering information about what was happening in rural and distant areas as it remained at the time the sole international body to still work in the country, though reports said the UN would soon meet in Doha to decide on the future of its work in Afghanistan. At the same time, the women who were still working at the UN offices would be barred from attending office, and would thus share the plight of their sisters in other spheres of life. A massive prison seemed to be building up to throttle all women in the country.

The last large-scale earthquake that devastated parts of Eastern and Southern Afghanistan had seen the international community rush in with assistance of medicine, food, funds, clothes and rescue equipment. India was the first country to jump in with humanitarian assistance; Afghanistan gratefully accepted the help, and Pakistan agreed to facilitate quicker passage through its territory. Since then, India and Taliban Afghanistan have grown relatively accessible to each other; and the re-opened Indian mission is doing its best to keep the gingerly-placed relationship going.

In the meantime, the United States was embarrassingly re-visiting the old debate over the timing and appropriateness of the American withdrawal of troops by President Joe Biden. On 7 April 2023, the Biden administration defended its action in leaving Afghanistan, blaming the immediate past President Donald Trump for creating conditions that 'severely constrained' the successor administration and led to the chaotic withdrawal from the traumatically suffering country as the Taliban entered its capital. The White House released on the day a 12-page document spelling out the conditions that led to the US exit from Afghanistan in August 2021 and sent related classified documents to various Congressional committees. The report placed much of the blame on the previous Trump administration, saying that President Biden was 'severely constrained' by Trump's decisions regarding the country. 'The Trump administration had negotiated a withdrawal agreement with the Taliban that Biden pledged to honour. (See '*Tortuous Negotiations*') The report criticised the Trump administration for lack of proper planning to carry out the deal with the Taliban. The report noted that when Biden took office on 20 January 2021, 'the Taliban were in the strongest military position and controlling nearly half of the country.' At the same time, the US had only 2,500 troops left in the country, which was the lowest since 2001 (after the US and European nations had taken control of Afghanistan). However, Trump who was preparing to contest in the next presidential election rejected the report outright. 'These morons in the White House, who are systematically destroying our country, headed by the biggest moron of them all. Hopeless Joe Biden, has a new disinformation game they are playing—Blame 'TRUMP' for their grossly incompetent SURRENDER in Afghanistan', on his Truth Social Platform.

The unwholesome situation arising out of the action of the Biden administration and Trump's vituperative response in consequence could only be a very minor incident in the annals of the Taliban Afghanistan as we examine its history since 15 August 2021. The most overpowering fact in these annals is the enslavement of Afghanistan as the fundamentalist terror group's reign was stepping into the completion of its second year in power. More years may roll out before there is a positive turn for the better for the Afghan people or a more responsive Taliban government or its demise under unpredictable circumstances may bring this about. Judging by their history and record there is very little hope that the Taliban may become a responsive administration one day soon. This leaves the unforeseeable circumstances under which the Taliban may be made to quit, and once more a democratic, elected government takes their place.

Most scholars of Afghanistan seem to suggest that any future involvement of the United States in resolving the quagmire that is today's Afghanistan would be risky. At the same time, the world continues to look for American leadership as far as Afghanistan is concerned. At one time, Russia was emerging as another pole in this respect, taking various initiatives to help out the situation; but after its invasion of Ukraine, that additional arm of assistance is presently weakened and of little value. Almost the entire world appears to have forgotten or, at least, relegated this South Asian country to the background, its attitude betraying no sense of urgency for the sake of the enslaved people of Afghanistan. Nothing more can be thought of in the present circumstance; and an insisting void solely remains for the time being.

ACKNOWLEDGEMENTS

At the end of 1996, my newspaper, Hindustan Times, transferred me from Colombo, Sri Lanka, to New Delhi, India; and quite consciously I jumped with considerable hunger into yet another conflict zone, Afghanistan, India's neighbour with whom it has had a close relationship for centuries. The preceding six years had been spent in covering a most relentless civil war in the midst of which citizens lived in splendour in the South and other citizens lived in utter misery in the North and East of the island-nation.

Since then, Afghanistan, this utterly anomalous and self-contradictory country, continued to attract me like a magnet, and incessant stories of developments and people's sufferings there have not allowed me to cast my eye on any other subject. The country's shattered social life, collapsed economy, a political system which has rudely transformed from a functioning democracy—howsoever defective it proved to be—to a medieval fundamentalist state which overnight shut its door on all modernisation. The people had long feared this day, and when the brusque medievalism came 'alive' in mid-August 2021, many of them refused to restrain themselves and fought back but were quickly subdued by the Taliban fighters who numbered a few thousands but were battle-hardened, well-armed, knew their targets, and were devoid of emotions. The civil resistance fizzled out though the military resistance continued in pockets in the North.

This history raised several basic questions about what the Western world, as led by the United States, desired for Afghanistan. According to this dispensation, Afghanistan was a ripe case (in the post-Taliban 1.0 period beginning at the end of 2001) for experimenting with regime change and to install liberal democracy. Iran had changed from absolute monarchy to a religious theocracy.

The Arab countries, suffering from a conspicuous lack of liberal democracy, were all monarchies, and Egypt—which had thrown out a monarchy and embraced military dictatorship and popular democracy—had somehow managed never to return to monarchy but had not achieved anything beyond a defective form of democracy. It was against this infertile background that after the Taliban and Al-Qaeda were ousted but not eradicated from Afghanistan, the democratic world celebrated, in December 2001, the installation of the interim administration of Hamid Karzai, the first of the 'moderate' Pashtun leaders known among his countrymen as an American puppet. Washington and its 'good' allies jumped in with billions of dollars for rebuilding of a new democratic liberal government and nation, under the guidance of America and the global fraternity, pushing out the medieval state founded on the shari'a (Islamic law) so out of place in the twenty first century that it beggared description. The long interregnum of twenty years, during which a very weak and corrupt government presided over a fast changing society in which women in particular, tasted freedom and their rights for the first time in many years and which enabled them to live down the scars of the first Taliban regime (1996-2001). They grabbed the opportunity to educate themselves, worked out of home and excelled in music, arts, various cultural disciplines and dared to dream of another life, more beautiful than the one they had hitherto known.

But even this period of relative nation-building at the popular level came to an end when the Taliban Islamic Force returned to power in Kabul in mid-August 2021 and resumed its unfinished job of establishing an emirate—a Muslim state based on strict Koranic values—its path obligingly paved by an American-trained, funded and equipped Afghan National Army. A bitter US President, Joe Biden, while announcing his decision to withdraw American troops in their entirety from Afghanistan, described the irony of the changeover in the following words:

> American troops cannot and should not be fighting in a war and dying in a war that (Afghan) forces are not willing to fight for themselves. We spent over a trillion dollars. We trained and equipped an Afghan military force—incredibly well-equipped, a force larger in size than the militaries of many of our NATO allies. We gave them every tool they could need. We paid their salaries, provided for the maintenance of their air force—something that the Taliban don't have. The Taliban do not have an air force. We provided close air support. We gave them every chance to determine their own future. What we could not

provide them was the will to fight for that future.¹

While the new rulers are looking pretty confident of achieving all their objectives, the world at large is still searching for the most effective way to deal with this group of people who have been called 'messianic terrorists'[2] for good reasons.

Readers will soon realize that much of this narrative will deal with issues that concern women and girls, human rights, citizens' privileges, and a strong desire among Afghans to catch up with the rest of the world.[3] The Taliban have not yet found an effective means of dealing with this changed mindset in the country they are ruling; and much of the conflict and events that are taking place is due to this hiatus between the rulers and the ruled. The core of the conflict in Afghanistan lies in the fact that while Afghans desire to be 'modern' in a positive sense, the Taliban have, on the other hand, reaffirmed their faith in the most fanatical interpretation of Islam. Yet, their mindset too has changed, and the change is subtle. At times, they appear to be quite accommodating, but soon enough, they reveal by their words and deeds that they have not really

---

1 US President Joe Biden's speech announcing the full withdrawal of American troops at the White House on, 16 August 2021 following the Taliban takeover of Afghanistan.
2 The reference is to Peter Tomsen's encyclopaedic book 'The Wars of Afghanistan: Messianic Terrorism, Tribal Conflicts, And The Failures of Great Powers', Public Affairs, New York, 2011.
3 A resonance of this sentiment or desire was found years later in the Indian state of Karnataka when, with the hijab issue raging in Feb-March 2022, Muslim girl students called a press conference to announce that 'Our priority is education.'

changed, and that they are determined to make Afghanistan a perfect shari'a[4]-specific Islamic state. What this means will be discussed in the following chapters. This book would not have been published with the kind of urgency I bestowed upon it had my friends not insisted on answers from me on Afghanistan once the country pushed its way up in the world media with the return of the dreaded Taliban in Kabul on 15 August 2021. While thanks are due to all my interested friends, I take this opportunity to acknowledge in particular my debt to the following: eminent Afghan liberation fighter and diplomat Masood Khalili who, as his country's representative in New Delhi, helped me understand Afghanistan from different angles and who taught me to admire his friend and leader the legendary Commander Ahmad Shah Massoud; Dr Zahir Tanin, then editor, Afghanistan and Central Asia, BBC, Persian Service, who helped me understand the role of the ethnic minorities in Afghanistan. Despite our brief interaction, I continue to benefit from his elaboration of the intricacies of that particular aspect of the country; Sandip Banerjee, a former corporate executive, who read up my earlier book "Afghanistan

---

4 The Oxford Companion To Politics of the World defines shari'a in the following words: It is the generic term for Islamic law and has to be distinguished from fiqh, jurisprudence, and qanun, which refers to law as statute and as legal rules in actual operation in the contemporary Middle East (the reference book was published in 1993). Strictly speaking, the shari'a derives from two written sources, the Quran, the Book revealed to the Prophet Muhammad in the 6th century CE, and the sunna, which is a compilation of the words and deeds of the Prophet. In actual fact, the shari'a was formed in later centuries through arduous and systematic scholarship, developed by jurists of competing schools. Although formally based on the Quran and the sunna, the shari'a generated a logic of its own as jurists had to articulate a system with internal coherence, responsive to social interests, needs and customs. The Oxford University Press, Oxford, 1993, p.826.

From Terror To Freedom" (2003), to learn about the country and would frequently ask to be updated on my progress on the new book; Anita Kelles-Vitenen and Heikki Hirvonen, both of whom interacted with me following the upheaval in Afghanistan through 2021 and ignited my interest in the complexities of European politics in the wake of the February 2022 Russian invasion of Ukraine—despite no apparent similarity in the two cases, I was impressed to find that Afghans in particular were avid observers of the Russia-Ukraine war and frequently compared their leadership with that of Ukraine— and as a result helped me to look afresh into several new angles of that domain of politics; Baladas Ghoshal, an eminent academic, who sharpened my desire to write extensively on Afghanistan following the Taliban's takeover and who played an important part in the publication of my first book on the country; Arindrajit Lahiri, a prominent development banker who has boundless interest in the politics of Afghanistan as in Ukraine; Ganapathyluxmi Narasinhan, a veteran corporate executive; and Saugata Chatterjee, a senior banking executive who also delves deep into politics of various kinds. I leave unnamed the scores of friends who continue to discuss Afghanistan with me whenever there are major developments in that country. In particular, I recall the sharp and informed questions that I received from my friends in the Calcutta-based Lake Morning Walkers Group who, to my delight, used to bombard me with stimulating inquiries in the wake of particular developments. Finally, I hope that the book I have eventually come up with will satisfy my readers' interest in the subject to a reasonable level. Shortcomings found in this narrative shall of course have to be addressed by myself alone. I thank Vitasta Publishing

India Pvt. Ltd., New Delhi, for accepting my offer with much care and understanding.

My two trips to Afghanistan in the post-Taliban period were both sponsored, the first one in June-July 2002 by Nahzat-e-Milli Afghanistan led by Commander Massoud's brother Ahmad Wali Massoud, and the second by the Interim Government of Afghanistan in September 2002. I was assured of full funding by the Afghan ambassador in New Delhi and my friend, Masood Khalili. The entire trip passed off smoothly thanks to an energetic tarjuman (interpreter), member of a large tribe of educated young men who had returned from exile in Pakistan and who were thriving at the time in Kabul as hundreds of journalists from all over the world were arriving at every hour. Their first visual contact with post-war Kabul was happening at the airport itself as burnt tanks, blown-out planes, and heaps of destroyed arms and ammunition lay everywhere inside the airport, most of these swept close to the peripheral walls, while makeshift cabins had been put up to function as arrival-departure lounges and immigration and custom offices. The scene was so dramatic and traumatizing that like me every other visitor must have felt mesmerized by it. The Kabul airport itself presented a disturbing scene of massive destruction. One of the last battles that the Taliban 1.0 fought with American and international forces before being driven out of the capital was fought here; and the tell-tale marks were very much visible, leaving an indelible impression in the minds of all visitors. The Taliban and Al-Qaeda leadership had by then escaped and taken shelter in the Tora Bora caves further in the East. Their eviction from this location finally signalled the end of that first period of the medieval darkness they had plunged

Afghanistan into. Fortunately, the Taliban's return to power did not lead to any repetition of that episode of two decades back.

When my maiden trip came to an end, I had by then travelled across the country with the interpreter and a driver, upon a sturdy vehicle and I was escorted thus to the head office of Ahmad Wali Massoud's political party Nahzat-e-Milli Afghanistan in a Kabul district. It was a two-storey white-washed long building. On the first floor, in a large hall, we saw several cupboards and large wooden tables where several Afghans talked incessantly and eagerly, judging by their gestures. The languages used were Dari and Pushto. We were asked to sit down at a table; and soon a party functionary came, opened a cupboard and took out a large wad of cash. My interpreter was asked to count the money; after counting, he said, 'There are US$12,000.'

Then the party man took the money back and handed it over to me. We bade good-bye and left the party premises. A few days later, when I called on Wali Massoud for an interview, he asked if I was satisfied with the money. I had left Delhi with just $100 in cash; and now all my expenses had been met. Of course, the bulk of the money went to the interpreter, the driver and the vehicle for petrol. I was naturally happy and conveyed my thanks to him. These memories flooded my mind as I went through Steve Coll's fascinating account of how millions of dollars were shipped to Afghan mujahideen during the war with the Soviet Red Army, the civil war, and lastly the war with the Taliban Islamic Force. The Pentagon and the CIA may have kept their accounts professionally audited but at the Afghanistan end, chaos, lack of accountability and plain looting appeared to have prevailed over the long decades of warfare.

My second trip in less than three months of the first was also sponsored, by the Interim Administration headed by the country's first elected President Hamid Karzai—an election still in the making following the Bonn Agreement in December 2001—and had the blessings of the Indian Ministry of External Affairs. While I knew of the Afghan government's sponsorship, I never knew that the Indian government had chosen me to represent my government for the occasion in Kabul. This became clear when I was seated on the rostrum at the first annual commemoration of the assassination of Comander Ahmad Shah Massoud; I discovered that I was sharing the dais with ministers from France, Italy, Germany, Iran, and Turkey. There was another surprise in store for me. While I had left Delhi with the safe impression that my job was to deliver an address on the late Commander Massoud, a week later a senior journalist from the Indian capital who was part of an Indian media delegation hosted by the Afghan government told me, 'Do you know what the External Affairs Ministry Secretary told me when I asked who was representing the Government of India? He said it was Apratim Mukarji.' 'What?' I exclaimed in complete surprise. 'Yes, this is the truth. In fact, everybody in our media team was astonished when we heard that instead of sending a senior government official they had decided on you. But you were never told?' 'No, I was never even given a hint,' I replied. Much later, as the same journalist and I were spending a pleasant evening on the roof of the Indian ambassador's residence in Kabul, the latter's eyes twinkled at me and he asked, 'So you see how we utilised your service without your knowing anything about it.' I responded by saying that in that case I should have been given an official designation, properly briefed and asked to look up certain high functionaries of the Afghan government. 'That would have been cumbersome and Kabul's consent would have been required. As things turned out, you have called on the most important functionaries for interviews, and thus you have further helped bring our two countries closer to each other.' This could be a rare case of camouflaged diplomacy by a rank outsider and non-diplomat but blessed by unseen diplomats!

Lastly, I most gladly acknowledge my gratefulness to Vitasta Publishing Private Limited for deciding to publish this book so that the public is better-informed about the regime in Kabul at a time the global leadership seems clueless about what to do.